The Future of Capitalism

The Future of Capitalism

Facing the New Anxieties

PAUL COLLIER

HARPER

An Imprint of HarperCollins*Publishers*

HarperCollins books may be purchased for educational, business, or sales promotional use. For information, please email the Special Markets Department at SPsales@harpercollins.com.

Originally published in the United Kingdom in 2018 by Allen Lane, an imprint of Penguin Random House UK.

FIRST U.S. EDITION

Library of Congress Cataloging-in-Publication Data has been applied for.

ISBN 978-0-06-274865-2

18 19 20 21 22 LSC 10 9 8 7 6 5 4 3 2 1

for Sue

diverging lives, converging anxieties

Contents

PART ONE
Crisis

I

The New Anxieties

PASSION AND PRAGMATISM

Deep rifts are tearing apart the fabric of our societies. They are bringing new anxieties and new anger to our people, and new passions to our politics. The social bases of these anxieties are geographic, educational and moral. It is the regions rebelling against the metropolis; northern England versus London; the heartlands versus the coasts. It is the less educated rebelling against the more educated. It is the struggling workers rebelling against the 'scroungers' and 'rent-seekers'. The less-educated, toiling provincial has replaced the working class as the revolutionary force in society: the *sans culottes* replaced by the *sans cool*. So, what are these people angry about?

Place has become a dimension of the new grievances; after a long period during which geographic economic inequalities narrowed, recently they have been widening rapidly. Across North America, Europe and Japan, metropolitan areas are surging ahead of the rest of the nation. Not only are they becoming much richer than the provinces, socially they are becoming detached and no longer representative of the nation of which they are often the capital.

But even within the dynamic metropolis, these extraordinary economic gains are heavily skewed. The newly successful are neither capitalists nor ordinary workers: they are the well educated with new skills. They have forged themselves into a new class, meeting at university and developing a new shared identity in which esteem comes from skill. They have even developed a distinctive morality, elevating characteristics such as minority ethnicity and sexual orientation into group identities as victims. On the basis of their distinctive concern

3

for victim groups, they claim moral superiority over the less-well educated. Having forged themselves into a new ruling class, the well educated trust both government and each other more than ever.

While the fortunes of the educated have soared, pulling up national averages with them, the less-well educated, both in the metropolis and nationally, are now in crisis, stigmatized as the 'white working class'. The syndrome of decline began with the loss of meaningful jobs. Globalization has shifted many semi-skilled jobs to Asia, and technological change is eliminating many others. The loss of jobs has hit two age groups particularly hard: older workers and those trying to find their first job.

Among older workers, job loss often led to family breakdown, drugs, alcohol and violence. In America, the resulting collapse in the sense of a purposeful life is manifested in *falling* life expectancy for whites who have not been to college; this at a time when the unprecedented pace of medical advances is delivering rapidly rising life expectancy for more favoured groups.[1] In Europe, social safety nets have muted the extremity of outcomes, but the syndrome is also widespread and in the most broken cities, such as Blackpool, life expectancy is also falling. Redundant over-fifties are drinking the dregs of despair. Yet the less-educated young have fared little better. In much of Europe, young people face mass unemployment: currently, a third of young Italians are unemployed, a scale of job shortage last seen in the Depression of the 1930s. Surveys show an unprecedented level of youthful pessimism: most young people expect to have lower living standards than their parents. Nor is this a delusion: during the past four decades, the economic performance of capitalism has deteriorated. The global financial crisis of 2008–9 made it manifest, but from the 1980s this pessimism has been slowly growing. Capitalism's core credential of steadily rising living standards for all has been tarnished: it has continued to deliver for some, but has passed others by. In America, the emblematic heart of capitalism, half of the 1980s generation are absolutely worse off than the generation of their parents at the same age.[2] For them, capitalism is not working. Given the huge advances in technology and public policy that have taken place since 1980, that failure is astounding. These advances, themselves dependent on capitalism, make it entirely feasible for *everyone* to have become substantially better off. Yet a majority now expect their children's lives to be worse than their own. Among the American white working class this pessimism rises to an astonishing 76 per cent.[3] And Europeans are even more pessimistic than Americans.

The resentment of the less educated is tinged with fear. They recognize that the well educated are distancing themselves, socially and culturally. And they conclude that both this distancing and the emergence of more-favoured groups, perceived as creaming off benefits, weaken their own claim to help. The erosion of their confidence in the future of their social safety net is happening just as their need for it has increased.

Anxiety, anger and despair have shredded people's political allegiances, their trust in government and even their trust in each other. The less educated were at the core of the mutinies that saw Donald Trump defeat Hillary Clinton in the USA; Brexit defeat Remain in the UK; the insurgent parties of Marine Le Pen and Jean-Luc Mélenchon gain over 40 per cent of the vote in France (shrivelling the incumbent Socialists to under 10 per cent); and in Germany so shrinking the Christian Democrat–Social Democrat coalition to turn the far right AfD (Alternative for Germany) into the official opposition in the Bundestag. The education divide was compounded by the geographic divide. London voted heavily for Remain; New York voted heavily for Clinton; Paris eschewed Le Pen and Mélenchon; and Frankfurt eschewed the AfD. The radical opposition came from the provinces. The mutinies were age-related, but they were not as simple as old-versus-young. Both older workers, who had been marginalized as their skills lost value, and young people, entering a bleak job market, turned to the extremes. In France, youth voted disproportionately for the new-look far right; in Britain and the USA, they voted disproportionately for the new-look far left.

Nature abhors a vacuum, and so do voters. The frustration born of this gulf between what has happened and what is feasible has provided the pulse of energy for two species of politician that were waiting in the wings: populists and ideologues. The last time capitalism derailed, in the 1930s, the same thing happened. The emerging dangers were crystallized by Aldous Huxley in *Brave New World* (1932) and George Orwell in *Nineteen Eighty-Four* (1949). The end of the Cold War in 1989 appeared to usher in a credible prospect that all such disasters were behind us: we had arrived at 'the end of history', a permanent utopia. Instead, we are facing the all-too-credible prospect of our very own dystopia.

The new anxieties have promptly been answered by the old ideologies, returning us to the stale and abusive confrontation of left and right. An ideology offers the seductive combination of easy moral certainties and an all-purpose analysis, providing a confident reply to any problem. The revived ideologies of nineteenth-century Marxism, twentieth-century fascism and seventeenth-century religious fundamentalism have all already lured societies into tragedy. Because the ideologies failed, they lost most of their adherents, and so few ideologue politicians were available to lead this revival. Those that were belonged to tiny residue organizations: people with a taste for the paranoid psychology of the cult, and too blinkered to face the reality of past failure. In the decade preceding the collapse of communism in 1989, the remaining Marxists thought they were living in 'late *capitalism*'. The public memory of that collapse has now receded sufficiently to support a revival: there is a new flood of books on the same theme.[4]

Rivalling the ideologues in seductive power is the other species of politician, the charismatic populist. Populists eschew even the rudimentary analysis of an ideology, leaping directly to solutions that ring true for two minutes. Hence, their strategy is to distract voters from deeper thought through a kaleidoscope of entertainment. The leaders with these skills are drawn from another tiny pool: the media celebrities.

While both ideologues and populists thrive on the anxieties and anger generated by the new rifts, they are incapable of addressing them. These rifts are not repeats of the past; they are complex new phenomena. But in the process of implementing their passionate snake-oil 'cures', such politicians are capable of doing enormous damage. There *are* viable remedies to the damaging processes underway in our societies, but they derive neither from the moral passion of an ideology nor the casual leap of populism. They are built upon analysis and evidence, and so require the cool head of pragmatism. All the policies proposed in this book are pragmatic.

Yet there is a place for passion, and it suffuses the book. My own life has straddled each of the three grim rifts that have opened in our societies. While I have maintained a cool head, they have seared my heart.

I have lived the new geographic divide between booming metropolis and broken provincial cities. My hometown of Sheffield became the emblematic broken city, the collapse of the steel industry immortalized in *The Full Monty*. I lived this tragedy: our neighbour became unemployed; a relative found a job cleaning toilets. Meanwhile, I had moved to Oxford, which became the location of choice for metropolitan success: my postcode now has the highest ratio of house prices to income in the entire country.

I have lived the divide in skill and morale between families of hyper-success and families disintegrating into poverty. Aged fourteen, my cousin and I were in tandem: born on the same day, the children of uneducated parents who had won places in grammar schools. Her life was derailed by the early death of her father; shorn of that authority figure, she became a teenage mother, with its attendant failings and humiliations. Meanwhile, my life progressed through the stepping-stones of transformation, from school to a scholarship at Oxford.* From there, more steps led to chairs at Oxford, Harvard and Paris; lest this should not be enough for my self-esteem, a Labour government awarded me a CBE, a Conservative government a knighthood, and my colleagues in the British Academy awarded me its Presidential Medal. Once started, divergence has its own dynamic. By seventeen, the daughters of my cousin were themselves teenage mothers. My seventeen-year-old has a scholarship at one of the finest schools in the country.

Finally, I have lived the global divide between the rampaging prosperity of the USA, Britain and France, in each of which I have lived

---

* Like me, the famous British playwright Alan Bennett was the son of Yorkshire parents with little education. *The History Boys* recounts his story, so similar to mine, of social mobility from humble origins to Oxford. But he grew up in more fashionable Leeds. In order to emphasize the social gulf that he had crossed, he set his play not in *his* home town, but in *mine*. The first Act closes with the protagonist itemizing his disadvantages in a mounting crescendo: 'I'm short; I'm gay; and I'm from Sheffield!' He isn't, but I am. Indeed, Bennett set the play in my school: I am more authentically a 'History Boy' than Bennett himself.

in comfort, and the despairing poverty of Africa, where I work. My students, mostly African, face this stark contrast in making their life choices after graduation. Currently, a Sudanese student, a doctor who has been working in Britain, is facing the choice of whether to stay in Britain or return to Sudan to work in the office of the prime minister. He has decided to go back: he is exceptional, there are more Sudanese doctors in London than in the Sudan.

These three appalling cleavages are not just problems that I study: they are the tragedies that have come to define my sense of purpose in life. This is why I have written this book: I want to change this situation.

THE TRIUMPH AND CORROSION OF SOCIAL DEMOCRACY

Sheffield is an unfashionable city, but that only strengthens its people's bonds, and those bonds were once a powerful political force. The cities of northern England pioneered the industrial revolution, and their people were the first to face the new anxieties that it brought. Through recognizing that they had a common attachment to the place where they grew up, communities such as Sheffield's built co-operative organizations that addressed these anxieties. By putting affinity to use, they built organizations that reaped the benefits of reciprocity. Co-operative building societies enabled people to save for a home; another Yorkshire town, Halifax, gave birth to what became the largest bank in Britain. Co-operative insurance societies enabled people to reduce risks. Co-operative agribusiness and retailing gave farmers and consumers bargaining power against big business. From its crucible in northern England, the co-operative movement rapidly spread across much of Europe.

By banding together, these co-operatives became the foundation of the political parties of the centre-left: the parties of social democracy. The benefits of reciprocity within a community were scaled up as the community became the nation. Like the co-operatives, the new policy agenda was practical, rooted in the anxieties that beset the lives of ordinary families. In the post-war era, across Europe many of these social democrat parties came to power and used it to implement a range of pragmatic policies that effectively addressed these anxieties. Health care, pensions, education, unemployment insurance cascaded from legislation into changed lives. These policies proved to be so valuable that they became accepted across the central range of the political spectrum. Political parties of the centre-left and centre-right alternated in power, but the policies remained in place.

Yet, social democracy as a political force is now in existential crisis. The last decade has been a roll-call of disasters. On the centre-left, mauled by Bernie Sanders, Hillary Clinton lost against Donald Trump; the Blair–Brown British Labour Party has been taken over by the Marxists. In France, President Hollande decided not even to seek a second term, and his replacement as the Socialist Party candidate, Benoît Hamon, crashed out with merely 8 per cent of the vote. The Social Democrat parties of Germany, Italy, the Netherlands, Norway and Spain have all seen their vote collapse. This would normally have been good news for the politicians of the centre-right, yet in Britain and America they too have lost control of their parties, while in Germany and France their electoral support has collapsed. Why has this happened?

The reason is because the social democrats of the left and right each drifted away from their origins in the practical reciprocity of communities, and became captured by an entirely different group of people who became disproportionately influential: middle-class intellectuals.

The intellectuals of the left were attracted by the ideas of a nineteenth-century philosopher, Jeremy Bentham. His philosophy, Utilitarianism, detached morality from our instinctive values, deducing it from a single principle of reason: an action should be judged as moral according to whether it promoted 'the greatest happiness of the greatest number'. Because people's instinctive values fell short of this saintly standard, society would need a vanguard of morally sound technocrats who would run the state. This vanguard, the paternalistic guardians of society, were an updated version of the Guardians of Plato's *Republic*. John Stuart Mill, brought up as Bentham's disciple – and the other intellectual who built Utilitarianism – was reading *The Republic* in the original Greek by the age of eight.

Unfortunately, Bentham and Mill were not latter-day moral giants, equivalent to Moses, Jesus and Muhammad; they were weirdly asocial individuals. Bentham was so bizarre that he is now thought to have been autistic, and incapable of having a sense of community. Mill stood little chance of normality: deliberately kept away from other children, he was probably more familiar with ancient Greece that with his own society. Given such origins, it is unsurprising that the ethics of their followers are highly divergent from the rest of us.[5]

The weird values of Bentham would not have had any impact had they not been incorporated into economics. As we will see, economics developed an account of human behaviour as far from Utilitarian morality as it is possible to get. *Economic man* is utterly selfish and infinitely greedy, caring about nobody but himself. He became the bedrock of the economic theory of human behaviour. But for the purpose of evaluating public policy, economics needed a measure for aggregating the well-being, or 'utility', of each of these psychopathic individuals. Utilitarianism became the intellectual underpinning for this arithmetic: 'the greatest happiness of the greatest number' fortuitously lent itself to standard mathematical techniques of maximization. 'Utility' was assumed to result from consumption, with extra consumption generating ever smaller increments to utility. Were the total amount of consumption in society fixed, the maximization of utility would be a simple matter of redistributing income so that consumption was perfectly equal. Social-democrat economists recognized that the consumption 'pie' was not a fixed size and, since taxation would discourage work, the pie would shrink. Advanced theories of 'optimal taxation', and 'the principal–agent problem' were developed to address the incentive problem. In essence, social-democratic public policies became increasingly sophisticated ways of using taxation to redistribute consumption while minimizing disincentives to work.

It was soon proved that there was no mechanical way of moving from individual 'utilities' to statements about the well-being of society that met even basic rules of intellectual coherence. The profession nodded, yet carried on doing it. Most academic philosophers abandoned Utilitarianism as being riddled with inadequacies: economists looked the other way. Utilitarianism was turning out to be amazingly convenient. In fairness, for many questions of public policy it is indeed good enough; whether the deficiencies are devastating depends on the policy. For modest questions, such as 'should a road be built here?' it is sometimes the best technique available. But for many larger issues it is hopelessly inappropriate.

Armed with its Utilitarian calculus, economics rapidly infiltrated public policy. Plato had envisaged his Guardians as philosophers, but in practice they were usually economists. Their presumption that people were psychopaths justified empowering themselves as a morally superior vanguard; and the presumption that the purpose of the state was to maximize utility justified redistributing consumption to whoever had the greatest 'needs'. Inadvertently, and usually imperceptibly, social-democratic policies changed from being about building the reciprocal obligations of all citizens.

In combination, the result was toxic. All moral obligations floated up to the state, responsibility being exercised by the morally reliable vanguard. Citizens ceased to be moral actors with responsibilities, and were instead reduced to their role as consumers. The social planner and his Utilitarian vanguard of angels knew best: communitarianism was replaced by social paternalism.

The emblematic illustration of this confident paternalism was post-war policy for cities. The growing number of cars needed flyovers and the growing number of people needed housing. In response, entire streets and neighbourhoods were bulldozed, to be replaced by modernist flyovers and high-rise towers. Yet to the bewilderment of the Utilitarian vanguard, what followed was a backlash. Bulldozing communities made sense if all that mattered was to raise the material housing standards of poor individuals. But it jeopardized the communities that actually gave meaning to people's lives.

Recent research in social psychology has enabled us to understand this backlash better. In a brilliant book, Jonathan Haidt has measured fundamental values around the world. He finds that almost all of us cherish six of them: loyalty, fairness, liberty, hierarchy, care and sanctity.[6] The reciprocal obligations built by the co-operative movement had drawn on the values of loyalty and fairness. The paternalism of the Utilitarian vanguard exemplified in bulldozing communities breached both of these values and liberty – while recent research in neuroscience-enhanced social psychology has found that the modernist designs beloved of the planners reduced well-being by breaching common aesthetic values. Why did the vanguard fail to recognize these moral weaknesses in what they were doing? Again, Haidt has the answer: their values were atypical. In place of the six values held by most people, the vanguard had shrivelled its values down to just two: care and equality. Not only were its values a-typical, but so were its characteristics: Western, Educated, Industrial, Rich and Developed – or WEIRD, for short. Care and equality are the Utilitarian values: the WEIRD followers of the weird. At its best, education widens our empathy, enabling us to put ourselves in the place of others.* But in practice it often does the opposite, distancing the successful from the anxieties of ordinary communities. Armed with the confidence of meritocratic superiority, the vanguard readily saw themselves as the new Platonic Guardians, entitled to override the values of others. I suspect that had Haidt probed further, he would have found that, while the WEIRD were ostentatiously dismissive of hierarchy, what they meant by it were those hierarchies inherited from the past. They took for granted a new hierarchy: they formed the new meritocracy.

The backlash against paternalism grew during the 1970s. Potentially, it could have attacked the disdain for loyalty and fairness and restored communitarianism, but instead, the vanguard attacked the disdain for liberty, and demanded that individuals be protected from the infringements of the state by reclaiming their *natural rights*. Bentham had dismissed the notion of natural rights as 'nonsense on stilts', and in this I think he was correct. But politicians struggling to win elections began to find proclamations of new rights convenient. Rights sounded more principled than mere promises of extra spending, and, whereas specific promises could be questioned on the basis of cost and tax, rights kept the obligations needed to meet them

---

* Pinker (2011) has a brilliant account of how the spread of mass literacy in the mid-nineteenth century created a mass market in novels. By reading novels people learned to see a situation from the perspective of someone else – a training in empathy, and Pinker explains the demise in the previously popular spectacle of public hangings as a consequence.

discretely offstage. The co-operative movement had linked rights firmly to obligations; the Utilitarians had detached both from individuals, shifting them to the state. Now, the Libertarians restored the rights to individuals, but not the obligations.

This impetus to rights for individuals allied with a new political movement that also claimed rights: the rights of disadvantaged *groups*. Pioneered by African Americans, it was emulated by feminists. They too found their philosopher – John Rawls – who countered Bentham's critique of natural rights with a different overarching principle of reason: a society should be judged moral according to whether its laws were designed for the benefit of the most disadvantaged groups. The essential purpose of these movements was inclusion in society on an equal basis with others, and both African Americans and women had an overwhelming case for profound social change. As we will see, social patterns can be stubbornly persistent, and so equal inclusion was inevitably going to require a transitional phase of struggle against discrimination. Half a century later we are still in that transition, but in the process what began as movements for inclusion have hardened, perhaps inadvertently, into group identities that have become oppositional: struggle is invigorated by envisioning an enemy group.* The language of rights proliferated, encompassing those of the individual against the paternalist state; those of voters periodically sprayed with entitlements by politicians; and those of new victim groups seeking privileged treatment. These three sets of rights had little in common, but each was antipathetic to the inclusive matching of rights to obligations achieved by social democracy while it had adhered to its communitarian roots.

The Utilitarian cause was promoted by economists; the rights cause was promoted by lawyers. On some issues the two vanguards agreed, making them extremely powerful lobbies. On others, they clashed: Rawls and his followers accepted that some of the rights that would empower small but disadvantaged groups would make everyone else worse off and so fail on the Utilitarian criterion. In the contest between economic technocrats and lawyers, the balance of power initially lay with the economists: the promise of delivering 'the

---

* This being the common political strategy of fascism and Marxism.

greatest well-being to the greatest numbers' appealed to vote-seeking politicians. But gradually the balance of power shifted to the lawyers, wielding the nuclear weapon of the courts.

While the two ideologies became increasingly divergent, neither had much room for the ideas that had guided the co-operative movement. Utilitarians, Rawlsians and Libertarians all emphasized the individual, not the collective, and Utilitarian economists and Rawlsian lawyers both emphasized differences between groups, the former based on income, the latter on disadvantage. Both influenced social-democratic policies. Utilitarian economists demanded redistribution guided by need; gradually, welfare benefits were redesigned so that entitlement was unlinked from contributions, dismissing the normal human value of fairness. Those who had not contributed were being privileged over those who had. Rawlsian lawyers demanded redress guided by disadvantage. For example, the rights of refugees became the top priority for Germany's Social Democrats in the 2018 coalition negotiations. Martin Schultz, the party's leader, insisted that 'Germany must comply with international law, regardless of the mood in the country'.[7] That 'regardless of the mood in the country' was a classic expression of the moral vanguard; both Bentham and Rawls would have cheered Schultz on, but within a month he was ousted by a popular mutiny. Both ideologies dismiss the normal moral instincts of reciprocity and desert, elevating a single principle of reason (albeit different ones) to be imposed by a vanguard of the cognoscenti. In contrast, the co-operative movement was grounded in those normal moral instincts: a philosophical tradition going back to David Hume and Adam Smith. Indeed, Jonathan Haidt is explicit about this debt in seeing his own work as 'a first step in resuming Hume's project'.

While the intellectuals of the left were abandoning practical communitarian social democracy in favour of Utilitarian and Rawlsian ideologies, the parties of the centre-right either ossified into an ideas-light zone of nostalgia, or got captured by an equally misguided group of intellectuals. The Christian Democrats of continental Europe, exemplified by Silvio Berlusconi, Jacques Chirac and Angela Merkel, mostly took the path of nostalgia; the Conservative and Republican parties of the Anglophone world chose ideology. The philosophy of Rawls was countered by that of Robert Nozick:

individuals had rights to freedom which overrode the interests of the collective. This idea allied naturally with new economic analysis led by the Nobel Laureate Milton Friedman, that the freedom to pursue self-interest, constrained only by competition, produced superior results to what could be achieved through public regulation and planning, and formed the intellectual foundations of the policy revolutions of Ronald Reagan and Margaret Thatcher. While the new ideologies of left and right presented themselves as being diametrically opposed to each other, they had in common an emphasis upon the individual, and a fondness for meritocracy: the morally meritocratic elite of the left vied with the productively meritocratic elite of the right. The superstars of the left became the very good; those of the right, became the very rich.*

So, what had been so wrong with social democracy that both left and right abandoned it? In its heyday of the 1950s and 1960s nothing much was wrong with it. But although social democracy has been the dominant intellectual force in public policy, it was a creature of its time. Far from encapsulating universal truths – the hallmark claim of all ideologies – it was built on distinctive circumstances, and valid only conditional upon those circumstances. As circumstances have changed, its pretensions to universalism have been shattered. By the late 1970s, the time that the USA and Britain were as equal as they have ever been, the conditions for it were already crumbling; the mass revolt that swept Reagan and Thatcher into power was well underway. Social democracy worked from 1945 until the 1970s because it lived off a huge, invisible and unquantifiable asset that had been accumulated during the Second World War: a shared identity forged through a supreme and successful national effort. As that asset eroded, the power wielded by the paternalistic state became increasingly resented.

Just as its social underpinnings were undermined, so were social democracy's intellectual underpinnings. The omniscient Platonic Guardian social planner was mocked into oblivion with the rise of the new field of Public Choice Theory. This recognized that decisions

---

* Correspondingly, the anomalous individuals who were both very good and very rich, such as my old friend George Soros, became super-villains, distrusted by both sides.

on public policies are not usually taken by detached saints, but by balancing pressures from different interest groups, including the bureaucrats themselves. The selflessness of the planner could only be relied upon while the people involved in the decision were imbued with a passion for the national interest, as instilled into the wartime generation. Within philosophy, Utilitarianism still has pockets of adherents, but the withering critiques have accumulated.[8] They have been reinforced by the critiques of social psychologists like Haidt, revealing its values to be far from universal truths. The vast majority of mankind are not the selfish oafs depicted in Utilitarian economics, but people who value not only care, but fairness, loyalty, liberty, sanctity and hierarchy. They are not more *selfish* than the social democratic vanguard; they are more *rounded*.

As the new libertarianism of the right proved to be both more destructive and less efficient than expected, the left returned to power, but not to communitarianism. Instead, it was now controlled by the new ideologues. The new vanguard had probably supplanted the communitarians without even noticing that they had done so. But ordinary families noticed, not least because, divorced from communities, some of the policies favoured by the vanguard were damaging and unpopular. They ran the state from the metropolis, which was thriving, and targeted assistance on those groups judged to be most in need: the 'victims'. The new anxieties were hitting people who often did not tick sufficient of these boxes, despite the fact that their circumstances were deteriorating both absolutely and relative to the more fashionable 'victim' groups. A corollary of 'victim' status was that those included in it could not be held in any way responsible for their circumstances. Even when the working class ticked some of the victim characteristics, it merely entitled them to some extra consumption: that was the focus of Utilitarian redistribution. Concepts such as belonging, desert, dignity and the respect that comes from meeting obligations are so alien that they have been entirely absent from professional discourse. But, usually, victim status was withheld from the white working class: here is the impeccably WEIRD *National Review*, commenting on their falling life expectancy: 'they *deserve* to die'.[9] Evidently, although all victims are equal, some are more equal than others.

We are living a tragedy. My generation experienced the triumphant achievements of capitalism harnessed to communitarian social democracy. The new vanguard usurped social democracy, bringing their own ethics and their own priorities. As the destructive side effects of new economic forces hit our societies, the inadequacies of these new ethics have been brutally revealed. The current failures of capitalism, as managed by the new ideologies, are as manifest as were the successes of what they replaced. It is time to turn from what has gone wrong, to how it can be put right.

PUTTING IT RIGHT

Our politicians, newspapers, magazines and bookshops abound with smart-sounding proposals: we should retrain workers; we should help struggling families; we should raise taxes on the rich. Many of them are right in spirit, but address only one aspect of the new anxieties; they do not provide a coherent response to what has befallen our societies. They arc seldom developed into implementable strategies supported by evidence of their efficacy. Nor, other than those of the ideologues, are they explicitly grounded in an ethical framework. I have tried to do better. I have tried to combine a coherent critique of what has gone wrong with practical ways of healing the three divides that have riven our societies.

Social democracy needs an intellectual reset, bringing it back from existential crisis to something that can again be the philosophy across the centre of the political spectrum, embraced by both the centre-left and the centre-right. My inspiration for such a grandiose-sounding project is that over sixty years ago one hugely influential book did precisely that. *The Future of Socialism*, by Anthony Crosland, gave intellectual coherence to social democracy in its heyday. It decisively parted company with Marxist ideology by recognizing that, far from being the barrier to mass prosperity, capitalism was essential for it. Capitalism spawns and disciplines firms, organizations that enable people to harness the productivity potential of scale and specialization. Marx thought that this would cause alienation: working for capitalists in large firms would inevitably separate enjoyment from labour, while specialization 'chained [man] down to a little fragment of the whole'. Ironically, the consequences of alienation were most devastatingly revealed by industrial socialism: the culture summarized as 'they pretend to pay us, and we pretend to work'. Alienation is not the price society must pay in order to be prosperous; accepting capitalism is not doing a deal with the devil. Many good modern firms give workers a sense of purpose, and sufficient autonomy to take responsibility for fulfilling it. Their workers get satisfaction from what they do, not just from what they earn. Many other firms are not like this, and many people are stuck in unproductive and demotivating jobs. If capitalism is to work for everyone it needs to be managed so as to deliver purpose as well as productivity. But that is the agenda: capitalism needs to be managed, not defeated.

Crosland was a pragmatist; a policy was to be judged by whether it worked, not by whether it conformed to the tenets of an ideology. A core proposition of pragmatist philosophy is that, because societies change, we should not expect eternal truths. *The Future of Socialism* is not a bible for the future, it was a strategy fitted for its era. While being healthily suspicious of the arrogant paternalism of the vanguard, its view of well-being was as reductionist – equalized individual consumption. *The Future of Capitalism* is not a remake of *The Future of Socialism*. It is an attempt to provide a coherent package of remedies that address our new anxieties.

Academia has become increasingly compartmentalized into silos of specialism. This yields advantages in depth of knowledge, but the present task spans several of these silos. This book has only been possible because I have learned from collaborations with an exceptionally wide range of specialists of world-renown. The new social divergence is partly driven by changes in social identities; from George Akerlof, I have learned the new psycho-economics of how people behave in groups. It is partly driven by globalization gone wrong; from Tony Venables, I have learned the new economic dynamics of metropolitan agglomeration and why provincial cities can implode. It is partly driven by the deteriorating behaviour of firms; from Colin Mayer, I have learned what can be done about this loss of purpose. Most fundamentally, it is driven by the Utilitarian takeover of public policy; from Tim Besley, I have learned a new fusion of moral theory and political economy, and from Chris Hook-way, I have learned the philosophical origins of pragmatism.

While I have tried to integrate the insights of these intellectual giants as the basis for practical remedies, none can be held respons-ible for the result.[10] Critics will read the book searching for things to challenge, and will surely find them. But the book is a serious attempt to apply new currents in academic analysis to the new anxieties that have beset our societies. I hope that, as with *The Future of Socialism*, it can provide a basis on which the beleaguered centre of the political spectrum can rebuild.

Capitalist societies must be ethical as well as prosperous. In the next chapter I challenge the depiction of humanity as *economic man*: greedy and selfish. Shamefully, there is now indisputable evidence that students taught economics actually start to conform to this behaviour, but it is aberrant. For most of us, relationships are fundamental to our lives, and these relationships come with obligations. Crucially, people enter into reciprocal commitments, the essence of community. The battle between selfishness and reciprocal obligations – between in-dividualism and community – plays out in three arenas that dominate our lives: states, firms and families. In recent decades, in each, in-dividualism has been rampant and community in retreat. For each, I suggest how the ethics of community could be restored and enhanced by policies that rebalance power.

On the bedrock of this practical communitarian ethic, I turn to the divergences that have been ripping our societies apart. The new geo-graphic divide, between booming metropolis and broken provincial cities, can be tamed but it requires radical new thinking. The metrop-olis generates huge economic rents which should accrue to society, but to do so requires a substantial redesign of taxation. Restoring broken cities is feasible, but the record is poor. Neither the market nor public interventions have been very effective. Success requires that a range of innovative policies be co-ordinated and sustained.

The new class divide between the prospering educated and the despairing less educated can also be narrowed. But no single policy can transform despair: contrary to the Utilitarian fixation with con-sumption, the nature of the problem is far too deep to be solved by increasing consumption through higher benefits. Even more than with broken cities, a wide range of policies will be needed to change life-chances, not just for individuals but for their relationships. Its social interventions would aim to sustain families that are stressed, rather than assuming for itself the role of parent. Some of the problems of despair have been compounded by the self-aggrandizing strategies of those who are well educated and highly skilled. There is some scope for curtailing the most damaging; again, it is not just that consumption is excessive and needs to be curbed by taxation.

As to the global divide, the confident paternalist vanguard has been cavalier about globalization, seduced into anticipating a post-national future. Yet, individually rational private responses to global opportunities are not inevitably socially beneficial. For economists, well-founded opposition to high trade barriers elided into unqualified enthusiasm for liberalization. Trade does usually benefit each country sufficiently that whoever gets the gains *could* fully compensate those who lose out. But while economists were vociferous advocates of trade, they kept very quiet about compensation. Without it, there is no analytic basis for claims that society is better off. Analogously, well-founded insistence on the rights of racial minorities elided into the unqualified espousal of immigration. Yet despite the shared label of globalization, trade and migration are very different economic processes, one driven by *comparative* advantage, the other by *absolute* advantage. There is no analytic presumption that migration produces gains either for the societies that migrants join, or for those they leave; the only unambiguous gains are for the migrants themselves.

A MANIFESTO

Capitalism has achieved a lot and it is essential for prosperity, but it is not the economics of Dr Pangloss. None of the three new social cleavages can be healed by relying only on market pressures and individual self-interest: 'cheer up and enjoy the ride' is not only tone-deaf, it is too complacent. We need active public policy, but social paternalism has repeatedly failed. The left assumed that the state knew best, but unfortunately it didn't. The vanguard-guided state was assumed to be the only entity guided by ethics: this wildly exaggerated the ethical capacities of the state, and correspondingly dismissed those of families and firms. The right put its faith in the belief that breaking the chains of state regulation – the libertarian mantra – would unleash the power of self-interest to enrich everyone. This wildly exaggerated the magic of the market, and correspondingly dismissed ethical restraints. We need an active state, but we need one that accepts a more modest role; we need the market, but harnessed by a sense of purpose securely grounded in ethics.

For want of a better term, I think of the policies I propose to heal these cleavages as *social maternalism*. The state would be active in both the economic and social spheres, but it would not overtly empower itself. Its tax policies would restrain the powerful from appropriating gains that they do not deserve, but not gleefully strip income from the rich to hand to the poor. Its regulations would empower those who suffer from the 'creative destruction' by which competition drives economic progress to claim compensation, rather than attempting to frustrate the very process that gives capitalism its astonishing dynamic.* Its patriotism would be a force for binding together, replacing the emphasis on the fragmented identities of grievances. The philosophical bedrock of this agenda is a rejection of ideology. By this I do not mean to imply a ragbag of ideas thrown together, but rather a willingness to accept our diverse and instinctive moral values, and the pragmatic trade-offs implied by that diversity. The device of overriding values by resort to some single absolute principle of reason is doomed to be divisive. Accepting our diverse values is grounded in the philosophy of David Hume and Adam Smith. The policies in this book cut across the left–right spectrum that characterized the previous century at its worst, and is returning with a vengeance.†

---

* 'Creative destruction' is the process by which efficient firms drive out less efficient through competition in the market. It accounts for much of the gradual increase in average incomes. The term was coined by Joseph Schumpeter (1942), who described it as 'the essential fact about capitalism'. It is why all the other 'isms', however romantically appealing, are at best irrelevant. The future of our societies will depend upon reforming capitalism, not overthrowing it.
† The building blocks – pragmatism, prosperity, community, ethics and social psychology – all cohere. This is because they all go back to David Hume and his

The twentieth century's catastrophes were wrought by political leaders who either passionately espoused an ideology – the men of principle – or who peddled populism – the men of charisma (and yes, they were usually men). In contrast to these ideologues and populists, the most successful leaders of the century were pragmatists. Taking on a society mired in corruption and poverty, Lee Kwan Yew tackled corruption head on and turned Singapore into the most successful society of the twenty-first century. Taking on a country so divided that it was on the point of secession, Pierre Trudeau defused Québécois separatism and built a nation proud of itself. From the rubble of genocide, Paul Kagame rebuilt Rwanda into a well-functioning society. In *The Fix*, Jonathan Tepperman studied ten such leaders, searching for the formula by which they each remedied serious problems. He concludes that what they had in common was that they eschewed ideology; instead, they focused on pragmatic solutions to core problems, adjusting to situations as they went along.[11] They were prepared to be tough when necessary: their willingness to deny patronage to powerful groups was a hallmark of success. Lee Kwan Yew was prepared to gaol his friends; Trudeau denied his fellow Québécois the separate status they craved; Kagame denied his Tutsi team the customary spoils of military victory. Before their eventual success, they all faced intense criticism.

The pragmatism of this book is firmly and consistently grounded in moral values. But it eschews ideology and so is guaranteed to offend the ideologues of every persuasion. They are the people who currently dominate the media. An identity of being 'on the left' has become a lazy way of feeling morally superior; an identity of being 'on the right' has become a lazy way of feeling 'realistic'. You are about to explore the future of an ethical capitalism: welcome to the hard centre.

---

friend Adam Smith. As Smith's biographer Jesse Norman (2018) says, he was a pragmatist. Conversely, the origins of pragmatism are to be found in Smith: 'The implications of his Newtonian philosophy of science receives its greatest modern exploration in the work of Peirce,' the founder of pragmatism. The ethics of Smith and Hume was explicitly communitarian: as Norman is careful to make clear, they were not proto-Utilitarians.

PART TWO
Restoring Ethics

2

The Foundations of Morality: From the Selfish Gene to the Ethical Group

Modern capitalism has the potential to lift us all to unprecedented prosperity, but it is morally bankrupt and on track for tragedy. Human beings need a sense of purpose, and capitalism is not providing it. Yet it could. The proper purpose of modern capitalism is to enable mass prosperity. Perhaps because I was born poor and work with poor societies, I know that this is a worthwhile goal. But it is not sufficient. In a successful society people *flourish*, combining prosperity with a sense of belonging and esteem. Prosperity can be measured by income, and its antithesis is despairing poverty; flourishing is currently best approximated by well-being, and its antithesis adds isolation and humiliation.

As an economist, I have learned that decentralized, market-based competition – the vital core of capitalism – is the only way to deliver prosperity, but what are the founts of the other aspects of well-being? Whereas *economic man* is presumed to be lazy, purposive action such as work is important for esteem.* And whereas *economic man* is self-regarding, belonging depends upon mutual regard. A moral capitalism that supports esteem and belonging, alongside prosperity, is not an oxymoron. Understandably, however, many people think that it is; they judge capitalism to be fatally tainted by relying on the single drive of greed.

---

* Currently, the best practical measurement of well-being is by means of a ten-step scale depicting a 'ladder of life', from worst- to best-imagined circumstances. This turns out to be a more stable measure than direct questions about happiness, which are influenced by the mood of the moment. Results for the ladder of life are reported in the *World Happiness Report, 2017*.

Confronted by this criticism, supporters of capitalism often parrot the Marxist doctrine that 'the end justifies the means'. This is a fundamental mistake; a capitalism driven only by greed would malfunction just as badly as Marxism, generating humiliation and division but not mass prosperity. Indeed, capitalism is currently taking societies down that path. This book sets out an alternative in which the means are infused with moral purpose. That reset will take more than warm-hearted slogans crafted by the PR departments of corporations, or Davos man.

Part Two of this book sets out the ethical foundations upon which these solutions rest; while Part Three is about practical solutions to our widening social divisions. This chapter explores how our morals are linked to our emotions, how they evolve, and how things can go wrong.[1]

WANTS AND 'OUGHTS'

The glib supporters of capitalism who argue that the end justifies the means invoke Adam Smith's famous proposition in *The Wealth of Nations* that the pursuit of self-interest leads to the common good. 'Greed is good' became the intellectual underpinning for the zeal of the Reagan–Thatcher revolution. Smith's proposition is a valuable corrective to the naïve notion that an action is good only if well-motivated. But modern economics, which *The Wealth of Nations* launched in 1776, is built on a character who is utterly despicable. *Economic man* is selfish, greedy and lazy. Such people do exist and you will meet some of them. But even billionaires do not live that way: the ones I know are driven workaholics who have built their lives around some purpose much larger than their own consumption. Many economists are ready to admit these limitations, but protestations of innocence hit brutal facts: students of economics become distinctively selfish,[2] and the malign assumptions of the models we use to guide policy set the parameters for serious discussion.*

Yet Smith did *not* think that we are *economic man*.[3] He regarded the butcher and the baker not just as individuals pursuing their

---

* An example is the introduction of the bonus culture into public service.

self-interest, but as morally motivated people in a society. A computer predicts the behaviour of *economic man* from the axioms of rational self-interest. But we predict the actions of the butcher and the baker by putting ourselves in their shoes; it is known as the 'theory of mind'. Smith recognized that seeing a person from the inside not only enables us to understand them, but induces us to care about them and assess their moral character. These emotions of empathy and judgement he saw as the foundation of morality, driving a wedge between what we *want* to do, and what we feel we *ought* to do. Morality stems from our sentiments, not our reason. He set this out in *The Theory of Moral Sentiments* (1759). In it, we can find three distinct intensities of obligation.

The strongest obligations come from intimacy. They are most far-reaching and unconditional for our children and close kin, but spread around those we know. The weakest obligation is towards distant people in distress. In a famous passage, Smith uses the example of an earthquake in China: it would not be sufficiently emotionally upsetting to prevent an eighteenth-century Englishman enjoying his dinner. Despite social media and NGOs, the same is true of a twenty-first-century clubber going out for the evening. In *Refuge*, a book about the refugee crisis, Alex Betts and I invoked this obligation, calling it a *duty of rescue*. Smith related it to a sense of *impartiality*: we know, objectively, that in situations such as that earthquake we ought to help. In *The Bottom Billion* I invoked a different duty of rescue. A billion people face despairing poverty. You do not need to be a saint to recognize that we should do what we can to bring hope.

Between intimacy and duties of rescue are the emotions that Smith made the focus of his book: the gentle pressures such as shame and esteem that enable us to exchange obligations – I'll help you, if you'll help me. The trust that makes that feasible is underpinned by the emotions that discourage breaches. Why do people feel such sentiments – they are not part of the psychology of *economic man?* The answer, supported by evidence such as our regrets, is that people are better described by the term *social man. Social man* cares about what others think of him: he wants esteem. *Social man* is still rational – he maximizes utility – but he gets utility not just from his own consumption, but from esteem. Like greed and belonging, it is a basic drive.

The Nobel Laureate Vernon Smith saw that *The Wealth of Nations* and *The Theory of Moral Sentiments* are built on a common idea: the mutual benefit from exchange. The arena for exchanging commodities is the market. The arena for exchanging obligations is the networked group, the subject of this chapter. For two centuries, economists thought that Adam Smith had written two incompatible books and ignored *The Theory of Moral Sentiments*. Only recently has he been properly understood: there are not two Smiths but one, and his neglected ideas are profoundly important.[4]

People are motivated partly by the 'wants' of *The Wealth of Nations*, and partly by the 'oughts' of *The Theory of Moral Sentiments*. For each, Smith saw that the change from self-sufficiency to exchange was transformative, but his own assessment seems to have been that *The Theory of Moral Sentiments* was the more important, as if the exchange of 'oughts', trumped the exchange of wants. Are the 'oughts' just mental chatter? Isn't behaviour shaped only by 'wants', or greed, as the textbooks and the critics of capitalism, imply?

Social science now has evidence as to their relative psychological importance, and behavioural experiments find that 'oughts' matter as well as wants. Here is some ingeniously simple new evidence as to which is more important. People were asked to recall and rank those past decisions that they most *regret*. We all make mistakes, and the worst mistakes rankle; the responses were grouped into categories. We know what *economic man* would most regret: 'if only I had bought that house'; 'if only I hadn't messed up that interview'; 'if only I had bought shares in Apple'. Our regrets would be our failures to fulfil our 'wants'. Yet they barely register in this study. People make plenty of such mistakes, but they seldom dwell on them. The regrets that fester are overwhelmingly about failures to meet 'oughts', when we have let someone down, breaching an obligation.[5] We learn from such regrets to keep our obligations. Although our decisions are biased towards momentary folly, when we consider our actions 'oughts' usually trump wants.

Social psychology has also vindicated Smith's proposition that morality derives from values, rather than reason.[6] Jonathan Haidt has found evidence for just this dominance. People try to justify their values by citing reasons for them, but if our reasons are demolished we conjure up others, rather than revise our values. Our reasons are revealed as a self-deceiving charade, a sham called *'motivated* rea-soning'.[7] Reasons are anchored on values, not values on reasons; or, as graphically put by Smith, 'reason is the slave of the passions'. It gets worse for *rational economic man*. In what is already recognized as a major advance, in *The Enigma of Reason* Hugo Mercier and Dan Sperber show that *reason itself* has evolved for the strategic pur-pose of persuading others, not to improve our own decision-taking.[8] Motivated reasoning is *why* we developed the capacity to reason, and *how* we normally use it. Yet more fundamentally, the massive brain expansion of the past two million years has been driven by the need for sociality.[9] Far from Smith's ideas looking quaint, they sketch the future direction for economics textbooks.

Often, values complement each other, generating further norms. Fairness and loyalty, two of the values Haidt found to be common, jointly support the norm of *reciprocity*, which is what links our fundamental drive for esteem to the shame and guilt we feel when we breach an obligation. Experiments have shown that reciprocity is the sweet-spot at which even demanding obligations are sustainable. While the value of care underpins the duty of rescue, if those in a position to help form a group, they can harness fairness and loyalty to build mutual commitments: 'I'll help, if you'll help'. Just as we learn to prioritize wants, so we prioritize values. Through practical reasoning we refine values that at first sight conflict, letting the context reveal the compromise.

This was the thinking of Smith and Hume. Building on it, the philosophy of Pragmatism advocated this intertwining of the common moral values with practical reasoning. In its origin it is communitar-ian, seeing the task of morality as doing our best to fit our actions to the values of our community and the specifics of context.* We should

---

* Here is one of its founders, William James: 'A social organism of any sort what-ever, large or small, is what it is because each member proceeds to his own duty with a trust that the other members will simultaneously do theirs. Whenever a desired result is achieved by this cooperation of many independent persons, its existence as a fact is a pure consequence of the precursive faith in one another of those immediately concerned. A government, an army, a commercial system, a ship, a college, an athletic team, all exist on this condition, without which not only is nothing achieved, but nothing is even attempted.' (James, 1896) This chapter shows how such trust is built.

use practical reasoning to deduce the right action; it rejects ideology, no one value is overarching, absolute and timeless. In real communities, the relative importance of values evolves; pragmatism asks 'What, here and now, is most likely to work?'

In contrast, ideologies each lay claim to supremacy, derived from reason, over those who disagree with them. The custodians of the supreme ideology are a vanguard of the cognoscenti. Religious fundamentalists invoke a unique divine being as the ultimate authority; Marxists invoke the dictatorship of the 'proletariat' guided by a hierarchy;[10] Utilitarians invoke the sum of individual utilities and Rawlsians invoke 'justice', as defined by themselves.[11] Just as Pragmatism stands in contrast to ideology, it also stands in opposition to populism. Ideology privileges some 'reason' over the rich array of human values; populism dismisses practical reasoning based on evidence, making brazen leaps from passions to policies. Our values, intertwined with practical reasoning, combine the heart and the head. Populism offers the headless heart; ideology offers the heartless head.

Pragmatism has its dangers. The freedom to deduce moral actions situation-by-situation has to be bounded by our inherent limitations. Reasoning takes effort, yet our will and capacities are limited. Worse, we are tempted to fit reasons to our values. Worst, our judgements are no better than our knowledge. Pragmatists admit these limitations: our individual moral judgements are fallible. All societies have developed ways of coping: we use rules of thumb, some of which get codified into institutions. At their best, institutions encapsulate the accumulated social learning from a range of experience too vast to be known by an individual. For many moral decisions, it may be best to be guided by them. Those political philosophers most sceptical of the capacity for individual practical reasoning favour the accumulated wisdom incorporated in institutions: this is *conservatism*.* Those least sceptical favour the freedom that it offers: this is *liberalism*.† Both concerns are well based: the answer is balance.

* Not to be confused with the eclectic moral abominations implied by those who use conservative as a term of abuse.
† Not to be confused with the eclectic moral abominations implied by those who use liberal as a term of abuse.

HOW RECIPROCITY EMERGES

Reciprocal obligations are decisive for well-being, but how do they come about? Any account has to be consistent with evolution, including the cravings and values that undergird reciprocity. It is easy to see why the competition for food would select those with a predisposition to greed, winnowing out the altruists. But why do we also crave belonging and esteem? Why do we value loyalty, fairness and care, or indeed have any values at all? Evolution has been a brutal process of selection by advantageous traits, so selfish materialism looks to be what you needed: you can't eat esteem and belonging, and values cramp your style. *Economic man* sounds superficially like an amplified echo of the *selfish gene*.

Yet we know that this is wrong: the selfish gene does not produce the selfish man. For many thousands of years, humans could only survive by co-operating in a group: going it alone spelled death. Lacking the craving for belonging and esteem, *economic man* was too selfish to be allowed to remain in the group; he was banished. Natural selection winnowed out *rational economic man* in favour of *rational social woman*: we are hardwired to crave belonging and esteem as well as food. But where did the common values come from?

Early man lived in groups; networks in which people could interact, spreading common behaviour through imitation. When *Homo sapiens* came along we also lived in groups, and also imitated each other. We still do. People will unknowingly influence the behaviour not just of their friends, but of *their* friends, and the friends of their friends.[12] But *Homo sapiens* developed a uniquely powerful vehicle for interaction: language. Why was language such a massive advantage? Because only language can convey narratives. As people talk to each other, the narratives that circulate convey a range of ideas. This is the fundamental activity that distinguishes humans from other species. Descartes' *cogito ergo sum* is back to front: we do not deduce our world from ourselves, we deduce ourselves from our world. The atoms of humanity are not reasoning individuals, but the relationships into which we are born. We can learn from the freakishly rare anomalies of 'babes in the wood' – children reared by wolves. Do they, as in the Romulus and Remus mythology, grow up to found Rome? Updated from Rome to the present, we might think of it as the logical endpoint of the Ayn Rand hypothesis: if only people could grow up freed of the shackles of society, they would become Atlas-like independent-minded innovators. In fact, they become tragic creatures, unrecognizable as human beings. One celebrated instance was a nine-year-old child found in a French forest in the eighteenth century. Despite intense coaching he never even learned to speak, let alone to function as a normal person. Today's equivalents are the Romanian babies raised in state hostels in the communist era.

Through repeated exposure to narratives, children rapidly develop a sense of belonging to a group and a place. We acquire this sense long before we develop the capacity to reason. Family identity is established in the early years, and even something as large as national identity is generally formed by the age of eleven, whereas the capacity to reason develops later, at around fourteen.[13] I think of myself as a Yorkshireman. I grew up with a thousand narratives of Yorkshire identity and this narration echoes down the generations: writing this reminds me that each night I read *Daft Yorkshire Fairy Tales* to Alex, my eleven-year-old, in dialect.

Sheep lack the capacity for complex language, yet they also develop an awareness of belonging to a group in a place. Once this has developed, the shepherd's job is much easier because they will not stray from the hillside to which they have become bonded, a process termed hefting. We know that, once a flock is hefted, the knowledge of belonging is passed from ewe to lamb. This happens far too quickly to be genetic, it is learned behaviour. But although the hefting of a flock is far too rapid to be genetic, it still takes many generations to establish. Why are sheep so slow? At this point I offer an explanation that draws on social science, not shepherds.* The sheep in a flock face a co-ordination problem. Sheep imitate other sheep, and so for the flock to stay on the hillside, they all need to understand not to wander off, and not to follow any that do. We know from modern experimental psychology that the key to solving a co-ordination problem is 'common knowledge'; that is, the move from all knowing the same

---

* I do not discount an alternative explanation that sheep are pretty stupid.

thing, to all knowing that we know it.[14] A group can generate common knowledge either by common observation (everyone watching the same thing at the same time), or by a common narrative. I speculate that it takes sheep hundreds of years to forge common knowledge because they can only use common observation and so face a chicken-and-egg problem. They need to observe that all other sheep choose to remain on the hillside, but until sheep have learned it, the behaviour will not be there to observe; sheep must wait for a rare chance configuration of behaviour to occur in order to learn it. *Homo sapiens* can build shared belonging far more swiftly by using language to circulate the narrative 'we belong here'.*

Narratives not only tell us about belonging, they tell us what we ought to do – they give us the norms of our group. We learn these as children, along with the incentive of esteem we get for complying with them. When we internalize these norms as our own values, by complying we also get self-respect. Breaching a norm costs esteem; as we saw, when people behave like that they come to regret it. Some of our values are pre-linguistic: a group does not need language to evolve the instinct that parents care for their children. But the reciprocal obligations over large groups require co-ordination sufficiently complex to need narratives, and hence language.†

Narratives have a third function: we learn how our world works through stories that link actions to outcomes. Our actions become *purposive*. Experiments show that we rely more on stories than on direct observation or tuition. By joining them up into a *causal chain*, actions that are not in our immediate self-interest may then look rational, creating *enlightened* self-interest. At its best, this expands our knowledge. At its worst, it creates a rupture between reality and what we believe – narratives as 'fake news'.[15] True or false, stories are

* Sheep can say 'baa', and many other animals are able to use rudimentary language, but only humans have mastered the complex grammar needed to craft narratives. See Feldman Barrett (2017), Chapter 5.
† For a while socio-biologists thought that natural selection among groups might itself lead to innate pro-social values such as reciprocity, but the weight of research now suggests that this cannot explain our pro-social values. Bees can do it with only sign language, but that is because they have a different mode of reproduction. See Martin (2018) for a clear recent discussion.

powerful. In their devastating analysis of the financial crisis, two Nobel Laureates, George Akerlof and Robert Shiller, conclude that 'stories no longer merely *explain* the facts, they *are* the facts'.[16] What is true of financial crises turns out also to apply to the outbreak of mass violence. New research finds that the best way of predicting such outbreaks is to monitor the narratives circulating in the media.[17]

The three types of narrative – belonging, obligation and causality – fit together to forge a web of reciprocal obligations. Our narratives of obligation instil fairness and loyalty to tell us why we ought to meet those that are reciprocal. Our narratives of shared belonging tell us who is taking part: reciprocal obligations apply only over a defined group of people who accept them. Our narratives of causality tell us why the action we are obliged to take is purposive. In combination, they are a *belief system*, changing our behaviour. Belief systems can turn the hell of anarchy into community; from 'nasty, brutish and short' into 'flourishing'. Narratives are unique to *Homo sapiens*: we are not just apes.

People in the same network will hear the same narratives, and have the common knowledge that they all have heard them. Within a network, specific narratives of belonging, obligation and causality will tend to fit harmoniously. Those that are potentially disruptive may be kept out of circulation by a taboo, or squeezed out by being discredited.[18] Ideas get shuffled around so that they reinforce each other. Together, they link a shared identity to a goal and a proposition of how to reach it. 'The faithful' seek 'paradise' by 'praying often'; or 'Oxford professors' aspire to 'be a great university' by 'paying attention to teaching'.[19]

Belief systems can have some horrible consequences that are most apparent in nationalism, something I will tackle in the next chapter. But they also have an invaluable upside: the move from the selfishness of *economic man* to the obligation-driven person who recognizes herself as part of a 'we', and a community in which people view each other not with fear or indifference, but with a presumption of mutual regard. A world filled only by *economic man* would not be the triumphantly functional paradise envisaged by simple economics textbooks, where selfishness is apparently all that is needed. Those textbooks presuppose a society in which rules have already been agreed and are respected. ECON 101 starts where SOC PSY 999 and POL SCI 999 finish. Economists are belatedly recognizing this: the pioneers have been George Akerlof and his co-author Rachel Kranton.[20] But as it catches up, economics also brings some useful insights.

One such recent insight, with huge implications, concerns the evolution of ethical norms. It comes from Tim Besley, who takes his inspiration from biology: norms, like genes, get transmitted from parents to children.[21] But the process looks very different. Tim starts from an imagined society in which some people hold one norm, and others a different one. When people choose marriage partners they tend to hook up with those who share their norms, but Cupid occasionally messes up and the children grow up with parents whose norms differ. Whose norms do they adopt? Tim postulates a simple process that is an instance of ideas being shuffled around so as to avoid the mental stress of an awkward fit: children will tend to pick up the ideas of the happier parent. As to which parent is the happier, in a political system in which the majority gets its way, it tends to be the one whose ideas are the more widespread.[22] From this, two remarkable punchlines follow.

In natural selection, if an island has white cliffs, the birds that live on it will evolve to become white, no matter what range of colours they have when they arrive from other islands. An organism evolves to fit a habitat. In contrast, *norms* can evolve to be very different even in two identical habitats, driven by small initial differences in their incidence. The environment is the population, and people evolve to fit each other.* Where a society starts determines where it ends up, with initial differences being amplified. This clearly corresponds with the reality we observe in the world: different societies have very different prevailing norms, each of which is persistent in its own society. But it is the second punchline that is the killer. In natural selection, the population ends up with those characteristics that are 'best fitted' to the habitat. Given the white cliffs, birds do better by being white. But with norms there is absolutely no such presumption. They can end up being awful for everyone, despite being good

---

* The nearest analogy in natural selection is the phenomenon of 'niche construction', as when beavers adapt their physical environment.

for each individual, given the norms held by everyone else. To see how bizarre this is relative to natural selection, it is equivalent to all birds evolving to be blue because most birds were initially blue, even though, against the white cliffs, they are all more easily eaten by predators.* In combination, the two punchlines imply that a network of people may well end up in some stable configuration of norms that is nevertheless dysfunctional. It is stable (i.e. it doesn't undergo further change) just because each person is trapped by the norms held by everyone else.

These results have a potent implication: conservative political philosophy cannot be entirely right. Conservative philosophers revere the accumulated institutions of a society as encapsulating the wisdom of experience. But the institutions may have formalized norms that are highly dysfunctional. But this does not license the rule of reason: motivated reasoning can lead to disaster.

THE STRATEGIC USE OF NORMS IN ORGANIZATIONS

For the past few thousand years, most of us have not lived in small bands of foragers. Modern life is only materially possible because people work together in large organizations where we can reap the efficiencies of scale and specialization.

Three types of organization dominate our lives, each best suited for a different range of activities. The smallest, yet most fundamental, is the family: 86 per cent of Europeans share a household with others, and families are the crucible for most children. Although families are the norm, some ideologies are hostile to them. The socialist kibbutzim completely abolished them; communist Romania similarly detached many thousands of children from their parents, rearing them collectively. Both Stalinist Marxism and the leaders of

---

* Sometimes – as in niche construction – the habitat also evolves to fit the characteristics. Blue birds do not paint cliffs blue, but beavers alter the flow of a stream. But the way humans adjust norms is not analogous to niche construction: the habitat is nothing more than the norms of others.

fundamentalist sects encourage children to denounce their parents. Nor, as we will see, is capitalism currently helping families: in swathes of society families are disintegrating. Yet families dominate child-rearing for good reason. Nowhere has any alternative way of raising children proved successful.

When people work, they are usually organized into firms: scale is essential for modern levels of productivity. In the USA 94 per cent of people work in a group, and in Britain 86 per cent.* As with families, some ideologies are hostile to companies. Old romantics advocate a return to a society of artisans, peasants and communes. New romantics hyperventilate about the new e-platforms such as Amazon, Airbnb, Uber, and eBay that enable people to transact with each other directly. But Amazon and Uber have themselves become huge employers. In African societies most people work solo, as artisans or smallholders. It has its virtues, but in consequence productivity is chronically low, and so people are achingly poor. We need modern firms, and so do Africans: Africa is not only the least prosperous region, it is the least happy region.[23]

At the grandest level, many activities, such as regulation, the provision of public goods and services, and the redistribution of income, are best organized by the state. Here the numbers are even more dramatic: *all* prosperous societies are organized into states, and *all* stateless societies are extremely impoverished.† Again, some ideologies are hostile to the state. Marxists, who in practice imposed the most state-centric organization of society ever attempted, have a very different ostensible goal: the state is supposed to 'wither away'. But the anti-state ideology currently most influential is that of the Libertarians of Silicon Valley. According to them, bitcoin will supplant the state provision of money as users walk away from official

---

* These figures are underestimates because many people who are self-employed (the residual category) actually work for a firm, self-employment being a legal device to reduce liabilities.

† A few societies have achieved happiness without prosperity, the most striking example being Bhutan. But Bhutan is decidedly not an example of a stateless society. Rather, it is an unusual instance of a state that has prioritized purpose and belonging over income, notably through its emphasis upon the preservation of national culture. Its people are the happiest in Asia.

currencies. The supermen who own the new e-utilities will each individually determine how best they are used, ignoring or defeating state-imposed regulation. Globally enabled person-to-person connectivity will supplant the spatially bounded society of the nation state. 'Governments of the Industrial World, you weary giants of flesh and steel, leave us alone.' Liberated from government, we will all blend into one gigantic whole: 'privacy is no longer a social norm'.[24] The outcome will be both morally and practically superior. Alas, I fear not.

The Silicon Valley titans who have connected the world imagine that in doing so they are ushering in a global society that unites around their own Libertarian values. This is highly unlikely. The new technologies of person-to-person connectivity are displacing the networked groups that were driven by the chance of shared location, whether a local community or a nation. Membership of the new e-networked groups is by choice not chance: people prefer to network with others who share their views within 'echo chambers'.[25] They embody the process by which narratives generate our beliefs, increasingly detached from sharing the place we live in. Yet our *political* units are still defined by where we live. Our votes are counted place-by-place, and the public services and policies arising from our politics are provided and applied place-by-place. So, due to digital connectivity, the same process that previously produced wide variations in norms *between* polities is now producing wide variations *within* them. The ideas within our polities are becoming more polarized; the disagreements are becoming nastier; the hatreds that in earlier centuries pitched polity against polity are now pitching belief system against belief system within each polity. Hatreds between polities turned into mass organized violence. Hatreds within polities will have different consequences, but they could be grim.

Families, firms and states are the essential arenas in which our lives are shaped. The quickest way of building them is as hierarchies in which those at the top issue commands to those lower down. While quick to build, they are seldom efficient to run: people only obey orders if commanders monitor what subordinates are doing. Gradually, many organizations learned that it was more effective to soften hierarchy, creating interdependent roles that had a clear sense of purpose, and giving people the autonomy and responsibility to perform them. The change from hierarchy run through power, to interdependence run through purpose, implies a corresponding change in leadership. Instead of being the commander-in-chief, the leader became the communicator-in-chief. Carrots and sticks evolved into narratives.

In modern families, the parents are equals, and coax children into responsibilities. In firms and governments, hierarchies have radically flattened; for example, the Bank of England used to have six different dining rooms, a degree of differentiation now inconceivable. Leadership has not been abolished, but its role has changed. There is a good reason for the retention of leadership – the utopian alternatives invariably fall apart.

The people at the top of organizations in families, firms and states are more powerful than those beneath them, but usually they have responsibilities that far exceed their powers. To meet their responsibilities, they need other people in the group to comply, but have only limited means of enforcement. In my role as father, I try to insist that Alex goes to sleep at night. But raw power is hard work and not very effective: Alex reads under the bedclothes. In all successful organizations, whether families, firms or states, leaders discover that they can radically increase compliance by creating a sense of obligation. Alex wants to stay awake and read, but if I can persuade him that he *ought* to go to sleep, the challenge of enforcement is reduced. As this happens, my power is transformed into authority. More grandly expressed, this is the construction of moral norms for strategic purposes. The crucial power of leaders is not that of command: it is that they are positioned at the hub of a network. They have the power to persuade.* That leaders are using morality strategically to shape our lives sounds sinister. Yet it is usually the opposite: it is the healthy process that has enabled modern societies to be better places than all previous societies. They could be even better.

But how, practically, do leaders use language strategically to build obligations? Here is Robert Wood Johnson, the chairman of Johnson & Johnson doing it in 1943. He set out the company's moral principles,

---

* Nor is this recent: it was the celebrated punchline of the political scientist Richard Neustadt in his analysis of the power of the US President, formulated in 1960.

literally in stone: 'Our Credo'. It begins, 'We believe that our first responsibility is to the people who use our products.' Note the words 'we' and 'our', not 'I' and 'my'; this was to be the credo of everyone in the company. It went on to rank lesser responsibilities in descending order: to employees, to the local community and, lastly, to shareholders. The Credo has been sustained for three generations by the use of narratives: if you visit their website it is still organized around 'stories'. Has it made a difference to behaviour?

In 1982 Johnson & Johnson was hit by disaster. Seven people in Chicago died, their deaths being traced to poison that had been put into bottles of Tylenol, its best-selling product. What happened was sufficiently remarkable for it still to be used as a case study in business schools. Even before senior management had time to react, local branch managers had taken the initiative to remove all the Tylenol from supermarket shelves, promising the stores full recompense. This sounds less remarkable that it was because, since that episode, it has become standard practice across the business world. But until 1982 companies did not recall products; their practice had been to deny responsibility. Junior employees in Johnson & Johnson had the confidence to take this initiative, which committed the company to a liability of around $100 million, because they had understood from that Credo that their priority was to the users of Tylenol.[26] Their prompt action, which was subsequently fully endorsed by top management, was not only moral: it transpired to be good business. Contrary to predictions, the company rapidly recovered its market share.*

The sound bedrock of economics, accepted by Adam Smith, is the recognition that unreciprocated altruism is limited to duties of rescue: it is not an adequate counter to self-interest. Reciprocal obligations are vital, but they have to be built. This is what the narratives of

* The Johnson & Johnson belief system breaks down into three components: a shared identity built around a common moral purpose, defined in the Credo as providing high quality and affordable health products to customers; reciprocal obligations of employees to strive towards this purpose; and a causal chain leading to enlightened self-interest that this model underpins the sustainability of the business and the jobs of its workforce – as noted on its website, the company is one of the very few that has survived for a century. I am indebted to John Kay for this example.

belonging, obligation and purposive action do in combination.[27] I have sketched this as a sequence – belonging, then obligations, then purposive action – but sequence is not material; if a common action would lead to a good outcome for many people, that may be the basis for both shared identity and a common obligation.

Narratives are powerful, but there are limits to how far they can depart from reality: leaders are widely observed as well as widely heard, and so they cannot afford to contradict what they say by what they do. Their actions have to be *consistent* with their narratives; saying that you and I are all 'we' while favouring yourself over me gives the lie to the narrative of belonging. Saying that we all have a duty towards each other while behaving selfishly gives the lie to a narrative of obligation. The CEO of Johnson & Johnson could not have got people to take the responsibility for pulling Tylenol off the shelves on their own initiative if he had exploited them. Instead, his conduct was exemplary: he even received a Presidential Medal of Freedom, accepted on behalf of his workforce.

Just as leaders can undermine a belief system with incompatible behaviour, they can reinforce it by crafting their actions strategically. Suppose that your audience suspects that you do not mean what you say: the Credo says 'users before profits', but is that just there to sound good to users? What can you do about this suspicion? Michael Spence won the Nobel Prize for solving that one with his Theory of Signalling. Evidently, it doesn't help to say 'I *really* mean it', because you *would* say that even if you really didn't. Nothing you *say* can help, but you can *do* something. Specifically, you need to do something that if you really meant 'profits before users' would be unacceptably costly. The only actions that work are likely to be painful, even though you mean what you say, but that is the price you must pay to establish credibility. Signals reinforce the credibility of a belief system, but they do not make the narratives redundant: signals bring credibility, but narratives bring precision. They are complementary.

The transformation of power into authority is essential for building reciprocity across huge groups of people, such as everyone accepting the obligation to pay their taxes. Leaders are not engineers of human souls, but they can harness our emotions. The dangerous leaders are those who rely only on enforcement. The valuable ones are those who use their position as communicator-in-chief at the hub of their networked group – they achieve influence through crafting narratives and actions. All leaders add and refine the narratives that fit within the belief system of their group, but great leaders build an entire belief system.[28]

The most recent exemplar of leadership using narratives within a network is ISIS. Its leaders recognized the power of social networks to transmit potent new narratives. Narratives of belonging bound together young people who had previously identified themselves as Swedes, Moroccans, Belgians, Tunisians, Australians and many others into a new common identity of the Faithful. Narratives of reciprocal obligation locked them into brutal behaviour by the pressure of peer esteem. New narrative propositions built a causal chain giving purpose to compliance by linking their horrific behaviour to the material objective of a 'caliphate'. With ready supplies of cannon fodder, and Saudi money, ISIS rapidly became a significant player on the world stage, dismantled – as with fascism – only by overwhelming force. As a belief system, it is internally coherent, and so stable; each individual component viewed in isolation is so repellent that it creates a gulf between the group and everyone else, strengthening group identity.

ISIS used narratives strategically to take societies back to the twelfth century. Our leaders could use them to better purpose.

SOFTWIRED OBLIGATIONS

We started with the moral deficit facing modern capitalism: a society can do without morality because self-interest will get us to the nirvana of mass prosperity. 'Greed is good' because the stronger the appetite, the harder will people work, and so the more prosperous we will all become. We have come a long way from that proposition. We are *social* beings, neither *economic man*, nor *altruistic saints*. We crave esteem and belonging, and these underpin our moral values. Around the world we hold six such values in common, none of which is generated by reason. Care and liberty may be evolutionarily primitive. Loyalty and sanctity may have evolved as norms that supported the group; members would have followed them as norms, and internalized them as values because they were rewarded with belonging. Similarly, norms of fairness and hierarchy may have evolved to keep order in the group, being rewarded with esteem.

Our values matter because those actions required by them – our obligations – trump our wants. Remarkably, from this limited set of values we have learned how to generate obligations virtually without limit, by means of belief systems crafted by narratives and backed by signalling actions. These belief systems can be built consciously by leaders at the hub of networks: in families, firms and societies. Depending upon the specific content of the narratives, they can produce remarkably different group behaviour, each ultimately sustained by our common values and our common cravings.

All this matters for the choices that currently face our societies. Ideologies beckon: each severs morality from our common values. Each prioritizes reason, privileging one value over the others. As a result, each inevitably collides with some of our values and the psychological foundations on which they rest. If the pursuit of their overarching objective undermines belonging, it is no matter; if it plunges some people into humiliation, so what: all ideologies accept 'collateral damage', or 'broken eggs'. While they agree that reason is supreme, they disagree as to *which* reason it is. This guarantees that the path of ideology will lead to unresolvable social conflict. Ideologies are less likely to take us forward to their imagined utopias than back to lives that are nasty, brutish and short.

Populists also compete for our adherence. They glory in our values and cravings, but discard the centuries of social learning reflected in our practical reasoning and our institutions, and ignore our capacity to build reciprocity. They too would take us backwards.

This book proposes a different path: an ethical capitalism that meets standards that are built on our values, honed by practical reasoning, and reproduced by the society itself. That deceptively simple sentence packs a lot of controversial complexity. Ideologues would baulk at 'built on our values'; populists would baulk at 'honed by practical reasoning'. And what is implied by that phrase 'reproduced by the society itself'? I do *not* mean the timeless perfection of utopias, whether Plato's Republic, Marxists' paradise, or the triumphalism of 'the end of history' – they are ridiculous. By 'reproduced' I mean only that the norms of society should not inherently self-destruct. In the language of social science, we are looking for something that is *locally* stable. Periodically, society will be hit by shocks: a natural one like climate change, or an intellectual one like the emergence of a new religion. Such shocks can push society sufficiently far out of its local equilibrium that it heads off to completely different norms. But our norms should not collapse from the weight of their own contradictions.

We now have a coherent picture that shows us how individual behaviour is shaped by obligations, why it matters, why it might go wrong, and how it might be put right. Shortly I am going to apply these insights to the three types of group that dominate our lives: families, firms and societies. *I am going to show how the leaders of these groups could build reciprocal obligations that reconfigure capitalism to work with, rather than against, the grain of common values.*

My emphasis on reciprocal obligations contrasts with the prevailing political discourse, which has shrivelled morality to assertions of individual rights and entitlements; obligations have been shifted off to governments. Yet for one person to have a right, someone else must have an obligation. A new obligation forces a change in behaviour that enables a new right to be exercised: without some counterpart obligation, a new right is vacuous. Reciprocal obligations ensure this, each new right is married to its new obligation.

Rights imply obligations, but obligations need not imply rights. The obligations of parents to our children go way beyond their legal rights. Nor do the duties of rescue need to be matched by rights: we respond to a child drowning in a pond because of her plight, not her rights. A society that succeeds in generating many obligations can be more generous and harmonious than one relying only on rights. Obligations are to rights what taxation is to public spending – the bit that is demanding. Western electorates have mostly learned that discussion of public spending must balance its benefits against how it would be financed. Otherwise, politicians promise higher spending during an election, and the post-election excess of spending over revenue is resolved by inflation.[29] Just as new obligations are analogous to extra revenue, so the creation of rights is analogous to extra spending. The rights may well be appropriate, but this can only be determined by a public discussion of the corresponding obligations.

Detached from such an assessment, the process of teasing new rights from old texts is like printing money: individual rights shower down like banknotes. Unless we create new obligations to match them, something is going to get squeezed out to meet the deficit. If people begrudge the burden of obligations that meet new legal rights, those obligations that are not matched to legal rights, such as conventions of reciprocity, and some duties of rescue, may be eroded.

The focus on rights has privileged lawyers. Typically, lawyers start from some written text, such as a law or a treaty, and try to deduce from it what rights might be implied. Each decision then becomes a precedent for whether some other right might be implied. This process of specialist lawyers 'discovering' new rights implied by old texts has exposed societies to a creeping drift between what these lawyers 'discover' and what most people regard as morally reasonable. In a trivial current British example, a court has determined that schools may no longer use the words 'mother' and 'father', because this infringes the discovered right of a same-sex couple. Here, a new right created by a judge intended to benefit a handful of people destroyed fundamental narratives that assist millions of other families in rearing their children. In inflicting such widespread harm relative to benefit, the demand revealed the triumph of ideology over pragmatism; selfish assertions of right weaken mutual regard.

As we recognize new obligations to others, we build societies better able to flourish; as we neglect them we do the opposite. Capitalist societies have suffered from a process of neglect, the key symptom being the decline of social trust. The leading indicator of how trust will evolve in the coming decades is how it has already changed in American youth: today's youth will be tomorrow's adults, and trends in America blow across to Europe. Among teenage Americans trust has collapsed *by 40 per cent.** That decline has happened across all social classes, but is most pronounced among the poor. As Robert

* Specifically, the period is the past thirty-five years, during which they have been asked whether they agreed with the statement 'most people can be trusted'.

Putnam says, this reveals not mounting paranoia, 'but the malevolent social realities within which they live'.[30] Despite the promise of prosperity, what modern capitalism is currently delivering is aggression, humiliation and fear: the Rottweiler society. To achieve the promise, our sense of mutual regard has to be rebuilt. Pragmatism tells us that this process will need to be guided by context and evidence-based reasoning. That is where we are heading.

3

The Ethical State

States that link ethical purpose to good ideas have achieved miracles. My generation grew up through such a period, between 1945 and 1970. We experienced the rapidly rising prosperity achieved by states that purposively harnessed capitalism for the benefit of society. It wasn't always like that, and it isn't now.

As the child of parents who were young adults in the 1930s, I learned vicariously how badly the state had failed. Through their stories I grasped the tragedy of the collapse into mass unemployment. States, and the societies they reflected, had lacked the sense of ethical purpose to see full employment as their responsibility. They also lacked the ideas that would have shown them what to do about it. In consequence, they dramatically mismanaged capitalism. The ideologies of fascism and Marxism were waiting in the wings. Only in Germany and Italy did either of them manage to take hold, but that was enough to trigger a global cataclysm. Belatedly, shocked by the mass ruin of lives, states and societies found that sense of purpose. In the USA Roosevelt embraced the obligation of the state to provide jobs — his 'New Deal'. He was elected, because people recognized the New Deal as ethical. New ideas arrived: Keynes's *General Theory of Employment, Interest, and Money* provided the analysis to address mass unemployment. Governments were initially unreceptive, however; though the book came out in 1936, the escape from the Depression was because rearmament happened to boost demand. As Paul Krugman has wryly said, the Second World War was the largest economic stimulus package in history. But, post-war, Keynes's analysis was used to maintain full employment, gradually becoming inadequate with the rise in inflation in the 1970s.

States failed their people in the 1930s, and they are doing so again. Currently, the word 'capitalism' provokes widespread contempt. But behind the toxic word are the networks of markets, rules and firms that delivered both the miracle of 1945–70 and the tragedy of 1929–39. My generation missed the tragedy, lived through the miracle, and complacently imagined that continued miracle was inevitable. The present generation has learned that it was not. The new anxieties are rooted in economic divergence. There is a widening regional divide between the booming metropolis and decaying provincial cities; there is a widening class divide between those in prestigious and fulfilling jobs and those in dead-end jobs, or none at all.

Capitalism has generated these new anxieties, just as it did in the Depression of the 1930s. States are needed to heal these social cleavages created by structural change. But, as in the 1930s, states, and the societies they reflect, have been slow to recognize their ethical obligations to address these new problems, and instead of being nipped in the bud they have been allowed to grow to crisis proportions. States cannot be more ethical than their people, though they can reinforce reciprocal obligations, and they can gradually persuade us to adopt new ones. But if a state tries to impose a set of values different from those of its citizens it forfeits trust and its authority erodes. The ethical bounds of the state are set by the ethical bounds of its society. The current lack of ethical purpose in the state reflects a decline in ethical purpose across society: *as our societies have become more divided, they have become less generously disposed to those on the other side of the divide.*

As in the 1930s, the lack of purpose has been compounded by a lack of practical new thinking. In Part Three, I try to fill the void of innovative thinking, presenting practical approaches to healing those damaging cleavages. But first we must come to grips with the ethical failings of the state, and its roots in the ethical changes in our societies.

THE RISE OF THE ETHICAL STATE

The heyday of the *ethical state* was the first two post-war decades. States created an unprecedented array of reciprocal obligations in a magnificent epoch of ethical purpose. The extraordinary new extent of obligations of citizens towards one another, to be administered by the state, was captured in the neat narratives of 'cradle to grave' and 'New Deal'. From health care during pregnancy, to pensions in old age, by contributing to state-run national insurance people would protect each other: the guiding ethic of communitarian social democracy. It spanned the centre of the political spectrum. In America, it was the period of bipartisanship in Congress; in Germany, the 'social market economy'. In Britain, the flagship National Health Service was designed by a Liberal in a coalition led by a Conservative, implemented by a Labour government, and sustained by Conservative governments. In both North America and Europe, beneath the noise and smoke of political contest, between 1945 and 1970 the political disagreements between the leaders of the mainstream parties were minimal.*

But underpinning the successes of social democracy was an inheritance so obvious that it became taken for granted. The escape from the Depression by means of the Second World War had been far more than an inadvertent stimulus package: it had been an immense common endeavour in which leaders had crafted narratives of belonging and mutual obligation. Its legacy was to turn each nation into a gigantic community, a society with a strong sense of shared identity, obligation and reciprocity. People were ready-primed to comply with the social democrat narratives that linked individual actions to collective consequences. For the first post-war decades, rich people complied with rates of income tax that reached over 80 per cent; young men complied with military conscription; in Britain, even criminals complied with the implicit restraint necessary for an unarmed police force. This enabled a huge expansion in the role of the state: the social-democratic agenda.

Yet the social-democratic state was increasingly taken over by the Utilitarian and Rawlsian vanguards; the *ethical state* morphed into the *paternalist state*. This would not have mattered so much had the

---

* The term 'Butskellism' was used to characterize the essential equivalence of the leading thinker in the Conservative Party, Rab Butler, and the leader of the Labour Party, Hugh Gaitskell, in the 1950s.

new vanguards recognized that, unless shared identity was continu-ally renewed, this extraordinary legacy was a wasting asset. Far from doing this, they did the opposite. The Utilitarian vanguard was glo-balist, and the Rawlsians promoted the distinctive identity of victim groups. Gradually, the basis for the social-democrat agenda unrav-elled, and by 2017 across Western societies the social-democratic parties had been abandoned by voters; they were in existential crisis.[1] By applying the concepts introduced in Chapter 2, we are able to see why this happened.

THE DECLINE OF THE ETHICAL STATE: HOW SOCIAL-DEMOCRATIC SOCIETIES UNRAVELLED

The collapse of social democracy was due to a double whammy: the gradual erosion in mutual obligation collided with the greater need for it as changes in the structure of the economy left a mounting trail of damaged lives. The spectacular economic growth of this period came at the price of increasing complexity. In turn, this extra com-plexity needed more specialist skills, and these needed highly educated people, precipitating an unprecedented expansion in higher edu-cation. This massive structural change had repercussions for identity.

To see why this cocktail proved fatal for social democracy I am going to sketch a model. A good model starts from assumptions that simplify but are not surprising, yet reaches surprising results. Ideally, it crystallizes something that thereafter seems obvious but which hitherto you hadn't realized. Normally a model would be set out in a series of equations, but I will try to sketch this one out in a few sen-tences.[2] While fairly simple, it requires a little patience to grasp how it works. The reward is that it is quite revealing. The model starts with some psychology and then adds some economics.

The psychology is stripped down, but considerably less crude than the grotesque pathology of *rational economic man*. He died out dur-ing the Stone Age, replaced (as we've seen) by *rational social woman*, and I draw on the insights of Identity Economics, the field pioneered by George Akerlof and Rachel Kranton, as to how she behaves.

Suppose we all have two objective identities: our job and our nationality. Identity is a source of esteem, and each of these identities generates some of it. To specify just how much each generates, suppose that the esteem from a job reflects the income associated with it, and suppose that the esteem from nationality reflects the prestige of the nation. Now add a choice: *salience*. Although these objective identities of job and nationality are beyond our control, we can *choose* which of them to regard as most important. The identity I choose to make salient gears up its effect on my esteem. Imagine that it is like a card that doubles the esteem generated by whichever identity I place it on. Playing the salience card has a further effect: it divides us into two new groups, those who make their job salient, and those who make their nationality salient. In choosing which identity to make salient, I am also choosing to belong to one or other of these groups. I get further esteem from membership of this group, depending upon how much esteem the group has.

Bringing this together, each person is getting four servings of esteem. Some comes from our job; some comes from our nationality; an extra serving comes from whichever of them we have made salient; and a final serving comes from belonging to the group that, like us, has chosen this identity as salient. To be specific about this last serving, suppose it is simply the average esteem of each member of the group from the other three servings. So how do we decide which identity to make salient?* This is where we need the economics: our *rational social woman* gets her utility from esteem and she *maximizes* it: that's what we mean by 'rational'. We are now ready to apply this little model to post-war social history.

In the aftermath of the Second World War wage inequality is modest, and the nation is prestigious, so that even the most highly paid workers maximize their utility from esteem by choosing to make their nationality salient, rather than their job. If we sum the four servings of esteem we see that its distribution across society is pretty equal. Everyone is getting the same esteem from their national identity; because they all make this salient they all get the same

---

* Of course, we also take decisions about how to meet our 'wants', but we can keep this off-stage.

double portion; because everyone has chosen the same salient identity, they all get the same esteem from their salient identity group; so, the only differences in esteem are due to the modest wage differences.

Now watch this happy outcome unravel. Over time, with rising complexity, a growing number of people get a fancy education, a fancy job to match it, and a fancy wage to match their enhanced productivity. At some point, the most highly skilled switch their choice of salience from their nationality to their skill because that way they maximize their esteem.

As this happens, that final serving of esteem, the one generated by having chosen the same salient identity as many others, starts to diverge. Those who choose to make their job the salient identity, get more from their membership of the same-salience group. Conversely, those sticking with nationality as salient lose esteem.* This divergence itself induces more people to switch their choice of salience from nation to job. Where does it end?

It might seem that everyone ends up switching their choice of salience, and this is possible. But a more likely alternative is that those in less-skilled jobs continue to make their nationality salient. When we compare this ending to where society started, the skilled have peeled off from their nationality; among them are the Utilitarian vanguard. As a result of peeling off, they get more esteem than they did initially. In contrast, the less skilled who have kept their nationality salient lose esteem; since the most-esteemed people have peeled off, belonging to the group that makes nationality salient yields less esteem.

Like all models, this one is excruciatingly reductionist. But, without drowning us in a morass of detail, it does help to explain why and how our societies have come apart at the seams. Throughout, everybody simply maximizes their own esteem. But due to structural changes in the economy, a cleavage opens up. The skilled switch their salient identity to their work. When she interviewed Susan Chira, then foreign editor of the *New York Times*, Alison Wolf captured a

---

* This is not because pride in their nation declines, but because being in the group who make their nationality salient has become less prestigious now that the skilled have walked off.

perfect expression of it: Ms Chira told her 'work is fulfilling, *it's so woven with identity*'.[3] Meanwhile, the less educated, with less to enthuse about in their work, clung on to their nationality but began to feel marginalized.

Since the smug skilled get more esteem than the marginalized, they are keen to make clear to others that they indeed make their skill their salient identity. We can now use a key insight of Michael Spence's Theory of Signalling to tell us how they are likely to do it. To show convincingly that I have chosen to drop nation as my salient identity, I need to do something that I would not be prepared to do otherwise. I need to denigrate the nation. This helps to explain why social elites so often actively disparage their own country – they are esteem-seeking. It decisively differentiates them from their social inferiors. Since by exiting the shared identity of nation they reduce the esteem of those they leave behind, it would not be surprising if they generated resentment. I hope that some of this resonates as familiar.

The new class of well-educated people with skills included both those of the right, who had embraced the libertarian ideology of the freedom to gain from individual talents, and those on the left, who had embraced Utilitarianism or Rawlsian rights. The latter group not only shed their own national identity, they encouraged others to do so. People with some characteristic deemed to qualify for victim-hood were encouraged to embrace that as their salient identity.

REPERCUSSIONS FROM THE LOSS OF SHARED IDENTITY

This unravelling of shared identity had repercussions for how society functions. As identities polarized into skill versus nationality, trust in the people at the top of society began to collapse.[4] How did this come about?

Recall the big idea of Chapter 2. A willingness to help others is generated by combining three narratives: *shared belonging* to a group; *reciprocal obligations* within the group; and a link from an action to the well-being of the group that shows it to be *purposive*. Consequently, if shared identity unravels, it undermines the willingness of the fortunate to accept that they have obligations towards the less fortunate.

The foundation of most generosity is reciprocity. That is the big step that catapults us from the weak force of altruism and duties of rescue, to the far stronger force of reciprocity that induces people to comply with high tax rates. But reciprocity faces a co-ordination problem: if you have accepted that the obligation is reciprocal, then I am willing to accept that I have an obligation to you, but *how do I know that you accept the obligation?* And how do you know that I have accepted it? How do we trust each other to meet these obligations if called upon to do so?

We know from experimental social psychology that the answer is that we need common knowledge. We each need to know that the other knows that we accept this obligation, 'we know that we know, that we know' echoing back recursively. This is what shared narratives of belonging, obligation and purpose circulating in a networked group gradually build. The claimed boundaries of shared belonging define the limits of reciprocity, and our awareness that we share exposure to narratives reinforces this with a sense of the practical boundaries to common knowledge. Because narratives are expressed primarily in language, there is a natural upper limit to the size of the group that is difficult to surmount – a shared language.[5] But there is no equivalent lower limit: within a language group, identities can become highly fragmented. Breaches in shared identity both weaken the defined group to which reciprocity applies, and the practical feasibility of reciprocal obligations spanning separated groups.

There is not much doubt that our societies have indeed polarized into those earning above average incomes who have jettisoned national identity in favour of their job, and those lower down society who have clung on to it. Nor, after Trump, Brexit and Le Pen, is there much doubt that these two groups are conscious of this polarization.

The story so far: the part of the population that is skilled and educated has tended to sheer off from nationality as its core identity, leaving the less fortunate clinging to its diminished status. In turn, this has resulted in the weakening of shared identity across society. This has weakened the sense of obligation felt by the fortunate towards the less fortunate, and this has in turn undermined the narrative built following 1945, that the affluent should be willing to pay high redistributive taxes to help the poor. This is at least consistent with the very substantial decline in top tax rates post-1970.

Now we are ready to push one step further: the less fortunate part of the population recognizes this weakening of the sense of obligation among the fortunate. It would, after all, be quite hard to miss it, and it does matter for the poorer part of the population. This being the case, would it be likely to have any impact on the extent to which ordinary people trust their 'betters'? Just by posing the question the answer becomes evident: trust would decline. If the educated see themselves as different from the less educated, and with diminished responsibility towards them, those others would be foolish to continue to trust them as much as when they knew that everyone had the same salient identity. We trust people if we are confident that we can predict how they will behave. We have more confidence in our predictions if we can safely use the techniques of a 'theory of mind': I predict your behaviour by imagining how I would behave in your circumstances. But using this technique is only reliable to the extent that I am confident that we share the same belief system. If we have radically different belief systems, I cannot put myself in your shoes because I do not inhabit the mental world that shapes your behaviour. I can't trust you.

The Utilitarian vanguard even developed a theory that anticipated the decline of trust and proposed how to prevent it. Henry Sidgwick, Professor of Moral Philosophy at Cambridge and an ardent follower of Bentham, argued that the solution was for the ruling vanguard to conceal its true purpose from the rest of the population. The decline in trust could be prevented by deception.* Of course, the severe decline in trust since the 1970s has been reinforced by the revealed failure of the vanguard running public policy to address the new cleavages. But, as Sidgwick's ludicrously self-defeating proposition suggests, the roots of the problem are much deeper than just this failure of outcomes.

The decline in trust is not the end of the unravelling of social democracy. The next rung down the ladder is the implications of the decline

---

* A subsequent Cambridge professor, Bernard Williams, subjected this proposition to a withering critique, calling it 'Government House' Utilitarianism.

in trust for the ability to co-operate. In a complex society, myriad inter-relationships depend on trust. So, as trust collapses, co-operation begins to fray. People start to rely more upon legal mechanisms for enforcement of good behaviour (this is good news for lawyers but not necessarily for the rest of us). As the sense of obligation on the part of the skilled towards their fellow-citizens weakens, because they no longer share a salient identity, behaviour becomes more opportunistic. The skilled may even come to view the rest of the population as 'mup-pets', and take pride in their skill in fleecing suckers. This appears, from email revelations, to have been a sentiment circulating in the higher echelons of financial firms. As Joseph Stiglitz aptly depicted the business model of Wall Street in the years preceding the financial crisis, it was 'find suckers'. Evidently, this amplifies the underlying structural economic forces in society that are increasing inequality.

WHY WE ARE WARY OF SHARED NATIONAL IDENTITY

People are understandably wary of making national identity salient: nationalism has led to some truly terrible things. All identities implic-itly define the characteristics for exclusion, but this becomes toxic if the characteristics for exclusion are not merely implicit, but explicit and hostile: 'we' are defined as 'not them', and 'they' become an object of hatred – we wish them ill. Such identities are oppositional. In some contexts, oppositional identities can actually be healthy. Sports teams, for example, strengthen their performance by having a clear notion of a rival; so do many firms. Such competition benefits all of us, spurring people to greater effort – it is one of the underrated benefits of capital-ism. But, historically, the most damaging forms of oppositional identity have been large-group identities such as ethnicity, religion and nation-ality. They have led to pogroms, jihad and world war.

Few societies have suffered more from such oppositional identities than Germany. In the seventeenth century the Thirty Years War between Catholics and Protestants utterly devastated what had been a prosperous society. It was resolved eventually by the Peace of West-phalia, which in essence switched the salience of identity from religion to nationality. It indeed restored peace, but eventually took Germany into the hell of National Socialism, the Holocaust, world war and defeat. Unsurprisingly, most Germans now want a larger identity and so are enthusiastic Europeans.

But Europe is not just a lump of land on to which a polity can be fitted. As we have seen, the polity is better able to function if the units of political power coincide with shared identity. If they don't, then either identity needs to adjust to power, or power needs to adjust to identity. In all modern societies, political power depends upon very modest levels of coercion and a high degree of willing compliance. Willing compliance takes us back to the sense of obligation that turns power into authority. Without that sense of obligation, power faces only three options. One is to force people to comply by means of effective coercion – the North Korean option. The second is to attempt this option but to provoke reactive organized violence against the state – the Syrian option. The third is for power to recognize its limitations and retreat into theatre: power issues commands that it knows will be ignored, and those commanded find some means of avoiding compliance without causing too much offence. This has been the experience of the European Commission in trying to achieve compliance with its targets of fiscal discipline; only the Finns have never breached them.

People in modern prosperous societies have grown up with power already transformed into authority and so take it for granted. Having worked all my life in societies which are struggling to make this transformation, I have come to realize that it is valuable, challenging and potentially precarious. To build Europe as a polity depends on building a new large identity, but this is an extremely difficult undertaking. Common endeavours on such a scale are difficult to organize, and the vehicle for narratives of identity and obligation – language – is itself highly differentiated: Europe doesn't have a common language.* Potentially, the attempt to transfer authority to a central

---

* The European Schools were supposed to build a new European identity, at least among elite students. But new research suggests that students are so indoctrinated with the ideology that European identity is synonymous with liberal cosmopolitanism that they have come to think that those who disagree are not proper Europeans. Far from building shared identity, it is another process of elite divergence from the identities of their own societies.

entity with which few identify, strips power of authority, opening the way for fragmentation into regional identities and the collapse into individualism: the hell of *economic man*.

Indeed, rather than building larger identities, many people are retreating into smaller ones. After over five hundred years of being Spanish as well as Catalan, many Catalans now want to retreat into being only Catalan. After over three hundred years of being British as well as Scottish, many Scots now want to retreat into being only Scottish – the wee we in preference to the big we. After over one hundred and fifty years of being Italian, the Northern League would like to retreat into being 'Northern'. After over fifty years of being Yugoslavian, Slovenes actually achieved the dream of secession; the consequences for other Yugoslavians were catastrophic. As I write, the Catalans are inspiring the southern regions of Brazil to seek secession. And, most astonishing of all, Biafra is back. The secession movement that fifty years ago led to a murderous war in Nigeria is once more agitating. All these seemingly distinct secessions have one thing in common: *they are rich regions trying to exit obligations to the rest of the country*. Catalonia is the richest of the seventeen regions of Spain and objects to paying taxes to poorer regions. The campaign slogan of the Scottish Nationalist Party has long been 'it's Scotland's oil' (this, despite the fact that the oil is actually located way out in the North Sea). Northern Italy is the richest part of the country and the secessionist narrative points resentfully to the fiscal transfers to poorer regions. Guess which region of Yugoslavia was the richest? Guess which three regions of Brazil are the richest? Guess where the oil is in Nigeria? Behind the posturing narratives of the right to self-determination, these political movements are further manifestations of the unravelling of the social democratic state: resentment against the reciprocal obligations built across a vast shared identity. They, as much as capitalism, warrant the epithets of greed and selfishness. That they have avoided them is a tribute not to their purpose, but to their PR.

We need large shared identities, but nationalism is not the way to build them. Instead, it is being used by political populists to build a support base through narratives of hatred of other people who live in the same country. The entire strategy is to build cohesion within one part of society by creating rifts with other parts of society. The resulting oppositional identities are lethal for generosity, trust and co-operation. This is what educated people reject and they are right to do so. But, currently, they are not offering any alternative basis for shared identity. In effect, the educated are saying that they no longer identify with less-educated citizens. Instead, applying Utilitarian principles, they make no distinction between their less-educated fellow-citizens and foreigners. Since the powerful obligations – those that are reciprocal – follow only from shared identity, the implication is that they have no greater obligation to non-elite fellow-citizens than to foreigners living anywhere.

New survey evidence enables us to see this process of erosion underway. In Britain, the current media presumption is that younger people are more generously disposed to poor people within society than their parents. In a large random survey conducted in 2017, people were asked to choose between two opposing propositions. One was: 'People's obligation to pay their taxes is more important than their personal wealth'. This was juxtaposed against: 'People are rewarded for working hard by keeping more of what they earn'. Contrary to the media myth – but entirely consistent with the theory of shared identity as a wasting asset – the age group of the over-35s backed the obligation to pay taxes, whereas the 18–34s were more drawn to the individualistic ethics of keeping what you earn.[6]

As compliance erodes, rights become unmet and trust in government declines. This is the fierce trend sweeping across Western societies. Practically, the change in the structure of obligations, from reciprocity within the society to unreciprocated global obligations – or from national citizen to 'citizen of the world' – could mean one of three radically different things. Perhaps you might ask yourself which of them applies to you.

One possibility is that you remain no less generous towards poorer people than the generation who, between 1945 and 1970, built your national tax system on the presumption of shared national identity, but you now want to define the poor globally rather than nationally. This would have dramatic implications. On average, across the advanced modern economies, somewhere around 40 per cent of income is scooped up in tax and redistributed in various forms, such as direct transfers to poorer people, social spending that benefits poorer people disproportionately, and infrastructure spending that benefits almost everyone. So, you remain happy to have 40 per cent of the country's income scooped up in tax, but now want it to be distributed globally rather than nationally: you do not see anything special about your obligations to your fellow-nationals. Given global inequalities, this would produce a massive increase in aid flows to poor countries; a large proportion of the 40 per cent of income captured in tax would be sent to them. A corollary of this redirection of taxation towards the global poor would be that poor people within the nation would be radically worse off. You may dismiss that as morally irrelevant – their needs are less than those of the people you are now meeting – but they would be right to be alarmed.

A second possibility is that you remain as generous towards your fellow-nationals as the previous generations, but now want to extend the same degree of generosity globally. Now the implication is more dramatic: taxation will need to rise massively. The post-tax income of the skilled will need to fall very substantially to maintain the level of generosity to fellow-nationals while extending the same largesse to the global population. This is not something that one country could do alone, since much of its skilled population would emigrate, leaving their poorer citizens worse off. This is a policy of the headless heart.

The third possibility is that what you really mean by your change of salient identity is not that you have significantly increased your sense of obligation to people all over the world, but that you have reduced your sense of obligation towards your fellow-nationals. In this case you are in the happy position of being off the hook. Taxation can be reduced because that inconvenient 'ought' that nagged you into generosity has been silenced: 'you can keep what you earn'. They – your poorer fellow citizens – will be worse off. This is a policy of the heartless head.

The contempt of the educated for national identity muscles its way on to the moral high ground: *we* care about everyone; *you* are deplorable. But is this claim to the moral high ground really justified? Roll on a generation and imagine that the new identity of 'citizen of the world' has become sufficiently embedded that public policy fully reflects it.[7] The tax policies based on national identity have been supplanted. Which of these three interpretations of 'citizen of the world' above seems most likely to have prevailed? I suggest that it is likely to be some compromise between the first and the third: somewhat greater generosity towards the global poor will be more than offset by substantially reduced generosity towards the national poor.

THE CONUNDRUM

There is a conundrum currently facing modern, prosperous societies. The brute fact is that the domain of public policy is inevitably *spatial*. The political processes that authorize public policy are spatial: national and local elections generate representatives with authority over a territory. And the policies themselves ultimately have a spatial application: schooling and health care have catchment areas; infrastructure is spatially specific; taxes and benefits are administered spatially. We can not get away from this fact: *our polities are spatial*. Indeed, they are predominantly *national*. But our identities, and the social networks that underpin them, are becoming ever less so.

The social-democratic era from 1945 to 1970 was built on the exceptional history that expanded our sense of community to embrace entire countries. Our spatial identities and social networks have already withered as a result of the skill divide that came as a consequence of rising complexity. Now what we are beginning to experience is a further wave of assault on shared spatial identity as the behavioural changes consequent upon smart phones and social media take hold. Smart phones are at the extremity of individualism – the selfie indiscriminately posted to 'friends' in the hope of attracting an impressive tally of 'likes'. We see the withering of spatial community, and indeed we live it as we sit in public spaces, such as cafes and trains, surrounded by people who are proximate yet invisible as we peer at our screens. Space binds us through public policies, but it is no longer binding us socially. It is under assault both from substitute

61

communities of digital echo-chambers, and by a more radical withdrawal from face-to-face interaction into the isolation of anxious narcissism. My prediction is that unless this divergence between our polities and our bonds is reversed our societies will degenerate, becoming less generous, less trusting and less co-operative. These trends are already underway.

In principle, we could re-engineer our political units to be non-spatial. Presumably some of the techno-geeks of Silicon Valley have such a future as a gleam in the eye: the opt-in, opt-out polity with each individual free to choose regardless of where they happen to be living. Each could have its own currency – to each its own bitcoin. Each could have its own tax rates, welfare benefits, health scheme; there are schemes for floating islands outside any national jurisdiction. Does this sound attractive? If so, try to think what would be likely to happen. Rich people would be likely to opt into those artificial political entities that offered low tax rates. The billionaires are already doing this, detaching the legal location of their companies from where they earn their revenues, and themselves to Monaco. Conversely, sick people would opt into entities with generous health care, which would duly default upon their unviable liabilities.

The non-spatial political unit is a fantasy, so the only real option is to revive spatial bonds. Unfortunately, given that the most practical unit for most polities is national, we need a sense of shared national identity. But we know that national identities can be toxic. Is it possible to forge bonds that are sufficient for a viable polity yet not dangerous? This is the central question that has to be addressed in social science. On its answer rests the future of our societies.

The nationalists have come close to capturing the notion of national identity as their own intellectual property. Indeed, they appear to think that they are part of a continuous tradition of national identity, but they are not. In many societies, traditional national identity was genuinely inclusive of everyone in the society. Wittgenstein, an Austrian Jew living in Britain, recognized his clear obligation to return to Austria to fight for his country in the First World War. In contrast to this traditional form of nationalism, the new nationalists want to define national identity on criteria such as ethnicity or religion. This variant of nationalism is relatively recent, the heir to fascism, and this new definition of national identity would exclude millions of people who are citizens living in the society. Not only do the new nationalists quite explicitly intend to divide society into an 'us' and a 'them', they trigger a further division within their self-defined 'us' due to the many people who are offended by them. Their rise bitterly divides the society. Marine Le Pen did not unite France: she divided it two-to-one against her; Donald Trump has polarized American society down the middle. Hence, such nationalism is not even a feasible means of restoring the loss of shared identity which is giving it momentum; on the contrary, it would destroy any prospect of it. In turn, this would undermine trust and the co-operation that it facilitates, and mutual regard and the generosity that *it* facilitates.

The other group, the educated 'citizens of the world', are abandoning their national identity. They engage in the pleasures of signalling their social superiority while persuading themselves that this selfish behaviour is morally elevating. The stark conclusion is that both of these newly prominent groups of citizens threaten to undermine the shared identity built at such enormous cost.

We need a way out of this conundrum. In the potent image of Wittgenstein, who saw people trapped in confusing ideas, we need to let the fly out of the fly-bottle.

Enter patriotism.

BELONGING, PLACE AND PATRIOTISM

To function in a way that enables everyone to flourish, a society needs a strong sense of shared identity. The pertinent issue is not whether this is true, the cohesion-deniers are as foolish as the climate-deniers. It is demonstrated by the success of Denmark, Norway, Iceland and Finland, the happiest countries in the world; and by Bhutan, the happiest country in Asia. But, unfortunately, these five all build social cohesion by a strategy that is not available to most other societies. They have built shared identity around a distinctive common culture. I doubt whether the actual content of that culture is particularly important: *hygge* and Buddhist monasteries have little in common. But most societies either always were too culturally diverse for that to be a viable option, or have now become so. Rather than lamenting this aspect of our societies, we need to devise a workable strategy for rebuilding shared identity that is compatible with modernity.

The past methods that succeeded in building shared identity across an entire country are no longer useful. In prehistoric Britain, the shared identity may have been built by the vast common endeavour of Stonehenge – 'a unifying enterprise that reflected the vision of a single island culture'.[8] In fourteenth-century England it was built by war with France, binding together a radically unlikely amalgam: Normans; Anglo-Saxons, whose leaders had been slaughtered by Normans; Vikings, who had slaughtered the Anglo-Saxons; and Britons, whose culture had been eviscerated by Anglo-Saxon takeover. Across nineteenth-century Europe it was built by the myth of ethnic purity. In the mid-twentieth century it was built by war, and sustained by cultural idiosyncrasies; the Americans had baseball, the British had tea, the Germans pork-and-beer. As our societies have become multicultural, even baseball, tea and pork-and-beer are fading distinctions: none of these approaches is likely to give us a robust strategy.

One attractive-sounding strategy is to build shared identity around shared values. This approach is popular because everyone believes in their own values and assumes that they are the right ones on which to build shared identity. The problem is that an astonishingly diverse range of values can be found within any modern society; it is one of the defining features of modernity. If we require shared values, we end up with something powerfully exclusionary: 'if you don't share our values, get out.' Donald Trump and Bernie Sanders are both Americans, but I defy you to find *any* values that they both hold, but which differentiate America from other nations. The challenge could be repeated – with appropriate substitutions of political leaders – in most Western societies. The only values that everyone in a society adheres to are so minimal that they fail to distinguish a particular country from many others, and so do not define a viable domain within which reciprocal obligations might be built.

As national identity has become unfashionable value identity has intensified, and the result is ugly. It has been reinforced by the greater ease of restricting your social interaction to those with whom you agree – the 'echo-chamber' phenomenon. Far from being a route to social cohesion, these value-based echo-chambers are tearing Western societies apart. The level of insults, vilification and threats of violence – in short, of hatred – found in value-based networks now probably exceeds ethnic and religious abuse.

So, if values as the criterion for shared identity hit the same rock as ethnicity and religion, is there anything else? Should we instead try to make the citizens-of-the-world agenda viable by dissolving nations and shifting political power up to the United Nations? In reality, as the name United *Nations* implies, the organization presupposes that nations, not individuals, are the building blocks of political authority, for the evident reason that in most societies the nation is the largest feasible effective entity of shared identity. Were political power to become concentrated at the global level, people would not willingly comply with its decisions: power would not turn into authority. World government would come to approximate a global version of Somalia.

The answer to a viable and inclusive identity is staring us all in the face. It is a sense of *belonging to place*. Why, for example, do I regard myself as a Yorkshireman? Yes, I like the values: blunt speaking and a lack of pretension. But that really isn't it. Recently I was on a breakfast radio programme with Baroness Sayeeda Warsi, who was the first Muslim woman to become a British cabinet minister. It was the first time we had met, and a radio chat show where we were each supposed to talk about our new books is not a naturally bonding occasion. Yet I rapidly felt at ease with her: she had grown up in Bradford and spoke with the glorious accent into which I, too, had been reared, and which in me has been chipped away by half a century in Oxford. So, I suspect that I felt more at ease with her than she did with me. But essentially, we shared that sense of belonging to the same place, with its little markers of accent and vocabulary; I noticed that we both asked for our BBC tea to be 'mashed', not 'brewed'.

We can set such anecdotes into a framework of considerable generality. People have a fundamental need to *belong*. The key dimensions of belonging are *who?* and *where?* Both of these are set in childhood and usually endure for life. We answer *who?* by identifying with some group – this is what Identity Economics has focused on to date; we answer *where?* by identifying with some place as *home*. Ask yourself what you mean by *home*. For most people, it means the place where they grew up.

The most viable concept of nationality available to modernity is to bind people together with a sense of belonging to the same place. Place is layered like an onion. The inner core is our home; but much of the identity we bestow on our home is the region or city in which it is set. Similarly, the city gets much of its meaning from the country, and in Europe some of the sense of belonging extends to the European Union. The population of the typical country will look diverse, and hold diverse values: but they will share the location of their homes. Is that enough?

One reason to be hopeful is that place-based identity is one of the traits that are hardwired deep in our psyche by evolution. It is not one of the relatively recent softwired values added by language. Not only is place-based identity deeply ingrained, it is powerful. A standard concept in conflict studies is the ratio of attackers to defenders needed for attackers to win. Obviously this is affected by military technology, but in general, over the history of human conflict defenders fight harder than attackers, and so the ratio is around 3:1. Astonishingly, this ratio is the same across many species. Tracing these species back up the evolutionary tree, territoriality looks to have been hardwired for around the past 4 million years.[9] The instinct to defend territory has very deep roots; we are bonded to a sense of home.

So, from the genetic inheritance of our 'passions', we have a strong sense of belonging to place. But, as we saw in Chapter 2, the soft-wired values generated by narratives also matter. Narratives aid memory, enabling us to read our place not just as a snapshot of its current state, but as an evolution: our attachment to our city as it is now is deepened by our understanding of the layers of change by which it has become what it is. These memories are common knowledge to all those who grow up in the city, they reinforce our common identity.

Yet, for decades, mainstream politicians have consciously avoided narratives of belonging. Indeed, they have actively denigrated them. Our politicians are at the hub of national social networks, they are our communicators-in-chief. By actively undermining a sense of shared belonging, they have accelerated the decay of the reciprocal obligations on which our well-being depends. Their ethical narratives have overwhelmingly been Utilitarian or Rawlsian, instead, and they have seen themselves as being at the apex of the *paternalist state*. The narratives of belonging to your country have been left, by default, to the nationalists who have hijacked them for their own divisive agenda, and in the process, the *ethical state* has withered away.

In 2017 President Macron of France broke this pattern of negligence. He has pioneered a vocabulary to distinguish between two forms of nationwide identity: nationalism and *patriotism*, describing himself as a patriot but not a nationalist. Narratives of patriotism, defined as belonging to a common territory, can be used both to recapture belonging from the nationalists and to restore it as central to people's identity. A new survey of the British population offers further supporting evidence for the viability of this strategy. The survey tested the associations of the word 'patriotism' across the population, comparing it with many other political concepts.[10] The results are highly encouraging: the four top associations with 'patriotism' are 'attractive', 'inspiring', 'satisfying' and 'appeals to the heart'. In this, it contrasts with *all* the ideologies tested in the survey. Most strikingly, 'patriotism' gets these favourable responses across all age groups, and across people clustered into their otherwise disquietingly divergent political and social preferences.

Patriotism is also sharply distinguished from nationalism in how nations behave towards each other. The discourse used by nationalists, bragging about putting their country 'first', portrays international relations as a zero-sum game in which the winner is the one that is the most inflexible. Patriotism, as exemplified by President Macron, promotes a discourse of co-operation for mutual benefit. He is quite explicitly seeking to build new reciprocal commitments within Europe on economic matters, within NATO on the security of the Sahel, and globally on climate change. Yet Macron is working in the interests of France. When an Italian company tried to buy the nation's most important shipyard, he intervened to ensure that French interests were protected: he is not a Utilitarian. But crucially, in contrast to nationalism, patriotism is not aggressive.

As with all narratives, if actions are inconsistent with them, narratives of shared belonging to place will lack credibility. At the centre of the onion is the home: if our attachment to home is weak then the outer layers will also be enfeebled. One reason why younger people are losing a sense of belonging is that it has become far more difficult to buy a home. The share of home ownership among a population is a practical indicator of this inner core of belonging, and restoring home ownership requires intelligent public policy, as we will see later.

While place is the psychological bedrock of a shared sense of belonging, it can be supplemented by purposive action. A country is the natural unit for much public policy, and so our shared identity follows from the common purpose underlying actions that enhance our mutual well-being. Narratives of purposive action can set out how, by accepting the shared identity that defines the domain of reciprocity, meeting our obligations to each other can gradually make us all better off. Listen to what politicians are saying about purposive action, and categorize their narratives into those that build shared identity and those that undermine it. Evidently, during wartime, narratives of purposive action overwhelmingly imply mutual benefit and so reinforce shared identity; during the miracle period of 1945–70, the public narratives were predominantly of this form. Currently, our politicians are carelessly pumping out narratives of purposive actions that provide rationales for thinking of our interests as being opposed to those of some other group. They have actively encouraged people to form oppositional identities, and such identities are socially toxic. Each narrative of opposed interests may be true in isolation, yet cumulatively they become so corrosive that collective well-being deteriorates.

Politicians are, first and foremost, communicators. Building shared identity in a society with diverse cultures and diverse values is necessary for mutual well-being, but challenging: it is a primary duty of leadership. By shying away from narratives of shared belonging, whether of place or purpose, politicians have inadvertently compounded the erosion of the capacities of the paternalist states to meet their obligations. Fortunately, there is a lot of the future left.

4

The Ethical Firm

In the Britain of my youth, the most respected company in the entire country was Imperial Chemical Industries. Combining scientific innovation and size it developed huge prestige, and to work for it was a matter of pride. This was reflected in its mission statement: 'we aim to be the finest chemical company in the world.' Yet in the 1990s ICI changed its mission statement. It became: 'we aim to maximise shareholder value.' What had happened, and why did it matter?

Firms are at the core of capitalism. The mass contempt in which capitalism is held – as greedy, selfish, corrupt – is largely due to their deteriorating behaviour. Economists have not helped. Milton Friedman, Nobel Laureate, vociferously propounded the nostrum – first articulated in 1970 in the *New York Times* – that the sole purpose of a firm is to make profits. As Friedman's ideas spread through the echelons of management this view gradually became standard in business schools, and so filtered into major companies such as ICI. This had consequences.

If there is one feature of modern capitalism that people find most repellent, it is this obsession on making profits. Currently, when faced with the choice between 'The primary purpose of business should be to make profit' versus 'Making a profit should be only one consideration among many', the people who agree with Friedman are outnumbered three-to-one, a difference that is uniform across age groups and opinions about other matters.[1]

Who is right: Friedman or public opinion? A clue comes from what happened at ICI. Did its new Friedman-inspired mission statement motivate the company's workforce to new heights? Has any worker for any company ever got up in the morning, thinking 'today

69

I'm going to maximize shareholder value'? That change in mission statement reflected a change in focus by the company's board. Previously, it had tried to be a world-class chemical company, which implied paying attention to its workforce, its customers and its future. Now it tried to please shareholders with dividends. If you are under the age of forty you are unlikely to have heard of ICI. This is because the change of focus proved disastrous: the company went into decline and was taken over.*

Academic opinion now agrees with public opinion. In 2017 the British Academy launched 'The Future of the Corporation' as its flagship programme. Led by Colin Mayer, Professor of Finance at Oxford University and the former Dean of its business school, the programme's central proposition is that the purpose of business is to meet its obligations to its customers and its workforce. Profitability is not the objective; it is a constraint that has to be satisfied in order to achieve these objectives on a sustainable basis. Why has business gone so wrong, and how can public policy put it right?

THE ETHICAL FIRM OR THE VAMPIRE SQUID?

A great firm does not have to behave like a vampire squid.† Think of a large firm, perhaps Unilever, Ford or Nestlé. What do you think the typical employee of such a firm would tell you about its purpose? Do you imagine that they would say 'to make money for the owners'?

---

* Anecdotes sometimes strike home. In January 2018, I gave the annual public lecture at the central bank of Pakistan and used ICI as an example of a company that lost its sense of purpose. At the end of my talk a distinguished-looking gentleman approached; it turned out that he had been a senior executive with the company. I prepared to apologize for the limitations of my knowledge, but on the contrary he shook my hand and confirmed that shareholder value had become the management obsession in meeting after meeting. In his judgement, that loss of true purpose had destroyed the company.

† This was the image used to critique Goldman Sachs. Whether this was a travesty of Goldman Sachs, recent research suggests that it is not a travesty of squids. They transpire to have the intelligent, asocial, greedy malevolence that economists have wrongly attributed to humans.

Few firms truly run themselves on such a philosophy. The people who work for Unilever are more likely to tell you that they are working to provide affordable foods and soap, often in societies where poverty and disease make their contribution more valuable than the self-promoting activities of NGOs. The people who work for Ford are more likely to tell you about the features of the cars they are making. On a trip to Indonesia, I came across a group of Nestlé workers. They were running a dairy that had transformed the opportunities for local farmers. During a time when public order had broken down in the region, the farmers came to town and surrounded the dairy so as to protect it from looters. Such purposes are achievements in which people can take pride: firms are creating jobs through which people can contribute to their society.

But in some firms the workforce would indeed regard its purpose as to make money. One investment bank nakedly proclaimed this to its staff, displaying in the entrance lobby its mocking mission statement: 'we make nothing but money.' Encouraged by this wretched philosophy, its clever employees gradually evolved the logical refinement: 'we make nothing but money *for ourselves*.' This opened up possible strategies for the smartest employees that the company's Friedman-trained management had lacked the wit to envisage. It transpired that there was a highly efficient way for employees to make money for themselves. This was to commit the company to transactions on which the employee received a bonus, but which exposed the company to the hidden risk of a future loss. This behaviour of its employees duly bankrupted the company. Its name was Bear Stearns, and its bankruptcy triggered the financial crisis of 2008–9 that inflicted global costs on a scale only matched by the world wars.* The cost to the USA alone is estimated to have been around $10 trillion.

The fates of ICI and Bear Stearns illustrate a crucial point: a company needs a sense of purpose. CEOs can use their position to build

---

* Bear Stearns itself was rescued by JP Morgan at the behest of the US Treasury, but the knowledge that it was bankrupt triggered a run on a far larger bank, Lehman Brothers, which was seen to be too-big-to-bail, but turned out to be too-big-to-fail without consequences that proved to be disastrous.

that sense of shared purpose. It is indeed a core responsibility and competence of senior management. We've already seen it in action: Robert Wood Johnson building the Credo that articulated the purpose of Johnson & Johnson and proved vital decades later.

Fifty years ago, the most successful company that had ever existed anywhere was General Motors. It was highly profitable and enormous. Yet by 2009 it was bankrupt. Since its inexorable decline was so significant, it has been analysed in great detail, both as it unfolded (with management consultants repeatedly brought in to diagnose what was going wrong), and in retrospect. What killed GM? Toyota.[2]

As Toyotas started to penetrate the American car market, the initial assessment of GM's top management was that it was a localized problem. Only people on the coasts were buying Toyotas; the heartland market was still solid. So, the phenomenon was entirely explicable: people on the coasts were a bit weird, but it would gradually pass. Unfortunately for GM, this complacent diagnosis proved to be wrong, and the contamination spread to the heartlands. The new diagnosis was technological: the Japanese had robots. Toyota was remarkably co-operative throughout and invited GM to inspect their factory in Japan. The instruction from the CEO of GM to the team that visited the factory was 'photograph everything: if they've got robots, we'll have robots'. Once this strategy was fully implemented, it decisively established that, whatever it was that Toyota was doing to make a difference, it was not the robots. In the next phase, Toyota was sufficiently generous to propose that they and GM run a joint venture in California, making the same car. As these identical cars came off the assembly line, alternate ones were badged as GM and Toyota and marketed accordingly. By this stage Toyota had built a very strong reputation for reliability: their cars were virtually fault-free. Indeed, upon our arrival in the USA in 1998 my wife and I bought one, and twenty years later we are still driving it. This reputation was paying dividends in the market: the identical cars rolling off that Californian production line were selling for a $3,000 premium if they had a Toyota badge on them. So, if it was a difference in quality, what explained it?

Decades previously, Toyota had pioneered a new style of relationships with its workforce. Ordinary workers on the assembly line were organized into small teams called 'quality circles' and given the responsibility for quality control. (Ironically, the concept of quality circles had been devised in America. It was enthusiastically adopted in Japan, possibly because it chimed well with Japanese culture.) The key step was to ask each group to spot faults as soon as possible on its stretch of the line. The mantra promoted by management was 'faults are treasures'. If a worker spotted a fault, what should he do about it? The most dramatic step taken by Toyota management was to install Andon cords, hanging down all along the assembly line. Any worker on the assembly line who spotted a fault was to pull the nearest cord, which would instantly halt the entire line. By its nature, assembly line production is so integrated that stopping the line is spectacularly costly. In the Toyota factory, it cost $10,000 *per minute*. A worker who stopped the line unnecessarily would in just a few minutes inflict costs on the company well in excess of his productive value over an entire year. So, this policy indicated that the management really trusted their workers to work *for* the company, not against it. In other words, it depended upon workers having a sense of purpose that was well aligned with that of the company. I rather doubt that they were thinking 'I'm trying to maximize shareholder value.'

This was utterly different from the approach to quality control used by GM, which was the conventional one of checking a sample of completed cars. Eventually, a new CEO understood the problem: the culture needed changing. Confrontation between GM management and the United Autoworkers Union would be superseded by mutual trust. 'If they've got robots, we'll have robots' was replaced by 'If they've got Andon cords, we'll have Andon cords.' On the orders of the CEO, the cords were installed all along the GM assembly lines. The CEO could announce a change of culture, but the humble assembly line managers, who better appreciated the attitudes of the ordinary workers, knew what would ensue. Over decades, antipathies had accumulated that could not be dissolved overnight. Given the chance to inflict ruinous damage on the company, a few workers would be sure to take it. Those Andon cords would be pulled for spurious reasons, productivity would collapse, and the line managers would be held responsible. Facing reality, they tied the Andon cords up on the ceiling.* The CEO's attempt to change the culture ended in a highly visible demonstration that the management did not trust its workforce. Oppositional identities were intensified.

There was an equivalent story in relation to suppliers. Over the years, Toyota built a co-operative relationship with its suppliers: they both faced the common challenge of making better quality parts that would improve the final product. This required a long-term perspective. Over the market cycle, sometimes Toyota would have the whip-hand in dealing with its suppliers, and sometimes power would shift to suppliers. If each party exploited its temporary advantage, in the long run they would both lose out. Gradually, they learned to trust each other. In contrast, GM had prided itself on being the tough guy, squeezing suppliers to the limit whenever it could. By the time GM realized it needed to change it was too late. As with its workforce, GM found itself skewered by the established belief system within which it operated.

For many years, the workforce of Volkswagen, based in the city of Wolfsburg, would have told you that the purpose of their firm was to make really good cars. Oxford was once Britain's Wolfsburg: the home of the British Motor Corporation. The contrast between the cultures of their workforces echoed that between Toyota and GM. I recall watching, stunned, as the crowd at an international football match played in a German stadium, proudly waved banners with 'VW' before the television cameras. An equivalent display by BMC workers would have been inconceivable, and strikes eventually bankrupted the British company. But in 2016 Volkswagen was hit by a major scandal. Its diesel cars had been fitted with a device that scammed the emissions tests conducted in the USA. What had motivated the employees who had designed this device? Were they just thinking of a personal bonus? I doubt it. More likely, these employees had fully aligned with the purpose of the company, but had not accepted the purpose of the American legislation that had introduced the tests. Quite possibly, they regarded the legislation as a backdoor

* Contrast this action by the junior management of GM with that of the junior management of Johnson & Johnson during the Tylenol crisis and what lay behind that difference.

means of restricting American imports of German cars; or they simply approached passing the test as a tick-box exercise. Of course, they were utterly wrong to do so: they had failed to update their vision of 'a good car' to take pollution into account. Even in terms of their consequences for the company, their choices ended up being disastrous. But it is an insulting delusion of many people who, like me, have cushy jobs in the public sector to imagine that workers in the private sector are driven by greed and fear. The evidence suggests that job satisfaction is actually considerably higher in the private sector; for example, people are far less likely to use illness as a reason for not going to work.

So, there is nothing intrinsically dirty about capitalism. Profit is the constraint that forces discipline on a firm, rather than defining its purpose. But the stories of Bear Stearns, ICI and GM indicate that something has gone seriously wrong. What is it?

WHO CONTROLS THE FIRM?

The answer is that the power of control has become lodged with the wrong people. Capitalism gets its name because ownership of the firm is assigned to the people who provide it with risk capital. The rationale is that those who are taking the risk have both the greatest need for control and the strongest incentive to scrutinize the managers. This rationale has, however, gradually diverged further and further from reality.

If a firm fails, many people suffer; the risk-bearing extends well beyond people who have put in capital. The people who probably lose most are the long-term workers in the company, as they will have accumulated skills and reputation that are only valuable in that company. In addition, if the company is an important employer in the town, everyone who owns a house there will take a significant capital loss.

Customers will also suffer. At the trivial end, when Monarch Airlines went bankrupt in 2017, 100,000 people were stranded. At the more serious end, modern supply chains create interdependencies between firms through which a bankruptcy is transmitted like a virus around the global economy. That is why the bankruptcy of a medium-size investment bank like Lehman Brothers caused such devastation in the financial crisis.

Those who have provided the firm with capital in the form of loans will suffer losses, alongside those who have bought shares, but only the shareholders will have the power conferred by ownership. In contrast, the shareholders may not suffer at all. As a professor, I am entitled to a pension from a fund that covers all universities. The fund is financed by its shareholdings in companies, so if a company fails does my pension suffer? Thankfully not, because the responsibility passes collectively to the entire university system; according to the contract, even if some universities were themselves to fail, the liability would pass to whichever ones remained. How would the universities meet a shortfall? In the end, the liability for my pension is likely to pass to generations of students. To students reading this I assure you of my profound gratitude. But in return for bearing this risk how much control do you have over the management of the companies held by my pension fund?

The company has to be accountable to someone motivated to care about the long-term performance of the company, and sufficiently knowledgeable to spot management mistakes. If share ownership is highly fragmented, there is a free-rider problem: nobody has much incentive to understand whether the long-term strategy of the management is smart. In Germany, the banks play this oversight role, holding shares on behalf of their owners and getting actively involved in company management. In America, and much of the world, it is played by the families that founded successful companies and which retain a blocking shareholding. Only one country has implemented the full Friedman vision. Its companies are tied to profit by millions of shareholders, and they hold companies to account by selling their shares on the market unless profits keep rising. Britain has been the guinea-pig for an economic ideology. Britain's banks have steered well clear of involvement in company management. Founding families have shed their shares because of the design of taxation. Legal control of companies is exclusively in the hands of the shareholders, of whom 80 per cent are pension funds and insurance companies. They, in turn, adopt the mantra, 'If you don't like the company, sell the shares.' Their decisions are now based primarily on algorithms within computers, making sophisticated inferences from recent movements in stock prices: around 60 per cent of the stock-market trades are automated. The superstars are the finest mathematical brains in society, devising algorithms of genius to detect patterns of price momentum. What is missing is any direct knowledge of the company, its management, its workforce, and its prospects such as can only be acquired through long involvement with the company.

Why should the management of a company care whether a pension fund sells its shares? In Britain, the ultimate threat to management is to be taken over by a rival, and this becomes easier the lower the company's share price. Two chocolate companies – Hershey in the USA, and Cadbury in Britain – illustrate the contrasting consequences of ownership. The Hershey family has retained a blocking shareholding, whereas the Cadbury family, an exemplar of Quaker philanthropy, sold its holding on the market. When Kraft tried to expand its presence in the chocolate market it targeted Cadbury, and the pension funds duly sold their holdings: Cadbury ceased to exist as a separate entity. So, effective power lies with the board of the company to avoid this fate. Pre-emptively, the board will watch quarterly profits to determine whether to dismiss the CEO. The typical CEO is now in post for only four years.

Gradually, CEO pay has become increasingly tied to indicators of short-term performance. The problem is most acute in Britain and the USA, the countries in which financial markets are most 'developed' and where CEOs have the shortest tenure. Gradually, this has come to infect the way in which the CEOs of non-financial companies are rewarded. Reflecting the heightened risks, the pay of CEOs has accelerated far beyond the average pay in their companies. In Britain over the past thirty years, it has risen from 30 times that of their workers to 150 times; as such, they are a model of restraint compared with their American counterparts, whose pay has risen from 20 times that of their workers to 231 times. Yet during this period, judged by objective measures, there has been no overall improvement in company performance. The higher pay is evidently not for enhanced performance; nor is it just compensation for extra risk. The people on the compensation committees of major companies constitute yet another networked group. As with all such groups, narratives gradually build a belief system. Over time, as I set out in the previous chapter, our societies have fractured from national to skill-based identities. A microcosm of this vast process is that the peer group of a CEO has shifted from being the fellow-workers in his company to his fellow-CEOs in other companies. In consequence, the norms of the group on the compensation committee as to what might be 'fair' have crept upwards. An executive relates hearing the comment, 'He gets $5 million and I only get $4 million: *it isn't fair.*' At the heart of this is not even greed, many of these CEOs are not hedonists but driven workaholics. It is the changed source of peer esteem arising from redefined identities. The $4-million CEO may not have been thinking of what he could have bought with the missing million dollars, but of the condescending sympathy of his $5-million colleague when they next met at Davos.

The financial sector has practised what it preached. If short-term performance in companies should be incentivized by highly geared pay, they themselves should adopt the same model. Nor have they been coy about it. They have led the way in the upward march of CEO pay relative to that of their workforce; in banks, it has now reached 500:1, undented by the financial crisis. This changed the ethical composition of the people who clawed their way to the top. Deutsche Bank got Edson Mitchell as its CEO, who transformed the bank's culture from German staidness to one of wild excess: he 'hired mercenaries . . . they didn't care about ethics'.[3] There was an ethical vacuum: on Friday evenings, the trading teams would decamp to leer at pole dancers; prostitutes were hired to entertain the senior staff at Christmas parties; and Mitchell was openly contemptuous of obligations to family. What rapidly inflated to become the world's largest bank was being run by people whose ethics were more suited to the management of a brothel. Mitchell died in a plane crash; his bank has met an equivalent fate.

Lower down the food chain, fund managers are judged by the quarterly valuation of the shares in the portfolio for which they are responsible. Asset management appears to lend itself to such an approach precisely because performance is so readily measured using a single metric. But it is very difficult to design incentives to reward what is really desired. Asset managers are well rewarded for short-term performance, as a result of which they judge the firms in which they invest on the same criteria.

THE CONSEQUENCES OF VESTING CONTROL WITH OWNERS

Is this ultimately a wise strategy for a pension fund? Being in charge of a company has become a desperate struggle to keep quarterly profits rising until the stock options kick in and the CEO can leave with a golden parachute. So, what is the smart strategy for a CEO? Obviously, it is to make changes that drive up quarterly profits as much as possible, as soon as possible. Here is the assessment of Carolyn Fairbairn, Director-General of the Confederation of British Industries. She worries that 'there is a fixation on shareholder value at the expense of purpose'.[4] The CBI is the lobby group for Britain's major firms: its director-general is hardly a dreamy radical.

If a CEO has to drive up quarterly profits, how can it be done? Consider three options. Option 1 is to build a company like Johnson & Johnson, with good, trusting relationships between the firm and its workers, its suppliers and its customers. This pays off handsomely in the end, but the snag is that it takes a long time. Option 2 is to cut all expenditures that are not essential for production. This sounds as if it drives the company into efficiencies that are valuable for society, even if they are painful for the company itself. But since past CEOs will have already cut the fat, the largest remaining category of expenditure that can be cut most easily without rapidly affecting production is investment. Naturally, in due course, cutting investment will hit output, but 'in due course' the CEO may be out of a job anyway. Option 3 is not to waste time on any real decisions about production or investment, but to rearrange the company's accounts. Those of us who are not accountants imagine that the profession has established clear rules as to how accounts are drawn up, but in practice there are many grey areas that enable profits to be increased, decreased, or shifted from one subsidiary to another.[5]

Which of these would you choose were you a CEO? We can see

the consequences of Option 2 playing out in corporate America and Britain. Despite high profitability, companies are choosing not to invest. Striking evidence for this behaviour comes from the contrasting investment rates of companies whose shares are traded on stock exchanges and those whose shares are held privately and cannot be sold on markets. The investment rate of the companies whose shares are traded is 2.7 per cent; that of those whose shares are privately held is 9 per cent. In Britain, which has the largest financial sector relative to its economy of any major country, corporate investment in research and development is far below the average for advanced economies.[6]

Unsurprisingly, the quarterly profit-chasing companies have worse long-term records of performance – even on the yardstick of profitability – than companies that are able to take a longer-term perspective. But if the previous CEO has already cut investment to the bone, perhaps you would be driven to Option 3. By its nature, this is hard to detect except in those instances in which the scam has been pushed so far that it gets uncovered. Periodically, this happens. In the USA, the legendary case is that of Enron. Enron's British equivalents are Robert Maxwell, CEO of Mirror Group Newspapers, who had once been investigated by public officials and found to be 'unfit to run a public company', and Philip Green, CEO of BHS, who was actually knighted. Each of them stripped their company of its pension fund, leaving thousands of employees impoverished. Maxwell stepped off the back of his mega-yacht as the scam was about to be discovered; Green still has his mega-yacht, aptly renamed by his critics *The BHS Destroyer*. Perhaps mega-yachts should be considered leading indicators for 'creative' accounting?

Options 2 and 3 each have consequences that are seriously damaging for society. Major companies are run without adequate attention to the longer term; and the reported accounts of companies become untrustworthy.

It gets worse: so far, we have seen that CEOs are increasingly diverting their energies from the long-term process of building a great firm to short-term tricks. But the widening of pay differentials has made it harder even for those CEOs and boards who want to take that long-term approach. As the Johnson & Johnson, ICI,

Volkswagen and Toyota stories demonstrate, a key part of a long-term strategy is to persuade workers to identify with the firm. Narratives can only do their magic if they are not contradicted by actions. Telling workers 'we are all in this together' while paying yourself five hundred times more than your typical employee is likely to be met with a degree of cynicism. A worker on the production line may come to think, 'Since you are using your power to loot the company, I'm going to pull that Andon cord next time I want a break.' Do as I say, but not as I do, seldom works.

So is the current strategy of pension funds wise? Quite evidently, it isn't. They have a clear obligation to be able to pay decent pensions to their members as they come due. Whether they are able to meet these obligations depends upon one thing only – the long-term return on their assets. This depends upon the long-term performance of the pool of companies whose shares they hold. In aggregate, pension funds cannot outperform the market, and so their ability to meet their obligations depends upon the long-term performance of the firms in the economy. By diverting managements from this task, pension funds have reduced their own ability to meet their obligations.

WHAT WE CAN DO ABOUT IT

It is time to turn from this depressing litany of failings to practical solutions. Fortunately, these problems are not inevitable features of capitalism but the results of fixable mistakes of public policy. Public policy has gone wrong because of the trivialization generated by the strident rivalry of antiquated ideologies. The ideology of the right asserts faith in 'the market' and denigrates all policy intervention. Its solution is 'get the government off the back of business: deregulate!' The ideology of the left denigrates capitalism and condemns the managers of firms and funds as greedy. Its solution is state control of companies, and state ownership of the commanding heights of the economy. Both these fundamentalist ideologies are ill-founded, but between them they have set the terms of public discussion, impeding productive thought.

The starting point for a new approach is to recognize that the role of the large corporation in society has never properly been thought through. The boards that run large companies are taking decisions of overarching importance for society. Yet their present structure is the result of individual, unco-ordinated decisions, each of which happened to lead to some further decision that had not been anticipated. The system of corporate governance has lacked any process remotely equivalent to the intense and shrewd public discussion, embodied by the Federalist papers, that produced the American Constitution and its system of national governance. Public policies towards business have been incremental, and so have never properly addressed the fundamental issue of control. Any viable solution must begin with rebalancing the interests in which the power of control is legally vested.

CHANGING POWER IN THE FIRM

Currently, in the Anglo-Saxon economies, the law requires directors of companies to run the company in the interest of its owners. This, for example, is how the wording of Britain's Companies Act is usually interpreted, even though it would permit wider considerations.* In turn, the owners are exclusively those who hold shares in the company. This system is not intrinsic to capitalism: it arose because, in the early stages of firm growth during the eighteenth century, the binding constraint was raising enough finance for risky investments that needed a minimum scale. That world has been superseded. The risk of financial loss is now routinely addressed by diversification, information and checks on corporate governance. There is plenty of capital willing to finance risky investments (as evidenced by the dot. com boom, followed by the securitized mortgage boom). People are now willing to buy non-voting shares: they take the same risks as other shareholders but without the power of control. The largest

---

* John Kay has pointed out to me that the detailed language of the Act encourages boards to take a larger perspective, but when I mentioned this to the Chairman of a major company he shook his head, assuring me that he was legally required to attend only to the interests of shareholders. A culture interprets its texts.

undiversified risks are now probably those of long-serving employees, who have invested their human capital in a single company, and customers who have locked themselves into long-term structures of supply, yet who are usually unrepresented on the board. It is entirely possible to give either of these groups representation on a board and sometimes it happens; such companies are called 'mutuals'.

The most respected company in Britain is no longer ICI; it is the John Lewis Partnership. This enduring and hugely successful firm has a highly unusual power structure. It is owned by a trust run in the interests of its workforce. Reflecting this, workers receive a substantial share of profits as an annual bonus. Moreover, what is sauce for the CEO goose is seen to be sauce for the shop assistant: *the same percentage is paid to a shop-floor worker as to the CEO*. All workers have a say in how the company is run through a series of local, regional and national councils, electing 80 per cent of the company's governing council. John Lewis is an example of a mutual company, owned collectively by people with a direct interest in it, such as workers or customers, as opposed to shareholders. As new workers are hired, or the firm acquires new customers, they gradually accumulate entitlements, replacing those who had left. By design, ownership and control are vested in those who participate in the company and so have a direct interest in its performance.

Many companies used to have such a structure, but it is subject to one fatal temptation. Those in whom ownership and control is currently vested are legally entitled to convert the company from its mutual status to a one whose owners have shares that can be sold on financial markets. By doing so, the current vintage of 'owners' acquire the entire capital value of the firm at the expense of all subsequent generations of participants. In Britain, the scope for demutualization was created by a change in the law in 1986; underpinning the previous law had been social norms that recognized such a move as unethical. But the new financial culture of the 1980s weakened norms of obligation. Sometimes, temptation proved too great.

In the USA, one vintage of partners in Goldman Sachs, a group of people more renowned for their exceptional acumen than for their exceptional decency, seized the opportunity provided by the new ethics. This enabled them to escape the grinding poverty experienced by all previous vintages of partners. In Britain, most building societies (savings and loan associations, in American parlance) demutualized. The largest, the Halifax Building Society, had been a huge and enduring company, built over the course of 150 years from humble beginnings in a small town in the north of England to a financial giant that efficiently provided millions of people with mortgages, and millions more small savers with security. The change in owner-ship structure freed the management of this magnificent company from the deadweight amateur control of its users, handing what had grown to be the largest bank in Britain to the professional scrutiny of fund managers watching quarterly profits. John Kay was on the board and observed the results.[7] The liberated management decided that quarterly profits could be increased by broadening the business from the boring process of taking in the deposits of small savers and lending them on to people buying homes. The big money was in play-ing the market in financial derivatives. Kay pointed out that gambling on these markets could only make money if other players lost it, and asked why the Halifax thought that it was going to be among the winners. The CEO explained that the bank had recruited a particu-larly smart team of players. Kay's laconic comment on this brag was that he found it somewhat less credible once he had met the team. But despite his doubts, Halifax's profits surged on the back of this new strategy, and the CEO appeared vindicated. Then they tanked. The Halifax had to be rescued by another bank and massive losses gradually came to light. The professional fund managers had pre-sided over rampant management folly that within one generation had bankrupted a company that as a mutual had grown over the course of 150 years from tiny beginnings to a world-class business. But, per-sonally, I cannot complain. Long ago, my mother had opened a Halifax Building Society savings account for my pocket money, and I had never got around to closing it: so, I received a little windfall as my interest was converted into shares which I sold in time.

So, the evidence on outcomes supports giving legal force to the rep-resentation of worker interests on the boards of companies. Nor is such a change impractical: in Germany, the legal structure of companies has long required worker representation. Far from this having generated disaster, German companies have been outstandingly successful. But what is to prevent the workers and owners of a company conspiring together to exploit those interests that are unrepresented; most obviously, the interests of users?

THE HABITAT OF FIRMS: COMPETITION FOR SURVIVAL

Companies exist within a habitat, and each one finds a niche within it. The struggle for survival in this habitat is the discipline that compels these companies to serve the interests of their customers. Translated from biology to economics, the habitat is the marketplace, and the struggle for survival is competition; the force of evolution, by which species come to be well-adapted to their environment, has as its counterpart the benign dynamics of capitalism. In struggling against each other to survive, firms try to make their product cheaper and better, and we are all the beneficiaries.

The enemy of competition is vested interests. Vested interests use their power to build impediments to competition via a range of strategies. At the legal end of the spectrum is lobbying, which has grown into a huge sector that burns up resources in a quest for privilege. In the middle of the spectrum we find corruption: the abuse of public office to sell permits and court judgments, and to grant monopolies. Current revelations suggest that, in return for favours, former President Zuma of South Africa used his office to generate rents for the business empire of the Gupta family. At the extremity of the spectrum is the total capture of the state.

The centralization of power inherent in communism eliminated accountability and so left vested interests rampant. Most people recognize this: the same surveys that find capitalism to be tainted by corruption find that corruption is even more strongly associated with communism. As the grotesque lifestyle of the three-generation Kim dynasty in North Korea illustrates, the all-powerful state is not a check on vested interests, but rather their ultimate triumph. Communist societies removed the habitat of the marketplace, and the result was so dysfunctional that, despite intense political repression, their people voted with their feet. 'Build a wall!' did not start with

Donald Trump's attempt to keep foreigners out, but with the desperate attempt of communist regimes to keep their citizens in. I grew up with images of people trying to climb over the walls, but younger people have no such memory: they can only learn it from books, and the books give priority to other parts of history. My ten-year-old knows about Hadrian's Wall but not about the Berlin Wall: try it as a test on your children.

Ever since markets began, powerful people have tried to limit competition to their own advantage. Vested interests know far more about the nature of their advantage than public officials can possibly know. Being narrowly defined groups, they find common action in their own interest easier to organize than the diffuse common interest that they oppose. Competition overcomes these obstacles. Since firms in the same business have similar information, once they compete the vested interests will lose their advantage regardless of whether public officials know about them. Once the common interest recognizes the principle of maintaining competition, it can use it to repel each specific vested interest heist. The opponents of competition plead that it is unfair, destructive and ignores some imagined benefit provided by the incumbent. Behind these arguments there lurks self-interest: it is *motivated reasoning*.

It was the market, not public intervention that disciplined GM and Bear Stearns. But nevertheless, sometimes competition will not be sufficient. For these tougher circumstances, we need active public policies.

While vested interests try to create artificial impediments to competition, in some sectors of the economy there are technological impediments due to atypically powerful economies of scale. Scale economies are most pronounced when the activity depends upon a network. The provision of electricity requires a network of wires, the grid; the provision of water requires a network of pipes; the provision of train services requires a rail network. Sometimes it is possible to detach the service from the network: train companies can compete on a shared rail network; electricity generators can compete on a shared grid. But the network itself is a natural monopoly. The emergence of the e-economy has created new network industries that can extend to global monopoly. These firms need very little capital as conventionally defined – the tangible assets of equipment and buildings. Their value is an intangible asset: their networks.[8] Unlike tangible assets, these are very difficult for competitors to replicate; and, being immaterial, they have no fixed location subject to public policy. Facebook, Google, Amazon, eBay and Uber are all examples of networks that tend towards natural global monopoly in their particular niches. As unregulated, privately owned natural monopolies, they are highly dangerous.

The same process is underway less dramatically in many other sectors of the economy. The steady increase in complexity inherent in rising productivity has introduced some network features into other industries.[9] This, in turn, is enabling the top firms within each of these industries to become more dominant. Walmart has harnessed the new network features of logistics to retailing. The largest banks have reaped new scale economies in finance. The overall increases in productivity and corporate profits have become concentrated in such top companies.[10] While not as extreme as the natural monopolies, the gains from scale enable them to receive a premium over the return on capital earned by their smaller competitors. Competition in the ownership of shares in these companies drives up their price, enabling the original shareholders to capture this premium on scale as a windfall.

Where big is technologically super-profitable, either because it leads to the extreme outcome of a natural monopoly, or to the less dramatic exceptional returns of dominant companies, competition becomes impotent. We need some more targeted instrument of public policy. The conventional options are regulation and public ownership. Each has its limitations.

DO RULES RULE?

However well-intentioned are boards of directors, sometimes regulation is essential. A rule can ensure that all firms follow the same policy, whereas leaving the matter to the judgement of boards would result in variation. For example, it would be inefficient and inequitable if some firms did much more than others to reduce their carbon emissions.

However, when rules are used to address the problems of exploitative firms, the limitations are considerable. Regulation can aim either to break up natural monopolies, or to control the price they charge to consumers. Breaking up monopolies forces competition into the sector, but since the technological scale economies continue to push towards monopoly, policy intervention has to be sustained. Even then, by blocking the scale economies, policy imposes inefficiency. Price controls aim to restrain the company from exploiting the scale economies for its own benefit, forcing it to pass the gains on to consumers. Its limitation we have already encountered in a different context – asymmetric information. In its previous incarnation, it was about the gap between what the management of a firm knows, and what fund managers can find out. Now it is about the gap between what the management of a firm knows and what the regulator knows. The most spectacular asymmetries have been in financial markets, between the regulators and the banks, but the problem is endemic. The firm has far better knowledge of its costs and its market than can possibly be gathered by a regulator, and so the problem can never be fully resolved.

Arguably, the best policy response to the problem is to combine a best-guess at price control with contrived competition, through auctioning the right to the monopoly. An example of the benefits of auctioning rights comes from the British government sale of the rights to the 3G mobile phone network. Initially, the Treasury tried to work out a reasonable price for the network based on available information of its likely profitability, concluding that a price of £2 billion would be its target. Fortunately, it was persuaded by academic economists that the asymmetry problem was so severe that its estimate might be wrong, and so instead it put the network up for sale in an auction. The realized price was £20 billion. Evidently, whether the successful firm had paid £2 billion or £20 billion, it would have exploited the customers of the network to the maximum permitted extent, but at least this way what customers lost through monopoly exploitation was being captured by this windfall gain in government revenue.

An impediment to this is the credibility of government commitments. When firms bid on such contracts they will make mistakes, albeit not as large as those that would be made by a regulator since they have much better information. If the firm bids too much it will suffer squeezed profits and, at the limit, renege on the contract through bankruptcy. It will only be prepared to take this downside risk if there is a corresponding prospect of gains on the upside. Moreover, if all firms underestimate the potential for profit, the winning bid will turn out to have been too low.* But politicians have short horizons imposed by elections, and so if a firm that has won a contract to run a monopoly utility is seen to be making high profits there is a temptation to overturn the decision of the regulator. The more that firms fear that such interference is likely, the lower will be their bids at auction and so the higher the profit that the winner will make, and the more likely is political interference . . . Low credibility is a vicious circle.

If this were the only problem, the solution would be to shorten the length of the contract to match the political cycle; contracts would run from mid-term to mid-term to minimize the pressure from an impending election. But exploitative pricing is not the only dimension of company behaviour that matters. For a utility service such as water or electricity supply to be sustainable, the firm should use much of its profit to finance re-investment. But the shorter the horizon of the contract, the less inclined will the firm be to take socially desirable investment decisions. Potentially, the regulator can try to regulate investment, but this requires even more information than pricing: realistically, the regulator can have little idea as to which investments are desirable, nor how much they would cost. Regulation has its limits.

The problems of regulation are vastly compounded in regard to the global e-utilities. Such regulation would often need to be global, whereas the capacity to regulate has remained overwhelmingly national. International co-operation is made more difficult because the e-companies are overwhelmingly American, and so the American government is at best ambivalent. Here is the assessment of a

* The 'winner's curse' suggests that this will not be very common.

specialist antitrust lawyer, Gary Reback: 'Will the EU ever succeed in using antitrust law to rein in the power of the dominant American tech companies? No ... Their feeble antitrust enforcement efforts will never yield real results.' Moreover, it would be easy for the companies to portray any regulation that did manage to be effective as being anti-American. Rules do not rule.

So, given these inherent problems of regulation, the currently fashionable alternative is public ownership.

PUBLIC OWNERSHIP

Currently in Britain there is so much dissatisfaction with the regulated private utilities that large majorities favour nationalization to bring rail, water and electricity companies into public ownership. This is ironic since all the utilities were originally publicly owned monopolies, and the impetus for turning them into commercial companies was public dissatisfaction with their performance. However, the public memory of the inadequacies of public ownership is a decade more distant than memory of the Berlin Wall. Under public ownership, the utilities suffered from capture by their employees, reflected in a very high incidence of strikes, and politicized underpricing of services that caused under-investment. Current discussion has polarized around ideology: ironically, the left wants nationalized industries, but not a sense of nationhood; the right wants a sense of nationhood, but not nationalized industries.

In reality, some industries have worked better run by private regulated firms, and others worse, consistent with wide variations in the extent to which information is asymmetric. On reasonable measures, the railways are better, whereas water is worse. The evidence that rail is better under private management comes most clearly from usage: however much they grumble, people have voted with their feet. Rail usage declined every year in the decades of public ownership prior to privatization in 1998, and has increased, strongly, every year since. The evidence that water is worse comes primarily from the very high profits extracted as dividends.

SO, WHAT CAN WORK?

Since both regulation and public ownership have severe limitations, are there any other approaches that have not been considered? Here are three.

Taxation

In those sectors in which big is naturally more productive and more profitable, the exceptional gains from scale are a form of 'economic rent'. Such rents are an important concept in economics that will be central when I turn to the divergence between the metropolis and broken cities. What economists mean by the term is the return on an activity *beyond what is needed* to attract the workers, finance and enterprise on which it depends. If the rents evaporated, whoever has been capturing them would be worse off, but the activity would be unaffected. The private monopoly gains economic rents; so, less obviously, do the largest firms in those industries in which being the biggest implies being exceptionally productive. The future of taxation is to do a better job in capturing these rents. Unlike other taxation, by definition this does not discourage productive activity; instead, it is capturing something that has not been earned by the effort of work, the delayed gratification of saving, or the courage required for risk-taking.

In those industries where to be the biggest has come to imply the most productive, there is a case for differentiating rates of corporate taxation by size. The same data that academics have used to show that in some sectors big is more profitable could be used to design differential tax rates. The purpose would not be to discourage economies of scale, but to capture some of the gains for society. Ironically, we already differentiate taxation by size, but perversely: the new network monopolies such as Amazon benefit massively from being tax scams, avoiding the taxation of their terrestrial equivalents. Since the effects of taxation cannot be fully known in advance, the smart approach would be step-by-step, starting with modest new tax rates on size and evaluating the consequences. One consequence is pre-dictable: the big companies will lobby vigorously against it.

Representing the public interest on company boards

Many of the decisions of boards have consequences that extend beyond the firm but are not well suited for regulation, which is a crude sledgehammer that could easily do a lot of damage. An example is the bias of CEOs towards spending too little on investment: a regulation requiring firms to invest a certain proportion of their profits would replicate some of the worst features of Soviet economic planning. A wise investment decision depends upon a wealth of detailed evidence and judgement that cannot be reduced to a few regulations.

The best way to overcome these limitations is not to strengthen regulation, but to put the public interest right in the engine room where decisions are being taken: the public interest needs direct rep-resentation on the board. This does not mean that companies should be run as charities, sacrificing the interest of the company for what-ever cause some representative of the 'public interest' takes a fancy. Although the overarching purpose of a company should be consist-ent with long-term benefit to society, the primary means by which it can do that is to focus on its core competence. But it does mean that board decisions should not sacrifice a clear and substantial public interest for a small benefit to the firm.

How can the public interest best be incorporated into the board? The law could be changed to make due consideration of the public interest mandatory for *all* board members. Being legally liable, if board members chose to ignore an important aspect of the public interest, they could face civil or criminal challenge in the courts. The law could be framed in such a way that the company would not be expected to bear large losses for small public gains, but where there was a reasonable presumption that large public losses were being inflicted for small corporate benefits, a court case could be brought. Knowing this, it would be a rash board that did not bother to hold a board-level discussion on such decisions, and summarize that discus-sion in the minutes. Case law would gradually build up from early judgments, and if the outcomes looked to be tilted too far in one direction or the other, the law could be revised.

There is already a precedent for this in the United States through the new category of Public Interest Companies. These are companies with a dual mandate: commercial interest and public interest, both of which the board must take into account. This is the right idea, but, as it is, Public Interest Companies will never amount to more than a small sliver of the corporate sector. Indeed, their very existence inadvertently emphasizes that all other firms are *not* to be run in the public interest. The current vintage of Public Interest Companies should more properly be seen as a pilot. By studying the behaviour of these companies, the idea can be refined to the point at which a revised mandate can safely be rolled out across the corporate sector.

Policing the public interest

Every regulation can be subverted by clever box-ticking; every tax can be reduced by clever accounting; every mandate can be fudged by motivated reasoning. The only defence against such actions is an all-seeing police force. This does not mean the prying *paternalist state*: it means ordinary people in their role as citizens.

Once a society has enough citizens who understand the proper purpose of companies, and have accepted it as a norm, we ourselves become the anchors of good corporate behaviour. Our responses to good and bad conduct become an instance of the gentle pressure of esteem and shame, the system that maintains the vast network of reciprocal obligations characterizing all successful societies. This gentle policing role does not require everybody to be part of it: there is a critical mass of participants above which the risks arising from corporate misconduct become too high to entertain. In any large company, many people will inevitably be in the know on important decisions. Only a few of them need to behave morally in order to force decent behaviour. Usually, if a few people point out that public interest is in danger of being sacrificed, nobody will want to take the exposed position that the public interest doesn't matter. In rare instances, even one brave person will be sufficient – the whistleblower. All firms have a large pool of decent people who would be willing to take on a new identity alongside their existing identities; they would feel proud to become guardians of the public interest. At the height of the banking boom, one of the largest investment banks decided to create a small unit for promoting social enterprise. Working in the unit would mean forfeiting the bonuses that were supposedly motivating the high-octane corporate culture, and the management wondered whether any of its staff would be willing to transfer into it. The four new posts were duly circulated within the company: one thousand staff applied. There is no shortage of well-motivated people working purposively in large corporations.

Encouraging your firm to have a decent sense of purpose is your contribution to society, but continuing to work for one which lacks purpose is personally soul-destroying. As we will see in the next chapter, well-being does not come from financial success. If you are working for a firm which lacks social purpose and you have no realistic prospect of altering it, then – if practicable – *change your job*. I have been blessed with some exceptionally talented nephews, but the one whom I currently most admire was working as a car salesman. His company wanted the usual tricks of the trade, akin to the Goldman Sachs leaked emails in which clients were referred to as 'muppets'. A young man with an acute sense of ethical purpose, he quit for a job that offered less money but provided more opportunity to help its customers. He tells me he is much happier.

These new identities, norms and narratives would make our society better and our lives more satisfying, but they must first be built. No single firm can do this. At a trivial level, were a firm to ask its staff to keep the firm focused on the public interest it would probably be greeted as just a new piece of PR. But a deeper answer is that the corporate culture prevailing in one company largely reflects that prevailing in others. Some societies manage to establish cultures of good corporate behaviour. Perhaps it was because Japan had a stronger culture of worker–firm co-operation than America that Toyota was able to adopt the American idea of trusting the workers on the assembly line to self-police the quality of their cars. Similarly, post-war German industrial relations policy was heavily influenced by what the British Trades Union Congress proposed would be a better way of conducting them than the confrontational British practice of the pre-war era. Post-war Germany got the industrial relations that British trades unions had learned from the failings of the British system. The aftermath of defeat broke the vested interests and enabled Germany to do the policy reset, whereas in Britain victory enabled them to remain entrenched.[11]

Rebuilding the reciprocal obligations of corporate behaviour is a massive public good that must be accomplished by government. Chapter 2 gave an outline of how new obligations can be built. We need to build a critical mass of *ethical citizens*. Ethical citizens are people who understand the purpose of companies and the vital contribution they can make to society; they recognize the norms implied by this purpose; and encourage businesses to meet those obligations through the twin pressures of esteem and disapproval.

Citizens are routinely fed so much well-meaning chatter by government that people have become habituated to dismissing it, so a necessary start is to re-establish credibility. We have already met the solution to the conundrum of how a suspicious audience can be convinced – *signalling*. To recap, a signal is something that reveals your true type to the suspicious audience. How does it work? Nobel Laureate Michael Spence saw that the only way was through an action that, were you the type that your audience suspects, would be prohibitively costly. Almost certainly, this will be an action that, even though you are not the rogue they fear, will be unpleasantly costly for you. You need to find an action that for you is a bearable cost of winning trust, whereas for the rogue it would be unbearable. Armed with this insight, what can a government do in the present situation?

Recall that citizens are currently contemptuous of firms, generally regarding them as greedy, corrupt and exploitative. This dominant narrative has to be changed, but if your first utterance is that firms are pretty useful for society many people will switch off. There are dramatic things you can do. Many people are rightly outraged that no banking executive went to gaol as a result of conduct during the financial crisis. This is because the behaviour that caused the crisis was not deliberately intended to ruin the company, but reckless. When a motorist kills someone through recklessness, we have a classification for it – manslaughter – which distinguishes it from the crime of murder, which is killing with intent. We need the equivalent crime for all systemically important companies: *bankslaughter*. The knowledge that, even once retired with a golden parachute, a former CEO could be dragged off the golf course and held responsible for past mistakes would likely concentrate the minds of those in positions of responsibility.

Once you have demonstrated some spine, you can move on to present a national strategy in simple terms. Perhaps start with the purpose of firms, to benefit society in ways that are sustainable and restore rising living standards. Explain why many firms have deviated from this purpose. Explain the government policies that will try to correct this state of affairs, and – most crucially – explain their limitations. Then invite people across society to take on this new role as *ethical citizens*. Like all successful narratives, change cannot be achieved overnight. It requires a sustained and consistent message across many different mouthpieces of government and, like all narratives, it can be fatally undermined by actions that are inconsistent with the words. But across most Western societies, the political leaders of 1945–70 governments succeeded in building many new reciprocal obligations. Although those narratives were not specifically about firms, they probably helped to account for the predominance of the *ethical firm*. Remember: back then CEOs paid themselves only twenty times what they paid their workers. They now pay themselves 231 times what they pay their workers: the *ethical firm* has given way to the *vampire squid*. Times have changed; they need to change back again.

5

The Ethical Family

The family is the most potent of all the entities that lift us beyond the individual. Husband and wife publicly bind themselves to reciprocal obligations. Sentiment also binds parents to their children. Parents care for their children, and often, many years later, children care for their parents, but the potential for reciprocity is seldom asserted as a right. While care received in old age is welcome, the care provided to the child is given unconditionally, rather than being framed as a deal. Yet offspring often see reciprocity as an obligation. A wonderful old Yorkshire joke exploits this little gap between an obligation and a right. A son's ethical inadequacy is revealed: 'Mother, you've worked hard for me all your life, now . . . go out and work for thy self.' The web of obligations can extend far beyond spouses and children. In ancient societies family obligations extended to what now seem very distant relatives, such as seventh cousins.

Even families are networks; in the typical three-generation nuclear family, the parents in the middle generation form the hub, though often they will be recirculating narratives handed down from earlier generations. The basic formula for generating moral norms from narratives is even more evident at the level of the family than in states and firms. Families are natural units for creating a sense of belonging because we are reared in them from our earliest moments. Physical proximity is reinforced through stories of belonging: they attach each new generation to the family, creating a 'we'. Tales of obligation point out duties; other stories link our actions to consequences. Like all families, mine abounds in these stories, peopled by heroes and black sheep. It's fun to recall them, placing each in its category: belonging, obligation and enlightened self-interest.

As in all networked groups, these narratives get juggled around until they form a compatible package, a belief system. The biological underpinnings of the family leave plenty of scope for rival belief systems to coexist, but as of 1945 one belief system was almost universal across Western societies: here I will call it *the ethical family*. By this I do not mean to imply that it is the only belief system that is ethical: it is indeed strikingly different to the values of many families today. I am simply putting a label to the ethical structure that was very widespread in families for a long period.

In the ethical family of 1945, the married couple forming the middle generation accepted mutual obligations towards both other generations, children and parents. This often implied a considerable burden, but since each person would pass through all three generations it was accepted as the phase of responsibility. The structure was a powerfully stable belief system: a shared identity defining the domain for a norm of discriminating reciprocity, supported by enlightened self-interest. The shared identity of belonging to the family was easy to establish since it was a daily lived reality, the domain of 'mutual regard'. The norms of reciprocal commitments were natural extensions of sentiments of affection. And the norms could be reinforced by a sense of purpose: if enough people complied, long-term material benefits for everyone followed – 'enlightened self-interest'.

As of 1945, almost everyone belonged to such a family. Yet, over the following decades, this changed profoundly. Across Western societies people began to shed obligations to their families. The divorce rate exploded, peaking in the USA around 1980 and a little later in the UK. But as the new divides between the educated and the less educated opened, the difference became stark.

Shocks destabilized the long-powerful belief system of the *ethical family*; as the ethical family faded it compounded social divergence – and that divergence had some ugly consequences.

SHOCKS AT THE TOP

The first shock to the norms of the ethical family was technological. The birth-control pill offered young women control over their lives:

sex could be separated from its previous consequence of conception. This eased the process of finding a compatible partner; temporary sexual relationships became less risky, and so the old and fraught 'wrangle for a ring' gave way to a vastly more reliable search process of cohabitation prior to marriage. In the astute lines of Larkin, 'Sexual intercourse began / In nineteen sixty-three'.

The liberation started with technology-aided sex, but soon went far beyond it. A profound intellectual shock liberated individuals from the constraints of many stultifying norms of the ethical family. Obligations to family gave way to new obligations to self: the obligation of self-fulfilment through personal achievement. Laws were changed to make divorce easier. An indication of the changes underlying easier divorce was that it was made blame-free: there was no longer a guilty party.

Unsurprisingly, the intellectual shock originated in the university campus and so primarily affected the new class of the highly educated. It challenged the notion of the ethical family at its foundation, that esteem came from meeting obligations. In place of the family, the new ethics put the self; in place of esteem from meeting obligations, the new ethics put esteem from self-fulfilment. The variant that appealed to women was feminism; the variant that appealed to men was *Playboy*. Actions that had previously been conceptualized as temptations to be resisted became reconceived as moments of self-realization to be grasped. In many families of the new class, one or other partner of a couple discovered that to fulfil themselves required a divorce.

As men and women adjusted to these new norms, the nature of elite marriage changed, aided by a further shock: the vast expansion of universities. This equalized the numbers of educated men and women and provided a further vast improvement in match-making. Women and men learned how to find partners with whom they would be compatible (something that has continued with the enhanced match-making of online dating). This was soon supplemented by the legalization of abortion, a second line of defence behind contraception. The previous norms of the middle-generation couple, of gender hierarchy and mutual obligations to the other generations, were replaced in most educated households by mutual encouragement to self-fulfilment through personal achievement.[1]

Cohabitation and assortative mating turned the educated into well-matched couples, and so divorce rates declined. High-achieving parents aspired to pass their success on to their offspring, and so the gender hierarchy that had reflected the gender imbalance in education gave way to mutual parental hothousing.

When I was a child I got no help with homework: no parental coaching or monitoring; no private tutors. My parents were in no position, either academically or financially, to do so. But fortunately for me, even elite children got little extra-school help when I was in school, so I could compete. Yet as an elite parent, I find myself teaching science to Alex, aged eleven, while my wife teaches him Latin, and we also pay for a tutor. All the other children in his class are similarly helped. There has been a radical shift in norms. The former system would probably have persisted had it not been hit by another shock, the vast growth of the middle class, and a corresponding increase in the intensity of competition for the top slots in university education. My own university, Oxford, takes a significantly smaller proportion of the British population as undergraduate students than it did in the 1960s; it has globalized its intake, which in practice usually means the children of foreign elites. Yet with the expansion of the British middle class, far more families want their children to go there. Once some parents started to give their children an advantage by hothousing them, others had to match them or see their children's opportunities further deteriorate: the old norms were shocked beyond the range of circumstances in which they were stable, and imploded. In consequence, child-rearing among the educated class became more time-consuming, and so couples cut back on the number of children they had, reducing family size.[2] Trophy wives gave way to trophy children: reader, I reared one.*

The new self-fulfilment of the educated class was a genuine increase in well-being for many of its participants, albeit that the epidemic of divorce left casualties. We all know of them: salient for me,

---

* For the minority of readers who lack a sense of humour, this play on Charlotte Brontë's phrase is a joke. While our eldest indeed has the accoutrements of a trophy child, he would be rightly outraged and incredulous at the implication that his parents contributed anything towards his achievements.

a wife who lost access to her son as a result of being abandoned by her husband for fulfilment with another woman, and a husband who lost access to his daughter as a result of being abandoned by his wife for fulfilment with another man. Those who prioritized their own fulfilment doubtless conjured exonerating narratives. However, even after the rate of divorce abated, it left its mark on social norms. For those educated people who remained single, for whatever reason, the ethical family norm of no children prior to a stable relationship was rendered void: if self-fulfilment required a child, so be it, at least in Western societies. In this respect, Japan parted company with other developed countries. There the pressure to rear trophy children was far fiercer than in Western societies. As a result, single-parenting could not compete with double-parenting, and so educated single Japanese women tended to keep pets in preference to rearing children of whom they might not be proud.[3]

The new hothousing of the younger generation had no counterpart vis-à-vis the older generation. In the ethical family, the old were commonly cared for within or alongside the household of the middle generation. My widowed grandmother lived next door to one of her children; my widowed grandfather lived with two of his children. I grew up with an elderly uncle in the next bedroom. Such household structures can still be found within some communities, but they are no longer common. Not only were the parents of educated couples less likely to be living with their offspring, whereas previously they may have been receiving some financial support from them, they were now far more likely to be providing it. In part, this reflected the increased affluence of the educated retired, but this was reinforced by a new inter-generational co-operation between grandparents and parents in the common objective of rearing a successful third generation. In consequence, the narrative of purposeful enlightened self-interest that had reinforced the norms of reciprocal obligations in the ethical family ceased to be true: meeting obligations to children no longer corresponded to equivalent obligations of adult offspring towards aged parents.

Similarly, mutual obligations eroded beyond the nuclear family. Extended families shrivelled under the pressures of smaller family size and the geographic mobility of the skilled. Again, I exemplify the change at its most extreme. I grew up with twelve aunts and uncles within five miles of my home; my children are growing up with none. The extended *ethical family* gave way to the nuclear *dynastic family*.

As the highly educated became a class, they developed a new form of family in which some of the reciprocal obligations were restored and even reinforced. We see this pattern in the data. Extramarital births in this class were rare in 1965: only 5 per cent; they are still only 5 per cent today.[4] After its initial surge, divorce declined; by 2010 its incidence was down to one-in-six marriages. With few extramarital births, and few divorces, the number of young children reared in single-parent well-educated families has also reverted to very low levels: they are now back to less than one-in-ten.

The new ethics of self-fulfilment through personal achievement came with some downsides, but these were as of nothing compared to the consequences of the shocks that hit the class of the less educated.

SHOCKS AT THE BOTTOM

Just as the Silicon Valley technocrats predicted that the new social connectivity would reduce hatreds, so the Pill and abortion were predicted to reduce unwanted children. We see the resulting surge in the sexual activity of the less-educated half of teenage girls in the data. In the 1960s only 5 per cent had intercourse before they were sixteen; by 2000 it had reached 23 per cent. In contrast, even by 2000, only 11 per cent of the girls who went on to become graduates had had underage sex.[5]

But the Pill only stopped conception if combined with prudent foresight, and this favoured the educated. Aborting a foetus turned out to be a decision that, while comfortable within the new ethical belief system of personal fulfilment, was fraught within the old one of family obligations, and this again favoured the educated. The result was an explosion in teenage pregnancies among the less educated due to couplings never intended to be enduring. Such a teenage mother had four potential options. One was the old model of marriage to the father – the shotgun wedding has a long tradition. Another old model was that she and her baby would continue to live with her parents; my great-grandmother had relied on that without dire consequence within her village. A third option was to ape the new model of individual fulfilment of some educated women and branch out as a single mother, and for this the paternalistic state offered financial support and social housing. A final option was to pioneer a new model of cohabitation: fathers were often less wary of cohabitation than of public commitment. Of course, a relationship can be stable without people being married, but most cohabitations do not lead to lasting relationships; the average one lasts only fourteen months.[6]

The final shock at the bottom was economic. With the decline in manufacturing, middle-aged men lost their jobs. Many less-educated households had never bought into the new ethics of self-fulfilment, and many couples had held on to the norms of the ethical family in which the husband was the head, his authority underpinned by his role as the breadwinner. This role had an awful implication: redundancy at work implied redundancy at home. Such a marriage went from being a tight network of mutual esteem to an asymmetric one; the wife kept her esteem but her presence amplified the husband's loss of esteem. Sometimes the husband sought to reassert authority through violence, sometimes he sank into depression. These were the wellsprings of divorce.[7]

Again, we see this in the data. As among the educated, there was an initial surge in divorce. But in contrast to the educated, among the less educated divorce kept on rising. By 2010 its incidence had reached one in three marriages, double that of the educated.

In place of the obligations towards children provided by the ethical family, the paternalist state stepped in with the 'rights of the child'. These new rights did not extend to the right to be reared from birth to adulthood by the two parents from whom the child was genetically descended. On the contrary, the 'rights of the child' obliged the state to remove children from birth parents if there were grounds for thinking that the child was being abused. In response to highly publicized cases in which children had died at the hands of their parents, the obligation was progressively tightened. For example, in the USA if a doctor saw that a child had an injury, unless they could satisfy themselves beyond reasonable doubt that it had *not* been caused by the parents, they were obliged to report it to the authorities, who were in turn obliged to remove the child from the parents. But, correspondingly, the 'rights of the child' required the highest standards to be met before these removed children could be adopted into another family, and a correspondingly exhaustive bureaucratic checking process to ensure that any placement decision by the authorities would be above public criticism. The inevitable consequence of a high rate of removal from birth parents and a low rate of placement with new ones was that increasing numbers of children found themselves in limbo: in Britain there are now 70,000 of them. In practical terms, limbo meant that the state paid couples to foster children on a temporary basis, often circulating them from one fostering couple to another. Quite evidently, fostering fails on all the important metrics of child rearing: the relationship is quasi-commercial whereas children need manifest love; it is explicitly temporary whereas children need permanence; and it cannot evoke a sense of belonging.

CONSEQUENCES OF SOCIAL DIVERGENCE

The consequences of this selective breakdown in family obligations were most profound for children. In the USA, where these effects are most pronounced, and which may become the cultural future of Europe, over half of all children are now likely to spend time in a single-parent family before reaching eighteen.[8] As implied by the preceding analysis, this is highly class-selective. Among the educated class, the upper-half of American households, family obligations to children have largely been restored and enhanced. In contrast, among the half with less education, single-parent – or no-parent – children have become the norm, accounting for two-thirds of all children in this group.

Does this matter? Unfortunately, it does. Despite the powerful and understandable taboo on stigmatizing one-parent families, social science has now demonstrated rigorously, and causally, that children do better if they are reared from birth to adulthood by two parents from whom they are genetically descended.[9] For many children, even one-parent families have ceased to be an option. The responsibility for child-rearing has increasingly shifted from parents to the state. Yet social paternalism has a poor record of success. This is unsurprising; state provision, whether in children's homes or foster care, suffers from the drawbacks implied by 'what money can't buy', as described in other contexts by Michael Sandel. Paying people to care for children can supplement parental care, but not substitute for parents.

Whereas in the less-educated half of the population many families are disintegrating into empty shells, among the more-educated half we are seeing a proliferation of dynasties. The new hothousing model adopted by educated households has dramatically increased parental input. As never before, the children of the educated are exposed to intensive and purposive interaction with their educated parents.

Cumulatively, hothousing makes a difference. It starts early. Indeed, the child's pre-school experience is now recognized to be decisive: by the age of six the differences in performance that appear after a decade of schooling can already be predicted. In short, what the family does in the few years before school is more important than what schools do in the twelve during which they are responsible.

The differences start with objectives and are then implemented through techniques. Parents who are single and poor are far more likely to be stressed – their priority is not hothousing but the more mundane one of containing chaos. Among those parents who dropped out of school, obedience is rated above self-reliance by almost four-to-one; among those with postgraduate education, this is reversed. Such stress-induced parental behaviour has been found to impair children's non-cognitive development, which we now know to be at least as important as cognitive skills.[10] But cognitive skills also start to diverge early on. The earliest measured divergence is in language: hothousing involves talking to young children. A celebrated study found a class difference of 13 million words by kindergarten. The words themselves differ: the children of professionals hear eight times more encouraging words than discouraging ones; the children of those on welfare hear only half as many encouraging words compared with discouraging ones. Then comes reading. Parental reading fosters child development and is the biggest single factor explaining differences in readiness for school. And then, of course, there's money. The shift to hothousing has massively increased spending. But since the 1980s, whereas such spending by an American household in the top tenth of incomes has doubled to $6,600, among those in the bottom tenth it has fallen to $750; the biggest divergence has been for the decisive period of pre-school.

The same pattern of wide and widening divergence continues during the school years. In the USA, by 2001 the gap between the income classes for maths and reading levels was around a third larger than a generation earlier. Not only is the same pattern continuing, but it is being driven by the same process: the underlying differences between families.

The most dramatic consequence of this divergence between the educated and uneducated classes is a recent discovery about American children made by Robert Putnam, whose work has been seminal. Grouping children according to their cognitive abilities, he analysed their chances of getting into college. Of course, we would expect the children of the educated class to stand a better chance of getting into college since they are likely to inherit higher cognitive abilities. But Putnam found that those children of the educated class who are *in the bottom national group* of cognitive ability have a higher chance of getting into college than those children from less-educated families who are *in the top group*. The new hothousing rears not only trophy children, but camouflaged clots.

The trends towards rising social inequality and stagnant or falling social mobility are recent, and the numbers essentially track the change from my own generation to the next. But the most worrying news is that these observed changes are liable to understate, by a considerable margin, the true persistence of social inequality. In a remarkable recent book, wittily entitled *The Son Also Rises*, Gregory Clark studied the transmission of family inequalities over many generations.[11] Usually, social mobility is measured only by comparing one generation with the next, but he hit on the clever technique of using rare surnames, which can be more easily traced over the centuries. Evidently, what he was usually tracing here was the male line, which for most of history implies that he was tracing the role of the head of the household. What he found is that success is highly persistent, often over centuries. Clark shows that the conventional estimates of social mobility, based only on the transmission from one generation to the next, are radically inconsistent with such enduring inequality, and he provides a plausible explanation for the bias. Some asset is being passed down the generations without being dissipated. What can it be? It is unlikely that financial wealth can cascade in such a way: it only takes one rogue to dissipate a fortune and the cliché of rags-to-rags in three generations rests on this insight. He comes down to two assets that cannot be dissipated. One is genetic, but even though genetic inheritance is important, over several generations exceptionally useful genes are liable to be diluted by mating. The other possibility is what Clark refers to as family culture. This is shorthand for the norms and narratives of the belief system that shapes behaviour in the networked group of the family. Being at its hub, the head of the household is well placed to induce continuity. We know that elite parents put considerable effort into the transmission of their culture,[12] and perhaps particularly to those attributes conducive to success, even though the specific attributes will change over time.

The same technique of tracing rare surnames can be used to measure the other end of the social spectrum, families that get stuck around the bottom of society from one generation to the next. Clark found the same pattern of persistence over many generations: failure is being transmitted down the generations. Since indebtedness cannot be inherited, cascading lack of financial wealth is an implausible explanation. Indeed, for most of history most people have had no such wealth so most people have had the same monetary inheritance – nothing.

Clark explains why the conventional measures of social mobility based on adjacent generations are likely to exaggerate it. Simplifying to bring the point out, suppose that success in each generation was due only to family culture and luck. Each generation inherits a family culture and draws a ticket out of the hat called 'the wheel of fortune'. If family cultures pass down the generations intact, the only source of social mobility is luck. But the change in luck between the first generation and any of the subsequent generations is the same whether we take the adjacent generation or one that is distant. In this deliberately exaggerated example, the social mobility we observe between the first generation and the second would be the same as that between the first generation and the twelfth. Measuring only the former might give the illusion of a mobile society.

RESTORING THE ETHICAL FAMILY?

Some aspects of the ethical family were a stultifying veneer for relationships of power and abuse. We are well shot of them. But other aspects of the 'liberation' from it were little more than selfishness masquerading as self-discovery. Similarly, the juxtaposition of Utilitarian concern about 'the poor of the world' and denial of responsibility for family was less of a moral awakening than the easy pleasure of moral posturing: Dickens skewered such attitudes through the character of Mrs Jellyby, in *Bleak House*.

More fundamentally, the triumph of individual fulfilment through personal achievement over meeting obligations to family is beginning to look psychologically flawed. In a profoundly subversive book, *The Road to Character*, David Brooks starts from the familiar celebration of fulfilment through achievement only to turn the tables on it, suggesting that the future trend will be towards a restoration of fulfilment through meeting obligations to others.[13] The seductive proposition that we find ourselves through focusing on ourselves is opposed by a powerful counter-narrative, which is perhaps best expressed by Dietrich Bonhoeffer in *Letters and Papers from Prison*, his testimony while awaiting death at the hands of the Nazis: we find ourselves through 'losing ourselves' in the struggles of the other people in our daily lives. Freedom is not found in servitude to the self, but in escape from the self. Bonhoeffer and Brooks have the new evidence of social psychology on their side. Our regrets about insufficient personal achievement are dwarfed by our regrets of obligations that we failed to meet. The distinguished psychologist Martin Seligman has conducted a sustained programme of research on the attainment of well-being. His conclusion is unambiguous: 'If you want well-being, you will not get it if you only care about accomplishment . . . Close personal relationships are not everything in life, but they are central.'[14] The replacement of the *ethical family* by the *entitled individual* is revealed to be more tragedy than triumph.

Seemingly a world apart from this, a major breakthrough in economics showed that 'weaker' could be 'stronger'. In order to benefit from making credible commitments, it may be necessary for a person to shed some power. Being able to make commitments was an instance of enlightened self-interest. Fancily expressed, a 'commitment technology' solved the 'time-inconsistency problem': the discoverers received the Nobel Prize. The commitment technology to solve inflation was to give central banks independence; that which solved child-rearing was marriage. Paradoxically, over the same period that Western societies were establishing the commitment technology that tamed inflation, they were systematically tearing up the commitment technology that had defended the right of children to be brought up by the people who conceived them. Just as politicized central banks create an initial sugar-rush of printing money, so tearing up the bonds of marriage created the sugar-rush of liberation. In many Western societies, marriage is tainted by its religious associations, and so we need a purely secular equivalent. This is not revolutionary: in all Western societies marriage preceded Christianity and religious and secular forms of public commitment can readily coexist. In each case the commitment technology draws its strength from the public and explicit acceptance of mutual obligations: esteem and shame are the force on which it draws. If you recall, a commitment technology is in the self-interest of those who use it. It is 'enlightened' self-interest in the same sense as previous instances – it infuses compliance with purpose. Once you understand the true causal chain that leads to desired consequences, mutual compliance becomes rational. Just as enlightened self-interest complements and reinforces other reciprocal obligations, so the economic insight of the value of public commitment complements the psychological insight on the value of meeting those obligations.

Between them these insights can powerfully counter the somewhat jaded aspirations of fulfilment through achievement. But this does not address the new reality of the shrunken domain of the family, the transformation from the extended *ethical family* to the nuclear *dynastic family*. How might this be countered? Fortunately, there is one magnificent consequence of technological progress that can offset this process: increased longevity.* While families have shrunk horizontally, they have grown vertically, and many families now span four generations instead of three. The most senior generation in such a family commands an extended span. If each generation has two children, any surviving senior will encompass four nuclear families and twenty people spread across the three younger generations. Such patriarchs and matriarchs need not retreat into fossilized purposelessness: give them a role, that of regenerating the force of esteem that polices the obligations of the extended ethical family.

A PERSONAL POSTSCRIPT

Ten years ago, my wife and I faced a moral choice. In a further twist in the spiral of divergent fortunes, the infant grandchildren of my cousin were taken into 'care' by the paternalist state (a euphemism of Orwellian proportions). Given the current norms of the new British educational elite, we faced no social pressure from the community to take them in ourselves, and our families had a correspondingly undemanding understanding of our responsibilities. I wish I could say that we did not equivocate. It is hard in retrospect to reconstruct the filaments of thought, but one important influence was what that senior generation would have expected of us. Even in death, they exerted a fierce moral pressure on self-respect. Another potent influence, given our long exposure to African culture, was our respect for the African norm of the extended ethical family. Fortuitously, the state made it easy, since new legislation provided a route for the extended family to bypass the excruciating process of adoption. Assisted by unanimity of official and family opinion, we flew through the process in a mere eight of the crucial early months in a flurry of forms, checks and cheques. During that entire year, in a country of 65 million people, only 60 children were adopted through the standard

* A development of which I am becoming increasingly enthusiastic.

route: hence that statistic of 70,000 children stuck in the limbo of transient foster care, a number which has been rising every year.

When our two toddlers came home, our African friends reacted with a 'welcome to the club' shrug. Our British friends told us we were 'bold', in the *Yes Minister* usage, implying 'you'll regret this'. Ten years on we are far from regret, but clearer on family obligations. What we stumbled into should be as normal in our societies as it is in Africa. But in an affluent and ethical society what we did should not even be necessary.

6

The Ethical World

What might an *ethical world* look like? The ideologues each have their own prescriptions. Utilitarian ideology would demand a paternalist global government tasked with arranging fiscal transfers to achieve 'the greatest happiness of the greatest number'. Rawlsian lawyers have become increasingly influential in United Nations assertions of 'human rights'. Joining the cacophony are the emoting celebrity populists: Angelina Jolie, a spokesperson for the headless heart, wants 'global peace'.

If, instead, we apply the core precepts of Chapter 2, we can conceive of an *ethical world* analogous to that of an *ethical state*, an *ethical firm* and an *ethical family*.

> *Precept 1* Recognition of obligations to other societies that are not dependent upon reciprocity: the *duties of rescue*. These cover obligations to groups such as refugees, those societies facing mass despair, and those lacking the rudiments of justice.
>
> *Precept 2* The construction of more far-reaching *reciprocal obligations* among those countries willing to go further.
>
> *Precept 3* This reciprocity is supported by a recognition of common membership of a group, based on common purposive actions that further the *enlightened self-interest* of each participant.

The international situation of 1945 was about as far from such an ethical world as could be imagined. There were four longstanding nightmares. My parents' generation had spent a third of their conscious lives in global warfare. They had lived through the collapse of the prosperous global economy into which they had been born, into an opportunistic race of beggar-thy-neighbour protectionism that had led to mutual impoverishment. They had lived through an era of empires – British, French, Russian, Japanese, Austrian, Portuguese, Belgian, German, Italian – that were unravelling under the pressures of their manifest ethical absurdities. And they had lived through the horrors inflicted by fascist and Marxist ideologies that had taken control of Germany, Russia, Spain and Italy. In addition to these inherited disasters, the end of the Second World War bequeathed two new ones: the prospect that the aggressive new communist regimes that controlled around a third of the world would attempt to take over the rest of it; and the immediate reality of a huge pool of refugees resulting from the dislocation of Central Europe.

The political leaders of the time might reasonably have felt over-whelmed by a sense of 'don't start from here'. But instead, they began to put together an ethical world, using these three core concepts. They recognized those obligations towards other societies that arise irrespective of whether they are reciprocated – *duties of rescue* – and began to meet them. They began to tap the vast, unexploited poten-tial of *reciprocal obligations* between nations by building new purpose-specific clubs. They reinforced the clubs by causal chains that replaced the opportunistic pursuit of immediate self-interest by *enlightened self-interest*. This was an astounding achievement, and it paid off: the world gradually transformed for the better.

But the lucky generation of leaders who inherited that success did not understand the process that had produced it. The smart Pragma-tism that had built success out of the ashes of catastrophe gave way to the appealing narratives of Utilitarian and Rawlsian ideologues who have gradually undermined their inheritance. The current world is nowhere near as unethical as that of 1945, but there is again much work to be done. That story of remarkable achievement, deteriora-tion and the task ahead forms the structure of this chapter.

BUILDING AN ETHICAL WORLD

The fundamental insight of leaders in 1945 was that the opportunistic behaviour of individual nations had to be replaced by common obligations enforced by peer pressure. But peer pressure depends upon recognition of shared identity, something that had been lacking in the 1930s. New clubs of members willing to accept reciprocal obligations were gradually built; shared belonging around purposive actions.

The most pressing priority was international security. In response to the climate of fear created by the Soviet Union, a new club was formed in 1949 – the North Atlantic Treaty Organization (NATO). The central principle was reciprocal security guarantees among its members. The shared identity was of democracies facing a common threat. There were a few free-riders, but the new obligation was reinforced by an all-too-credible narrative of enlightened self-interest: hang together, or be hanged. Actions matched words, the key moments being the Cuban Missile Crisis of 1962, and the deployment of cruise missiles in the early 1980s. The new reciprocal obligations were successful in keeping the peace while the many internal tensions of communism accumulated.

While the Soviet Union was the new threat, within Europe Germany remained the old fear. France had fought three deadly wars against Germany in a mere seventy years. Enlightened self-interest was yet more obvious, but impeding it were the hatreds that the wars had produced. The solution was a realistically slow process of modest but repeated common endeavours, beginning in 1951 and expanding into the EEC. As with NATO, the central principle of the club was acceptance of reciprocal obligations.

To unwind the beggar-thy-neighbour protectionism of the 1930s, another new club was formed: the General Agreement on Tariffs and Trade (GATT). Between 1947 and 1964 it concluded six rounds of reciprocal trade liberalization. Again, the key driver was enlightened self-interest; everyone recognized where protectionism had led.

In response to the Great Depression of the 1930s, a further new club of nations was established. The International Monetary Fund (IMF) was a public bank into which a defined membership paid, undertook to abide by a set of rules and supervision, and in return were entitled to loans in the event of crisis. It was, in effect, a giant mutual insurance system.

The common principle of reciprocity underpinning these clubs was reinforced by the Organization for Economic Co-operation and

Development (OECD), which was designed to create peer pressure. It encouraged comparisons through league tables (such as the PISA ranking of educational performance), and by peer reviews of national policies.

These purpose-specific clubs, each with its defined and limited membership, reciprocal obligations within the group, and credible enlightened self-interest, gradually transformed the world. Each came to fruition at its own speed, but their cumulative achievement was astounding.

NATO delivered spectacularly in 1989, with the disintegration of the Soviet Union and the end of the Cold War. Within Europe, the EEC gradually anchored countries such as Spain, Greece and Portugal to democracy while deepening trade integration, enabling the poorer members to catch up with the richer ones. By its final round in 1986, the GATT had laid the foundations for the huge economic gains of the subsequent expansion of global trade. The IMF backstopped crises, its largest bailout during this entire era being for a British political crisis in 1976, averting the prediction of a *New York Times* headline that said, 'Goodbye Britain, nice knowing you'. The country was saved because Keynes and other British officials of a previous generation had established the IMF for just such an eventuality. They should be national heroes.

Alongside these clubs of reciprocal obligations, global leaders built new organizations designed to meet duties of rescue. Again, they were smart. Rather than leave these duties of rescue to each individual affluent country, they built global institutions that used the principle of reciprocity among those affluent nations to enforce new norms of meeting their duties to others. The UNHCR was launched to provide care for refugees; the World Food Programme was launched to provide food during famines; the World Health Organization was launched to provide improved health in the poorest societies. But the apex organization was the World Bank. Its membership was divided into two groups: affluent countries, which disciplined each other into contributing, and poorer countries, which were recipients of the pooled finance.

At the time, these were unprecedented collective responses to the duty of rescue, noble actions that complemented the rise of the reciprocal obligations. No one questioned that any of these duties of rescue should be met, and met collectively. In retrospect, this lack of controversy was remarkable.

In parallel to the new clubs and duty of rescue organizations, the global leaders of 1945 resurrected a proto-world government: an assembly of nations. In place of the failed and defunct League of Nations, founded after the First World War, came the United Nations, whose Security Council was intended to police world order. As with the League of Nations, and despite huge goodwill, it has seldom been effective. The five Permanent Members of the Security Council were a sufficiently small group for reciprocity to be feasible, but the ideological polarization between the USA and the USSR made it impossible to build the trust necessary for enlightened self-interest. Paradoxically, the United Nations achieved its greatest successes by turning itself into a club of the excluded: the 'Club of 77' formed by those countries lacking an effective voice in the club-based organizations.

THE EROSION OF THE ETHICAL WORLD

The clubs had worked by reciprocity, underpinned by the norms of loyalty and fairness. As pragmatism gave way to ideology, these were displaced by the norms of care and equality favoured by the WEIRD, and the consequent demands for the inclusion of all based on need. In response to this noble ambition, the clubs expanded both their membership and their aspirations.

NATO grew from its original twelve members to its current size of twenty-nine, taking NATO eastwards. Whereas the original group had some genuine element of reciprocity, the expansion amounted essentially to an extension of an American security guarantee to countries lacking military capacity. The EEC expanded from its initial six-member club into an EU of twenty-eight. The domain of the rules was greatly expanded from trade and democracy to cover most aspects of public policy. The GATT dissolved itself into the World Trade Organization (WTO), with an expansion to near-global membership and a correspondingly vast expansion in its domain of regulation to agriculture, services and intellectual property. Similarly, the IMF expanded to near-global membership and increased its remit.

As the defined groups expanded, the glue that had enforced reciprocal obligations began to weaken.* In response, the organizations could either become less effective or turn themselves into quasi-empires run by an inner core of members who enforced the rules through penalties imposed on subject members. Some organizations took one route, some the other.

First the route to ineffectiveness. In NATO mutuality declined even among the original membership. Only five of the twenty-nine members now meet the club commitment to spend 2 per cent of GDP on defence. In response, American commitment has begun to weaken. But the classic instance of an effective club that morphed into an ineffective globally inclusive organization is the WTO. Whereas the GATT achieved six mutual trade rounds in its first seventeen years, the WTO has failed to conclude even a single round in twenty-three years.

Now, more controversially, the route to empire. The expansion of the EEC into the EU, and of the IMF from a mutual bank for a club to a global fund for poor countries, have changed both into quasi-imperial bodies, through which some governments tell other governments what to do. In the EU, enlightened self-interest, which had infused compliance with purpose, gave way to a wide range of prescriptive norms, set and enforced by an inner group that is currently at loggerheads with three groups of supplicants: eastern members, southern members and Britain. I do not wish either to pass judgement on the norms or to exaggerate the process; in other respects, the EU remains a club of immense value and has the potential to do yet more. But the EU is no longer unambiguously a mutually supportive club: it has increasingly become powerful countries telling other countries what to do.

The IMF morphed into a global fund like the World Bank, whose rationale was to meet duties of rescue. By their nature, duties of rescue are neither reciprocal nor conditional. But both organizations became dominated by an inner core of donor countries that turned duties into power. Donors first made support conditional upon the

* This was why the British Government was so keen on the enlargement of the EU.

adoption of particular economic policies. But this idea, bad enough in itself, rapidly got hijacked by politically powerful NGOs. Currently, Western aid is conditioned on environmental and human rights requirements, often so strict that they are not even met in rich societies. For example, all World Bank projects must have 'environmental impact assessments'. Hydro-electric projects became impossible to finance because NGOs considered that they infringed human rights. Even urban road-widening became blocked by Western human rights campaigners.* Carbon emission standards were imposed on World Bank projects in poor countries that were considerably higher than those practised in high-income countries – a matter of passionate resentment given the severity of Africa's power shortages.† Again, I do not wish to overstate the case: both organizations still do an immense amount of good and are our primary vehicles for doing much more. But they have been captured for a different agenda.

REBUILDING AN ETHICAL WORLD

We need both the reciprocal clubs and the duties of rescue to work. We need clubs because a paternalist world government is neither feasible nor desirable: its attempts to rule over us all would be overwhelmed by non-compliance. Rather than reviving the old clubs it might be easier to form a new, multipurpose club that reflected the realities of current economic and military power. Such a club should be able to find many opportunities for reciprocal obligations that are globally beneficial. The G20 has sufficient span, but in practice it is too large, disparate and spasmodic to be very effective, and it is beset by free-riding. The G7 is smaller and tighter, but now has the wrong membership, excluding both China and India. A smaller group composed of China, India,

* President Kim of the World Bank told me of his frustration that even when opportunistic squatters, who had moved on to land assigned for road-widening, were offered substantial compensation, the human rights lobby was sufficiently powerful to block it.
† As a retired and highly respected African president explained to me, 'I told my ministers that they should never say no to the World Bank or IMF: it was too dangerous. But nor should they ever actually do what they told us: we couldn't trust them.'

the USA, the EU, Russia and Japan would encompass enough of the global economy and military capacity that its collective interest would be to fix global problems even if non-members chose to free-ride. And each member would know that, if it chose to free-ride, the other members would do the same: each is too large to be a free-rider.

Forming such a club faces two challenges. One is that the six have nothing in common, while their individual geopolitical interests conflict. However, for looming global problems such as climate change, pandemics and fragile states, they will increasingly have a common interest. They will also come to recognize a common distinctive characteristic: they, and only they, are large enough collectively to fix these problems, while individually being too large to free-ride on the other five. The other challenge is the predictable opposition from the headless-heart idealists: what about the excluded? Yet it is very much in the interests of the excluded to have a group that is small enough to surmount the world's collective-action problem. Others can join in the commitments, as long as the six have informally agreed that each of them must act. The disparate characteristics of the six ensure that there is unlikely to be any issue on which the six agree but which disadvantages everyone else. That is the new club that we need. It will take years to form, but the underlying logic of effective action on critical global issues may gradually drive us there.

Alongside the clubs, we need organizations that meet our duties of rescue more effectively. This is my home turf: I have spent my entire adult life trying to encourage people in affluent societies to recognize that we have such duties to others. We have been doing a terrible job at meeting them; the temptation to grandstand has impeded practical effectiveness, as we can see from the examples below.

Refugees*

I begin with our duty of rescue to refugees. There are 65 million people worldwide who have fled their homes, driven by fear or hunger. A third of them become refugees. They strive to restore normality to their lives: to find somewhere to live that is familiar; to find a job to

---

* This section is based on Betts and Collier (2017).

support their families; and to cluster together with other people from their community. These are reasonable needs, but the government of the neighbouring country may struggle to meet them. Most likely, its own citizens are poor and are finding it hard to meet their needs.

Societies do have obligations to their neighbours that, being naturally reciprocal, can be greater than the non-reciprocal duties of rescue. But with a mass calamity as drastic as an exodus of refugees, there is also a global duty of rescue. A neighbouring haven has reason to complain if you leave it to struggle on its own. Although it should permit refugees to cross the border onto its soil, you are richer: the two of you should be able to co-operate in meeting their duty to neighbourliness and your duty of rescue. Here we can be guided both by the principle of the heart, which demands *solidarity* with the society that borders on the crisis situation, and the principle of the head, which tells us to divide up our responsibilities according to our *comparative advantage*.

The advice of the head is not complicated. The neighbouring society is best placed to provide haven. It is close and so easy to reach and to return from, and is probably sufficiently similar to provide a familiar setting; as I write, the latest refugee movement is from Venezuela to neighbouring Colombia. Affluent societies have the international firms that can bring in jobs, and the money both to help refugee households in the transition to self-sufficiency and to compensate the host society for any costs incurred. This, rather than the chaos of refugee policy of recent years, is the strategy of the future.

The HIV positive*

Usually, the potency of reciprocity within a society generates obligations to fellow-citizens that exceed those we have globally. But sometimes we have obligations to some citizens of another country that exceed those of their fellow-citizens. HIV sufferers in poor countries are in this category. With modern anti-retroviral drugs, people infected with HIV can lead normal lives for many years, at the cost of less than $1,000 per year. To their moral credit, Presidents Chirac of France and George W. Bush of the USA recognized that, if ever there

---

* This section is based on Collier and Sterck (2018).

was a duty of rescue, this was it. Without the money, thousands of identifiable poor people in Africa would be left to certain, imminent death. They saw that their countries were rich enough that people would be willing, collectively, to finance this life-giving expenditure.

So, what was the response of the WEIRD? Health economists, imbued with Utilitarian ideology, opposed this use of money. Completely overlooking the moral force of the duty of rescue, they argued that more life-years could be saved for the same money by slightly reducing risks of mortality through preventative interventions for a range of other diseases. It would be more cost-effective to let all the people with HIV die. Meanwhile, the headless-heart populists agitated against another obvious way in which lives could be saved. HIV is usually transmitted through sexual intercourse. If people could be persuaded not to have multiple partners, simultaneously the transmission rate would decline massively; this is what President Museveni of Uganda achieved through broadcasts to the nation. But campaigns for behaviour change were opposed because they might inadvertently stigmatize those with HIV by implying that potentially they had some moral responsibility for the consequences of their actions. Remember, victims cannot be moral actors.

The duty of rescue from mass despair

Currently, many African youth have a vision of hope: escape to Europe. This is a tragedy. It is manifestly unviable as a solution to mass despair, and the exodus of the brightest and best can often compound the problems of a poor society. In an ethical world, each society should be in a position to offer credible hope to its youth. The role of affluent societies is not to tempt a few bright young people to lives of marginality in our own societies, but to bring opportunities to the many remaining at home in their societies.

All duties of rescue begin with respect for those being rescued. Rescue is about restoring and augmenting autonomy, not about asserting authority over people. Instead of a pious ragbag of social and political conditions, international support should be aimed at attracting ethical companies to societies that are desperately short of them, while curtailing the activities of corrupt business. Fragile countries desperately need the jobs that modern firms can provide, but few decent firms want to go to them: small markets and high risks keep firms away. To change this, public money is needed to compensate firms for the public benefit they bring by creating jobs. In 2017, the World Bank and Britain pioneered using aid to support their agencies – IFC and CDC, respectively – that work with firms. The response of the headless heart populists was horror: aid was being diverted from their own photogenic priorities.

CONCLUSION

The head combined with the heart can pragmatically guide us to new reciprocal clubs that can address the looming global anxieties, and to provide effective redress for those in need of rescue. A previous generation of global leaders inherited a far more alarming situation and yet achieved both, bequeathing to the next generation a much better world, still far from perfect, but transformed. That inheritance lulled their successors into the indulgences of ideology and populism. We are now paying a price for the resulting weakening of the clubs and contamination of the duties of rescue. But if we return to a pragmatic approach, we can not only restore the *ethical world*, we can make it better than ever before.

PART THREE
Restoring the Inclusive Society

7

The Geographic Divide: Booming Metropolis, Broken Cities

London, New York, Tokyo, Paris, Milan. Around the Western world, the metropolis has been leaping ahead of the rest of the country, and this widening divide is there whether we measure it in incomes, jobs growth, or house prices. It is relatively recent, dating from around 1980; until then income differences between regions had been narrowing. America was typical; for a century, differences had been narrowing at a rate of nearly 2 per cent a year. Since 1980, however, alongside the surging success found in the metropolis, many provincial cities have suffered abrupt economic declines. New analysis by the OECD finds that, in the high-income countries, over the past two decades the productivity gap between the top regions and the majority has widened by 60 per cent. Britain is typical: the population has been drifting from north to south every year since 1977, and the income gap has continued to widen. In 1997, the total economy of provincial Britain was 4.3 times larger than that of London. By 2015 that had become 3.3 times.

Unsurprisingly, this has played out in a new political divide. The resentful grievances of the provinces have been met by the disdainful confidence of the metropolis: 'flyover cities', the American phrase of disdain, has recently been topped by 'shackled to a corpse' from the political commentator of the *Financial Times*, Janan Ganesh. Where, in these phrases, is empathy? Where is a sense of reciprocal obligation? They have been brutally dismissed, evaporated with the loss of shared identity that previously united metropolis and provinces. Reflecting this, the metropolis voted heavily against the insurgent campaigns of Trump, Brexit, Le Pen and Five Star, while the broken cities found them appealing.

So, what are the economic forces that have been driving this new divide, and what can be done about it?

WHAT IS DRIVING THE NEW DIVERGENCE?

Underlying the forces that are causing the new divergence are two simple relationships that date back to the industrial revolution. One is between productivity and specialization, and the common phrase for it is 'learning by doing'. When people specialize at fewer tasks they are able to develop deeper skills. The other relationship is between productivity and scale: the common phrase for this is 'economies of scale'.

To harness scale and specialization people need to cluster together in cities. For a company to operate at scale it needs to have a large pool of workers, a large pool of customers, and to be located near other similar companies. As workers specialize, they need to work near others with complementary specialist skills. Cities provide the proximity that enables all these connections. But connected cities need enormous investments in metros, roads, multi-storey buildings, airports and rail hubs. Until the 1980s, only the cities of Europe and North America were able to afford them.

The productivity pay-offs from this easy connectivity were staggering, and many cities developed a cluster of firms in some particular industry that enabled them to be world-beating. My own home city of Sheffield established such a constellation of specialist steel manufacturers, and a correspondingly highly specialized workforce. By around 1980 the typical worker in these cities was astonishingly more productive than workers in those parts of the world that lacked industrial clusters. Since incomes tend to correspond to productivity, people were astonishingly more prosperous too.

Starting around 1980, this situation was disrupted by two co-incident but distinct processes: an explosion in knowledge, and globalization. The explosion in knowledge turbo-charged the old relationship between specialization and urbanization, leading to spectacular growth in the largest cities. Globalization opened up new possibilities for harnessing the gains from scale, but also exposed the established clusters to new competition, sometimes leading to their demise.

The knowledge revolution and the rise of the metropolis

Since the 1980s the knowledge economy has expanded exponentially. This has been driven partly by unprecedented growth in the fundamental research conducted in universities and partly by a complementary expansion in the applied research conducted in firms. The potential to harness matter to human advantage is limited only by the fundamental laws of physics. We are still in the foothills of this process because mastering the material world is extremely complex. Discovery-by-discovery we are venturing into this complex world, which may gradually revolutionize productivity. But the only way that our limited human capabilities can master complexity is through our most able people becoming ever more specialized. The last person with any serious claim to know all that was known died sometime in the fifteenth century. Today, our cleverest people know vastly more about the one narrow area in which they have reached the knowledge frontier, and are correspondingly further from the frontier in all other areas. This is true not just of research, but of commercially valuable skills. For example, the law has become more complex, so that legal specialism has become more finely delineated. The expansion of universities has generated not only research, but the graduates who are equipped to master such skills.

But the fundamental relationship between specialization and cities still applies. Extreme specialization only becomes productive if different specialists are near each other. So, greater specialization requires larger clusters of complementary specialists, and access to a correspondingly larger pool of potential customers. In London, a specialist lawyer is close to colleagues with other specialisms, to clients in demand of her specialism, and to the courts. The same lawyer based in a small town would be idle for much of the year.

This clustering of specialisms depends on the metropolis offering excellent connectivity. London and its environs contain both of

Britain's major international airports; the capital has the high-speed Eurostar rail link, connecting to Paris and Brussels, running into it; it is the nexus of all of Britain's mainline railways, and of most of its motorways. It has the Underground: in Central London, the average worker can connect with any of 2.5 million other workers within 45 minutes. It is also the location of government, so any activity that depends upon proximity to public policy is best located there.

The removal of barriers to international commerce has geared up the benefits of clustering highly specialized people together by enlarging the potential market from national to global. The main market for the services clustered in London used to be Britain; now it is the world. So, the market now supports lawyers who are even more specialized, and their skill and productivity are correspondingly enhanced. In consequence, their earnings are spectacular.

In turn, a large population of very high earners creates a market for services to entertain them. Proximity matters: restaurants, theatres, shops crowd in to satisfy every whim of people flush with money but short of time. And this cluster of luxury attracts a further influx: the global rich. London, New York, Paris all have billionaire residents who made their fortune elsewhere but enjoy spending it in them.

Voila – the booming metropolis!

The globalization revolution and the demise of provincial cities

This does not describe what has happened in Sheffield, or Detroit, or Lille. I remember a visitor to the Sheffield of 1960 saying: 'Goodness, this is a prosperous city!' By 1990 nobody would have said that.

Clusters of world-beating firms, such as that in the Sheffield of the 1960s, had a large advantage over new competitors but they were not invulnerable. Sheffield had no natural advantage in steel production. The feature that had induced firms to cluster in the city had been its fast-running streams to power grinding wheels: by the twentieth century its only advantage was that the firms and skilled workers were already there. Each company stayed there because others were there.

The workforce was productive, but that was reflected in their wages, so firms were not especially profitable.

On the other side of the world, an emerging market economy, South Korea, was building a new steel industry. As it built its own cluster, it had a different advantage: much cheaper labour. By 1980, it had become a little more profitable to make steel in South Korea than in Sheffield, so Korean firms were starting to outcompete Sheffield firms in world markets. The Sheffield steel industry began to contract, and the Korean industry to expand. As Sheffield's cluster shrank, the gains from many interdependent firms being in close proximity, known as 'economies of agglomeration', diminished. As a result, costs went up. As the Korean cluster expanded, its costs fell. The result was explosive: Sheffield's steel industry, first noted in Chaucer's *The Canterbury Tales*, collapsed with astonishing speed. Skilled workers, themselves the sons of skilled workers, found themselves unemployed with no prospects of a skilled job. The human tragedy of this co-ordinated shock was sufficiently noteworthy to be memorialized in a film, *The Full Monty*. Its poignant, self-mocking humour against the backdrop of disaster well captures what happened. Being my home town I felt this experience bitterly, but it has been repeated across many once-prosperous cities, such as Stoke, where the pottery cluster pioneered by Josiah Wedgwood imploded. These, and all other examples, are dwarfed by what has happened to Detroit since the 1980s.

Do such cities recover? The ideologues of the right believe that, as long as governments do not interfere, market forces will address the problem. Unfortunately, this is merely an ideological belief. For actual knowledge, we need experts.

The market responds to the collapse of a cluster, but not by replacing it with a new one. Instead, the initial response is a sharp drop in the price of residential and commercial property. Home owners become trapped by negative equity, and struggle to move to the booming cities where homes are much more expensive. The fall in the price of commercial property indeed attracts some activities, but they are the stuff that forms the underbelly of the national economy: warehouses that serve the local region; low-productivity manufacturers that can only survive if their premises are very cheap; call centres that rely upon cheap premises and low-waged, casual labour. As the city fills up with such activities, property prices and wages partially recover, but the city has stumbled into a cul-de-sac. These activities are low skilled, and so the workforce is no longer participating in the ever-rising productivity of complex specialization.[1] The superstar firms in the metropolis remain at the technology frontier and so the metropolitan population benefits from rising incomes, but neither the technology nor the incomes trickle down to the broken cities. For example, new data for America shows that high-wage, high-technology jobs are becoming progressively more concentrated in the biggest clusters.[2] More fancily expressed, the rate of diffusion of technology from the leaders to the laggards has slowed.[3]

There, minus the exuberance of '*voila!*', is the broken city.

ADDRESSING THE NEW DIVERGENCE

The preceding analysis helps explain why, across the advanced economies, the metropoles are surging ahead while many provincial cities have suffered humiliating decline. What can be done about it? There have been plenty of familiar-sounding 'solutions'. Ideologues churn them out, though they lead up a blind alley of overconfidence.

In addressing the new divergence, the populists have the easiest time of it. Since the divergence is *new*, they propose putting the clock back to before it happened. Their policy for doing so is protectionism, to reverse the globalization of markets. Before readers sneer at this response, we should recognize that it is not self-evidently stupid. If in some important respects the past was better than the present for many people, it will indeed seem both feasible and safe to adopt the strategy of restoring the past economy. The same people have learned not to trust the breezy reassurances that if they accept further change everything will end up better.

Nevertheless, the strategy of putting the clock back is doomed to failure. The key reason why is that the Emerging Market economies, like South Korea, that have established the new world-beating clusters, have no interest whatsoever in putting the clock back. Globalization has enabled them to achieve unprecedented reductions in poverty. If

South Korea continues to dominate the steel industry, no amount of protectionism by Britain can restore the pre-eminence of Sheffield in the world market. At most it could deliver the *British* steel market to Sheffield, but this would not be large enough to restore the high productivity that Sheffield once had, and in the process the higher cost of steel in Britain would handicap all the industries that needed it.

While protectionism cannot restore Sheffield, a range of restrictive policies could potentially reverse the prosperity of London. Just as the Sheffield steel cluster proved to be vulnerable to relocation, so the London finance cluster could be demolished. Its flashy prosperity is an affront to the gritty endeavours of provincial England, and so demolishing it would be greeted quite gleefully in some parts of the country. But this too would be a foolish strategy. A metropolis such as London is even better than an oilfield – it need never be exhausted. Irritating as this golden goose might be, there are better strategies than wringing its neck. Unfortunately, at the time of writing, Britain is set to do just that through a Brexit strategy that could cause a co ordinated shift of the financial sector to other European cities.

Why not pick up the eggs instead? In other words, why not use revenues gained from taxing the metropolis to revive provincial cities?

Faced with that proposal, the ideologues will each be salivating. The right will pontificate about the disincentive effects of high taxation, while mumbling against turning the provinces into a giant Benefit Street full of scroungers: 'shackled to a corpse'. The left may overreach in its enthusiasm to fleece the City, inadvertently triggering an exodus of alarmed companies that unravels the economies of agglomeration.

Both have just enough truth on their side to convince their adherents, but not enough to be right. The truth perceived by the right is that turning provincial cities into Benefit Street cannot be the goal. Well-being depends upon dignity and purpose, not just on how much you can afford to consume. A strategy of supplementing unrewarding jobs with public benefits is not a substitute for creating jobs that require skills that a worker can take pride in having mastered. So, the goal is productive jobs, not public supplements to the earnings from unproductive jobs. The truth perceived by the left is that the strutting affluence of those milking the highly paid metropolitan specialisms is ethically offensive. These people think they earn their incomes; I am about to show that they don't.

The strategy I propose separates naturally into two halves: taxing the metropolis, and restoring the provincial cities. Each half depends upon a distinct analysis.

TAXATION AND THE METROPOLIS: 'WE'VE EARNED IT'?

Taxation should be guided by ethics and efficiency. Ethics matter both because of their intrinsic value, and because an unethical tax will meet resistance and evasion. Efficiency matters because taxes drive wedges between prices; for example, the price a consumer pays for a product becomes higher than the amount the producer gets. Such tax wedges distort the allocation of resources and so reduce efficiency.

What ideologies of left and right think they know about taxation has polarized and poisoned our politics. A dose of pragmatism is liberating: smart new taxes could beat existing taxes on both ethical and efficiency criteria.

The ethical rationale for a tax is probably more important for tax design than its efficiency. Tax administration depends critically upon voluntary compliance. The standard philosophical method for the analysis of ethical propositions is *practical reasoning*. Despite its centrality to tax policy, practical reasoning has not been part of conventional economic methodology. In consequence, economists have largely ignored ethical aspects of taxation. As advisors to ministries of finance, they quite often propose taxes that breach promises that they consider to have been foolish (and quite probably they are right in this judgement). Indeed, economists appear to think that they have addressed ethical issues merely by considering *income inequality*, which is analysed through the standard Utilitarian calculus.*
As Jonathan Haidt has found, for most people *fairness* means

---

* Each extra dollar of income is assumed to give less 'utility', so that a transfer from someone who has a high income to someone with less will increase total utility and so be an improvement.

proportionality and *desert*, rather than equality. Yet they have been ignored.[4] Forget desert: if the idle have less money than the hard worker, a transfer raises 'utility'. Forget entitlement: if someone who has built a pension retires with more money than someone who has spent their life on a beach, a transfer raises 'utility'. Forget obligation: by now you will get the picture. Utilitarian economists might caution that some transfers might have disincentive effects and so be *inefficient*, but they would not recognize them as *unethical*. This blindness to wider ethical considerations is an instance of the larger phenomenon: these people are WEIRD.

Once we accept that issues of desert should loom large in tax design it has powerful implications for the gains from agglomeration. The first person to spot this was Henry George, a nineteenth-century American journalist and political-economist. Once he explained his idea it became a sensation.

Henry George's big idea

George made an *ethical* case for the distinctive taxation of the gains from agglomeration. He saw why they were ethically distinctive and concluded that the appropriate policy was to tax the appreciating value of urban land.

You can grasp his insight by posing a sequence of questions. Start with *'who gets the gains from agglomeration?'* To think it through, here is a stylized version of the industrial revolution. Initially everyone is a farmer. Industry starts up in a new city, and people move to it to work in factories. As the cluster of factories grows, people become more productive than they were in farming. this extra productivity is what is meant by 'the gains of agglomeration'. The extra productivity is reflected in wages because firms compete with each other for workers. But in order to work in the factories, people have to live near them, and so they need to rent land from whoever owns the land on which the city is forming. So, the gains from moving to the city are the higher wage *minus this rent.** As long as this rent is less than the productivity difference between farming and industry, more people will move to

---

* To keep things simple, suppose that, apart from wages being higher than their

the city. But as they do so the rents get bid up. This process keeps on until rents rise to eat up the entire productivity difference. At that point, there is no further incentive to move; in economic jargon, we have reached equilibrium. But, more excitingly, we have reached a powerful punchline that answers our question: *all the gains from agglomeration accrue as rent to landlords.* For those at the rightward end of the political spectrum who may be growing a little uneasy, let me reassure you that this is not Marxism: George was not a socialist. But he was a smart economist; many years after he had died, two economists proved his conclusion as a theorem. They had the decency to name it 'The Henry George Theorem'.[5]

Henry George then went on to pose a second question, incomprehensible within a conventional economic framework: *'Do the landlords deserve to get these gains?'* Although incomprehensible to economists, this is perfectly comprehensible to everyone else. To answer it we need no theorem: what we need is practical reasoning. To see whether someone deserves an income we trace back to find one of their actions that generated the income which has accrued to them. But when we trace the gains from agglomeration, the actions that generated the gains were done by everyone who works in the city. By working in the city, each person has contributed to the overall increase in the productivity. The gains from agglomeration are generated by *interactions between masses of people*, and so they are a collective achievement that benefits everyone. This is something that economists refer to as a public good. So, what part have the landowners played in this process? For all that they have done, they might as well have been lying on a beach. Indeed, quite possibly that is how they have spent their time. They have received the income because they owned land where people happened to cluster. Their activity played no part in generating the gains from agglomeration. In the confusing vocabulary of economics, it is classified as an 'economic rent'.

The important point is that, by reasonable ethical standards, landowners are less deserving of the gain from the appreciation in the value of the land they own than if they had worked for it, or if it

---

previous incomes as farmers, people are indifferent between life in the city and life in the country.

reflected a return on the capital they had accumulated from saving. This is not to say they have no claim whatsoever. As the legal owners of the land they have a claim to the gains of agglomeration based on *entitlement*. But this collides with the collective claim of all the workers in the city to those gains, which is based on *desert*. Where there is such a clash of reasonable criteria, pragmatism invites us to compromise rather than to retreat onto a pedestal of dogma. And that is where taxation comes in. Suppose that the society agrees on some tax rate *for those incomes for which desert and entitlement coincide*: the farmer produces output that he both deserves due to his work and to which he is entitled due to his ownership of the farm. Suppose the agreed tax rate is 30 per cent. Then in deciding on a tax rate on income from the appreciation in land values that reflects the gains from agglomeration, we should set that tax rate significantly higher than 30 per cent. This would reflect the fact that the claim of the landowner to this income is significantly weaker than the claim of the farmer to his income. Moreover, only by taxing the gains of agglomeration, and using the revenues to benefit the entire city, can the workforce that has generated the gain receive some share of it – which on the above reasoning they deserve.

Henry George's idea was an early application of practical reasoning, resting on the distinction in *desert* between rent and other forms of income. He was careful to distinguish the rent generated by land appreciation from the income on capital, which he argued was ethically legitimate: his proposition was neither Marxist nor populist.

Were his views eccentric? On the contrary, his ethical common sense resonated: *Progress and Poverty* became the best-selling American book of the entire nineteenth century.

Unfortunately . . .

Henry George established a powerful ethical case for the heavy taxation of the appreciation in the value of urban land. Despite resonating with the public, his policies were never properly implemented. The people who were making fortunes from the ownership of land in the centre of big cities opposed taxing it. Rather than coming up with countervailing ethical arguments, their approach was to use some of their exploding wealth to buy political influence. In Britain, the man who owned much of central London, the Duke of Westminster, was conveniently sitting in the House of Lords: he became the richest man in the country. In the USA, a man whose core business was New York land deals is currently President.

It is never too late to introduce such a tax. The electorate is far better educated than it was in Henry George's day and so it should be easier to build a political coalition that overcomes the resistance of vested interests. Further, since the 1980s there has been a surge in metropolitan growth, reflecting the large increase in the gains from agglomeration. Recall that this results from the leap in complexity and its concomitant deepening of skill differentiation. Thus, there are now far larger gains of agglomeration available to be taxed than in Henry George's day, and so it has become ever more ridiculous that public policies have not done anything about it. Instead, we have been trapped in the gridlock of the old ideology-driven tax disputes.

But the 'unfortunately' that heads this section is not a lament about the current deficiencies in public policy. It is that the same rise in complexity that has powered the new metropolitan gains from agglomeration has also invalidated Henry George's Theorem. His proposition that we can capture these gains through taxing land is no longer correct. The case for taxing the gains remains very powerful, but to do so requires a smart redesign of taxation. The analysis underlying the last two sentences is new: my colleague Tony Venables and I stumbled upon it as a result of working on something seemingly unrelated (which happens surprisingly often with academic discoveries).[6] I will try to give you a sense of the excitement of making a new discovery. The ideas can be presented quite simply: indeed, that is how we stumbled upon them. You can reach the frontiers of economic thought on this topic by thinking through two simple scenarios:

Scenario 1: A metropolis in which workers have differing skills and differing needs for housing

The first scenario is a variant of our farmers-and-industry story, except that this time it is people with differing skills and housing needs who each decide whether to move to a metropolis. The high connectivity provided by the metropolis makes skills more productive: the more highly skilled you are, the more that being in the metropolis raises your productivity. But as people move to the city, the rents get bid up as previously. So, who moves and who stays put? Pretty clearly, the people who gain most by moving are single people with very high skills. So, the specialist corporate lawyer who works long hours in the office and spends her free evenings out on the town before returning to her bedsit is hugely more productive than if she worked in a small town, and she will not be spending much of her correspondingly spectacular income on rent. It is often useful in economics to look for the people who are indifferent between two choices, in this case between moving to the metropolis and staying in a small town. We know that for them the gain in productivity will be precisely offset by the extra rent they need to pay, but who will they be? Some will only be semi-skilled: they are single and only need a bedsit, but their earnings are not much higher than in a small town. Others may be highly skilled, but because they have a large family they need a lot of housing and the rent eats up their extra earnings. These people are important for the analysis (in economics they are termed *marginal*) because they are only just willing to live in the metropolis; if landlords were to charge a higher rent these people would leave and the landlords would be short of tenants. These 'marginal' people determine the rents that landlords can charge. That corporate lawyer will be paying the same rent for her bedsit as the semi-skilled singleton who rents the neighbouring one. We have arrived at the punchline: that corporate lawyer has been able to capture some of the gains of agglomeration.

Generalizing, because of the differences in skills and housing needs, many of the gains from agglomeration no longer accrue to landlords, but stick with those highly skilled singles who don't need much housing. When Tony Venables and I simulated what might happen in a metropolis like London or New York, we found that around *half* of all the gains from agglomeration end up with such people rather than with landlords. Once we allowed for a further layer of differences, this time among smaller cities, the share captured by landlords fell even further. The key implication is that no matter how heavily the government taxes landlords, it cannot get hold of most of the gains of agglomeration.

This is bad news, because the ethical argument for taxation remains powerful. To see this, I am going to sketch the second scenario.

Scenario 2: A metropolis that needs the rule of law

This scenario has a few more steps towards realism, and it packs a more powerful punchline. There are two products, food and services, and many countries. Food can be produced anywhere, but services can only be produced in those countries that have the rule of law. You can think of this as a proxy for many other aspects of good governance. In turn, the rule of law depends upon ordinary citizens co-operating and working together to support it. If each citizen just sits back and leaves it to others, that is, if everyone free-rides, the public good of rule of law is absent. In this scenario, in most societies people free-ride and the rule of law is rare. In consequence, only the few societies that have the rule of law are able to produce services; in the rest, everyone just produces food.

The gains from agglomeration apply to services but not to food, so in the few societies that have the rule of law there is going to be a metropolis in which these services are produced. Because not many countries are able to make services they are going to sell at a premium over food in world markets, so the service-exporting countries are going to be more prosperous than the food-exporting countries.

Next, we explore who in the service-exporting countries benefits from this prosperity. Suppose that in all countries there are two types of workers: those who are atypically smart, and everyone else. Suppose also that being smart is no help in farming. In contrast, being smart is potentially valuable in producing services, but it depends upon how many smart people are clustered together: an isolated smart worker in services is no more productive than a farmer, but the more that the smart people congregate in the metropolis, the more productive they all become. Finally, we add the usual story about rents: as smart people crowd into the metropolis, the rents go up.

So, who gets the gains from agglomeration, and do they deserve them? As in the previous scenario, the gains are shared between the workers living in the metropolis and the landlords. We could tease out quite what this division will be, but for present purposes it doesn't matter. The punchline is that in this scenario only one group unambiguously deserves to get them, because only they are responsible for the actions that have been essential for the generation of the gains: namely, the ordinary citizens across the society who collectively sustain the rule of law. But they do not get *any* of the gains. Some of the gains accrue to the smart workers in the services sector, and the rest accrue to the landlords. Since the group that has an unambiguous ethical claim to a share of the gains gets nothing, there is a strong case for taxation. But, as in the previous scenario, land taxes alone will not hit the gains that accrue to the smart metropolitan workforce.

These two scenarios have a significant feature in common, that the smart workers who capture the gains of agglomeration sincerely believe that they deserve them. Their belief is anchored on the fact that their earnings are high because their productivity is high. In turn, they believe that their productivity is high because they have developed a highly skilled specialism (scenario 1), or because they are atypically smart (scenario 2). There is indeed enough truth in these propositions that, given how convenient they are to such people, it is understandable that they believe them. But they are not the *whole* truth. The productivity of the metropolis depends upon public goods that have been provided by the entire nation, such as the rule of law and past investments in the infrastructure for connectivity. These provide some benefits for everyone, but they disproportionately benefit skilled metropolitan workers. More fundamentally, the gains of agglomeration are, by their nature, *collectively* produced. They are the result of interactions between millions of workers, not merely the outcome of the individual effort of each highly paid worker. The super-skilled deserve to retain a *share* of their high productivity. But they do not deserve all of it. Nor do they deserve as large a share as someone who is not based in the metropolis and whose productivity is not so augmented by others.

The efficiency case for taxing the gains
of agglomeration

So far, I have only considered the ethics of taxing the gains from agglomeration. But there is another aspect of taxation that excites economists: efficiency. Economists are right to be excited about it, and on the taxation of the gains from agglomeration the profession at last has some valuable insights to offer.

The key insight is the concept of *economic rents*. They are any payments that accrue to someone for doing something that exceed what would have induced them to do it. On our previous criterion of ethics, the concept is irrelevant. Just because a star tennis player would be willing to play for less than the tournament prize money she wins does not delegitimize her keeping it. The star player earns economic rents on her exceptional talent, but since that talent is hers, so is the income arising from it. But when we switch from ethics to efficiency the concept of economic rents becomes really useful. By definition, taxing the rent does not affect the decision to work, and so the revenues do not come at the cost of inefficiency. The gains of agglomeration are economic rents: on the criterion of efficiency, they are the ideal target to tax.

In the simple scenario in which all the gains of agglomeration accrue to landowners it is evident that in taxing their gains we do not change their behaviour in any way that retards the city. You may recall that we left them on a beach: once we tax them they may need to work like the rest of us. But even in the other scenarios, taxing the rents is efficient. The corporate lawyer in her bedsit will lose some of that spectacular excess of her income over her rent, but as long as we leave her better off than working in a small town she will keep working in the metropolis. Similarly, in our other scenario, we can tax the smart workers producing services in the metropolis without changing their behaviour as long as we leave them better off than working as farmers.

In terms of tax efficiency, finding economic rents are the equivalent of finding the Holy Grail: revenue without collateral damage. If this sounds too good to be true, brace yourself: it is about to get even better. For this we need another handy economic concept – *rent-seeking*.

Rent-seeking is a menace; here is an example. Suppose that a legislature passes a law that grants a monopoly to a group of producers. Why did the legislature do such a thing? Because the legislators were lobbied and coaxed with rewards. The regulation generated rents; the lobbying was *rent-seeking*. The distinguished economist Anne Krueger showed that lobbying, and other rent-seeking, will increase up to the point at which one extra dollar spent on it yields one extra dollar of rent. The resources devoted to rent-seeking are a total waste.

The gains from agglomeration are rents: so, do they attract rent-seeking? Economists have never posed that question and there is a simple reason for their neglect. If the Henry George Theorem is right and the gains accrue only to landowners, then there is no scope for rent-seeking. Land is in fixed supply and so not amenable to lobbying or any other action. But the Henry George Theorem is wrong. In a metropolis, most of the gains of agglomeration accrue to those people with high skills and little need for housing. Suddenly, many opportunities for rent-seeking open up. People elbow their way into jobs by lobbying well-connected relatives; they pay tutors for the extra study that gets them more credentials; they go to hundreds of interviews. Or they squeeze their need for housing by delaying marriage, or delaying children. Each of these is a form of rent-seeking. Behaviour gets distorted in the competition to capture the lucrative rents of agglomeration. The rent-seeking does not increase the overall size of the pie, it just inflicts a collective loss of well-being upon mid-career people scrambling against each other. Potentially, these losses from rent-seeking are massive.

By taxing the gains of agglomeration, we reduce the pressure for rent-seeking. Getting that job in the metropolis would still be worth doing, but since it would be less lucrative, people are less likely to be driven to extreme measures. Delaying having children in order to be able to remain in a pricey London or New York City apartment might become a sacrifice too much. The economic rents of agglomeration in our thriving big cities are currently staggeringly large. Not only is the scramble for them probably inflicting damage on the people who are scrambling, but its sheer momentum may blind people to the irreversible damage they can do to their own lives.

Putting it all together: how can the gains of agglomeration be taxed?

As a general idea, taxing economic rents is now being recognized as wise. The most influential recent advocate is Robert Solow, Nobel Laureate and the founder of the theory of economic growth, who has argued that economic rents have increased, and that taxation should be shifted to them and away from earned income. With this reassurance, I will now bring the two blocks of argument together. Taxing the gains from agglomeration is a smart policy on grounds both of ethics and efficiency. Each of these criteria matters, and there are few other taxes that satisfy them both.

On ethical grounds, the case for taxing the gains of metropolitan agglomeration is unusually powerful. Usually with a tax the best we can hope for is to say that the burden is fairly shared, but in this case, taxing the rents is necessary to better align gains with desert. Similarly, on efficiency grounds, usually the best we can hope for with a tax is that it does little collateral damage. Few enough taxes are able to satisfy even that modest-sounding condition, but taxing the gains of agglomeration may even *increase* efficiency, by curbing rent-seeking.

The pertinent question is how, in practical terms, can the gains be taxed? Recall that they are spread between city landowners and skilled city workers. Capturing these gains through taxation therefore requires differentially high taxation of these two groups.

A sensible starting point is to capture the appreciation in the value of land and property. This is best done as an annual charge as a percentage of land and property values.* The revenues from such taxes should accrue *nationally*: they will be needed to finance redistribution to other cities that have been hard hit by the same forces that have benefited the metropolis. Currently, instead of being taxed more heavily than other sources of income, the appreciation in metropolitan land values is taxed more lightly. In many countries, Britain

---

* It is better to have an annual tax than a one-off tax on the gain in value, because when a one-off tax is introduced, developers postpone investments that would increase land value, and instead put resources into lobbying for the tax to be removed, blaming the tax for killing investment. With an annual tax, this strategic incentive to postpone – technically the 'option value' – is greatly reduced.

being one of them, it is barely taxed at all. This is a mis-design of the tax system of monumental proportions. In the nineteenth century, politicians agonized over 'the undeserving poor'. Politicians of the twenty-first century should be agonizing over the legacy of our policy negligence; we now have many thousands of 'the undeserving rich'. Unfortunately, not a few of them are politicians. The right wants to protect the rich; the left wants to roast them. We need to discriminate among them. Some are hugely useful to society, others have merely captured the fruits of collective effort.

But the crux of our analysis is that much of the rents do not accrue to landowners, they accrue to skilled metropolitan workers. Capturing these rents requires a tax innovation: tax rates need to be differentiated not just by income, as at present, but by the combination of high income *and* metropolitan location.

Metropolitan workers with only modest skills do not capture any of the rents of agglomeration. A large majority of those with modest skills work in the provinces, and so the pay of a modest-skilled worker in London who makes the morning coffee for the lawyer is going to be set in the provinces, plus the additional amount needed to cover the extra rent payable on a London bedsit over that of a provincial bedsit. So, the basic rate of tax that is levied nationally on those with modest incomes is equally appropriate for those working in the metropolis. But the high-earning corporate lawyer in her bedsit does capture rents of agglomeration that should be shared with others. So, she should pay a higher tax rate than were she working in the provinces, where she would not get the rents. This is not cranky: if she worked in New York City, she would already pay an extra 8 per cent income tax than if she earned the same amount in a smaller city. She pays it by dint of *working* there, even if she *lives* outside the city boundaries. If she works in London she doesn't – but she could. At modest rates of taxation of economic rents, few employment decisions would be changed and so the tax would be much less damaging than current taxes. The challenge, which is entirely feasible to solve with modern techniques of fiscal analysis, would be to work out how high the supplementary tax on high incomes of metropolitan workers should be before the efficiency costs are comparable to current taxes. The difference between what New York does already and this proposal is only on where the tax accrues. In New York City, the revenues from that 8 per cent income tax accrue to New York City; in my proposal, they would accrue to the nation to benefit the recovery of cities like Detroit and Sheffield.

What all this means is that the basic rate of tax, which is the only one paid by most people, would continue to be applied nationally. But each tax rate applicable to higher incomes would carry a metropolitan supplement that would target the rents of agglomeration captured by that skill group. Since the gains of agglomeration are far greater for the most highly skilled, the supplements would be progressively larger at higher levels of income.

Since tax administrations know where people live and work, this is in practical terms surprisingly straightforward: indeed, as in the New York example, many taxes are already geographically differentiated.* The most likely obstacle is the disproportionate political influence of wealthy city-dwellers, not least through being heavily over-represented in legislatures. Despite their high estimate of their moral self-worth, this proposal for an ethically just and economically efficient tax is likely to be greeted with self-righteous outrage. But recall, since we are taxing economic rents, the predictable arguments about disincentives and desert are self-serving: prepare for an avalanche of 'motivated reasoning'. Taxation is not only analytically warranted: it is a fitting response to the new urban arrogance.

REGENERATING PROVINCIAL CITIES: 'SHACKLED TO A CORPSE'?

How can cities like Sheffield, Detroit and Stoke be revived? The purpose of taxing the metropolis is not to finance welfare benefits for the inhabitants of these places, but to meet the costs of restoring them as clusters of productive work. As we have seen, the market

---

* In the USA, income taxes vary between states and cities. In the UK income tax rates now differ between Scotland and England. The current proposal differs from these designs not in administration, but in the assignment of the resulting revenues.

will not replace a broken cluster with a new one; instead, the city fills up piecemeal with low-productivity activities. But why can't market forces generate a new cluster, and, if markets can't do it, why should we think that government can?

A successful cluster is the common location of many different companies, some of which are in competition with each other. Being clustered together enables them to reap common economies of scale and so they all benefit from lower costs. Once a cluster is formed, market forces maintain it: no firm wants to leave because it knows that tomorrow the other firms will still be there, not somewhere else. But *forming* a new cluster is far more demanding. Precisely because companies are interdependent, a single company will be much more inclined to move to a new location if it expects many others to make the same decision. But how can the company know whether others will do so? If the pioneer goes ahead, yet another firm may join it as the second firm in the cluster, and if that happened yet another firm might decide to become the third. But there is no market mechanism for generating and revealing these decisions. The formation of clusters faces a co-ordination problem and so it needs a co-ordinator. Silicon Valley co-ordinated around Stanford University; what might work in less-favoured places?

Private-sector solutions to co-ordination

The co-ordination problem arises because the decision of each firm depends on each other firm. In economics, these effects are known as *externalities*; because they affect other firms rather than the firm itself, they are not taken into account in its decisions. But there *are* market solutions to this interdependence: think local, or think big.

Think local . . .

One sector of the economy has a natural role in the co-ordination of companies: finance. At its best, the financial sector hoovers up information about firms and allocates capital with a view to future opportunities. A bank whose business was legally restricted to a particular city would understand that its own future depended upon the success of the local economy. The bank would itself internalize the effects that were external to each of the firms that it was financing. In order for this not to be suicidal for the bank, it would need to learn a lot about the opportunities and interdependencies, firm-by-firm. It would thus be very different from the financial sector institutions described in Chapter 4. Are such banks a fantasy? On the contrary, prior to a legislative change in 1994, they were the norm in the USA. In Britain, we have to go further back, but names such as The Midland Bank and The Yorkshire Bank are testimony to a localized past, and local banks are still common in Germany. Potentially, the policy change to global banks could have enhanced the finance potential for cities needing a new industry, by giving access to a wider pool of capital. But in practice, global banks have little incentive to invest in local knowledge. When a city starts to contract, their local branches are instructed to reduce credit and the recovered money is moved to other cities. A return to localization would give the financial sector the incentive to perform its socially useful role: generating and judging information about the real economy.

Think big . . .

The need for co-ordination can be surmounted by means of a mega-firm: a firm like Amazon that is so big that it reaps sufficient scale economies of a cluster entirely with its own operations to justify being a pioneer. The firm is a cluster in itself, and its location will suck in an entourage of supporting suppliers. In most industries, being that big is not beautiful: the cluster efficiencies are liable to be offset by the difficulties of managing an elephant. So being big enough to be your own cluster is rare. There are far fewer such firms than there are broken cities whose mayors would like a mega-firm to come to them. The problem of which broken cities succeed in attracting the mega-firms also has a market solution, but not a pretty one. A smart mega-firm seeking a new location will organize an auction in which cities bid against each other for the prize of getting the firm. The value of the prize is the gains from agglomeration that will accrue to the city from the new cluster. New research that compares cities that win these auctions with those that lose confirms that these gains are real.[7] Auction theory tells us how much the winning bid will be: it will be equal to the prize.* So, the market 'solves' the co-ordination problem facing a broken city by handing all the gains of a new cluster to the mega-firm that creates it. As I write, Amazon is conducting an auction among American cities for a new head-quarters location. The company is sufficiently big to revive a broken city, and sufficiently ruthless to extract these benefits for itself.

Public-sector solutions to co-ordination

The government as the co-ordinator of business decisions sends shudders down the spines of market fundamentalists. But I am writing this section in Singapore, and from my desk I have a panoramic view of an outstandingly prosperous city that has been achieved by public planning. When I first visited the city in 1980 it had just raised the minimum wage in order to drive out what the government recognized was a doomed sector – garments. The strategy met with scathing critiques from the market fundamentalists: minimum wages would just create high unemployment. In America and Europe, the government as co-ordinator indeed has an embarrassing history of politically skewed interventions, but East Asia is a valuable correct-ive: co-ordination can work. Singapore's founder, Lee Kwan Yew, also understood both the economics and the ethics of agglomeration. His policies reflected this: 'I saw no reason why private landowners should profit from an increase in land value brought about by economic development and the infrastructure paid for with public funds.'[8]

Here is an approach that superficially seems the least distorting. If the metropolis is to be subject to supplementary taxation, then why not use the revenues to finance correspondingly reduced taxation of firms in broken cities, thereafter leaving it to the market to determine which firms move where? This, however, does not address the co-ordination problem, and it fails for the same reason that the market works to *maintain* clusters once they have formed, but not to *establish* them. Knowledge that firms going to a broken city would pay

---

* It may even exceed the value of the prize, in a phenomenon known as 'the winner's curse'.

reduced taxes does not help a pioneer firm know which firms will move, where they will move, or when they will move. Mayors would still have no option beyond bidding for mega-firms. But the mega-firm auction would now have an added twist. Since all broken cities would have this fiscal advantage, they would still have the same incentive to bid against each other to win the auction. As before, the mega-firm would capture a payment equal to the value to the city of the prize, but now it would also get the tax subsidy as a bonus. So, what might work?

Compensate pioneers

Broken cities need to attract firms that are dynamic enough to start a new cluster in their wake. Such pioneering firms are scarce, however, because, unless other firms follow them, they are likely to go bankrupt. Even if other firms do follow, the pioneer will still be at a disadvantage relative to these later entrants. When pioneer firms look for the skilled workers that they need, they are unlikely to find them. How can local workers have such skills when there have been no firms that use them? So, the pioneer will have to bring skilled workers from elsewhere so that they can gradually train its local employees, which is likely to be expensive. But if a second firm decides to set up shop in the same city, it will have an easier time recruiting the skilled workers it needs – it can poach some of the workers that the pioneer has trained. As a result, the second firm's set-up costs will be lower than the pioneer's, enabling it to have a higher return on capital.

In other words, pioneers of clusters face what is known as a *first mover disadvantage*. This is distinctive: more commonly, pioneers enjoy *first mover advantage*, but this applies to pioneers of new *markets*, and new *technologies*. Being the first in a market entrenches the firm ahead of subsequent entrants because it builds brand loyalty – think of Hoover; being the first to a technology allows the firm to patent it – think of Apple. But if the firm is pioneering a new *cluster* that will sell what it produces in an established market using an established technology, the pioneer bears the costs that later firms avoid.

For a broken city, however, a cluster pioneer is socially valuable.

So, what can be done about this? Since the pioneer generates externalities, this public benefit should be compensated with public money. As a principle this is straightforward, but to implement it requires competent specialist public agencies. How is this best administered?

Development banks

It is one thing to allocate money to a good objective; it is another to spend it effectively. The agencies that channel public money into investment in firms are development banks, and their mandate is to invest in the private sector to promote some public objective. All major governments have them: the European Union has an enormous one, the European Investment Bank; Japan and China have equivalent agencies. A development bank that was mandated to focus on reviving provincial cities is a potential vehicle for spending the revenues raised from the new taxes on the metropolis. Some development banks have been highly successful in achieving their objectives, others degenerate into troughs of corruption: everything hinges on them having a clear mandate, high standards of public probity, and a motivated staff who believe in the mandate and who face realistic scrutiny. That word 'realistic' is critical. Investment in building clusters is a risky and long-term undertaking; whether an investment is successful or not will often not be known for years, and there will be many failures. Unless this is understood by politicians and the public to whom the bank is answerable, it will become too cautious to be effective. A development bank that is trying to revive a broken city, financing activities with the potential to make local workers highly productive, will need to be bold, informed and engaged. As with the venture capital model, its staff will sometimes need to get involved with day-to-day management, and sometimes even highly motivated staff who work on a project for years will end up facing failure. The bank can only be judged on its overall portfolio and its long-term record.* But given the general inadequacies of conventional financial

---

* These ideas reflect my conversations with Diana Noble, the CEO who rebuilt CDC into the most purposive of the development banks working to bring firms into poor countries.

markets (discussed in Chapter 4), with the right staff they are worth trying.

Preparing for firms: business zones

Pioneering firms will only come to the city if there is a suitable place from which to operate. Firms can buy an abandoned building and adjust it to their needs, but business zones provide the dedicated space and infrastructure that a cluster is likely to need. Many businesses find it useful to be close together. Quite possibly, in losing its previous cluster, the city has been left with a district of derelict factories. Public money can finance an agency for the city that cleans the district up and administers a new business zone.

A key issue for such agencies is the price that they pay for the land. Once the agency enters the market, derelict land suddenly becomes more valuable. Not only is it bidding to buy, but the prospect of creating a cluster raises the future value of the land. Evidently, since the agency is responsible for this increase in value, it – and not the landowner – should capture the appreciation. In Britain, this principle was incorporated into the Development Corporations Act of 1981. However, judges are not trained in economics or public policy, and smart barristers try to bend the meaning of the words used in the legislation – a classic instance of rent-seeking by means of 'motivated reasoning'. In the past smart barristers have succeeded in this looting of the public purse: the interpretation of the law used for land valuations has become a compromise between its value without the agency, and its value with the agency, and landowners are usually able to capture a substantial part of the uplift in value that should accrue to the agency. This is rectifiable, but the drafting of legislation should take care to pre-empt the corrosive effect of barristers and the limited abilities of judges to appreciate, or even care about, the public interest.

Investment promotion agencies

The agencies that create and manage business zones look inwards, towards the city and its facilities. Investment promotion agencies look outwards, towards firms that might come to the city. If the market worked seamlessly, as the ideologues of the right suppose, investment promotion agencies would be a waste of money. The Irish know otherwise. Ireland in the 1950s was one of the poorest parts of Europe. To change that the Irish government pioneered an agency to encourage investment, which has been amazingly successful in attracting international firms and jobs.* The agency built a team of people who researched likely industries, forged connections with potential firms, and courted one of the larger ones as a potential 'anchor' investor.

Once such a firm expressed interest, the Irish Investment Authority then worked with it, learning how to anticipate the problems it would face in operating in Ireland. Having gained some understanding of the firm's business, it tried to address these future problems in advance, advising other public agencies such as local government what they could do to help. Its relationship with the firm did not end once the firm had made its investment. The employee of the agency who had been tasked with getting to understand the firm's business remained close to it, trying to spot further opportunities. More than half of the foreign investment in Ireland came from such subsequent expansion.

Clearly, the investment agency and the agency managing the business zone need to co-ordinate with each other, as each has information useful to the other. But their roles are sufficiently distinct to justify being separate agencies.

Knowledge clusters: local universities

Most provincial cities now have universities and they should play a prominent role in their city's recovery. That Sheffield has managed to recover from the collapse of its steel industry owes much to the good fortune of having two respected universities in the city. Some academic subjects are well suited to generating knowledge that has business applications. Knowledge is one of the activities that particularly lends itself to clustering: often knowledge advances when someone links two previously distinct recent advances, and so proximity to other researchers helps. Nor does knowledge simply flow from basic research to

---

* I would like to thank Professor John Sutton, Dean of the Economics Department at the London School of Economics, doyen of industrial economics (and proud Irishman), for the knowledge on which this section is based.

applications. Often it is when basic research is applied that people learn where they should be looking for further advances, so proximity to businesses that are applying knowledge helps both the businesses and the universities. The links between Stanford University and Silicon Valley, and between Harvard-MIT and the prosperity of Boston, are the iconic manifestations of this process.

Academics can, however, be pompous advocates of research uncontaminated by use. Of course, a prosperous society should be spending resources on such knowledge, but universities in broken cities should recognize their obligation to their community. Local universities need to refocus on those departments that have a realistic prospect of forging links with businesses. This is another potential use for public money.

Universities not only generate knowledge that has business applications, they also teach students; whether these students are equipped to be productive depends both upon what they are taught and how well they are connected to potential employers. At their worst, the universities in crisis-hit provincial cities focus their teaching on subjects that are disconnected from prospects of skilled employment. They are producing people with the academic credential of a degree, but not with a skill. Young people are lured into debt that their qualification does not equip them to repay.

The obvious location for the formation of new skills in a broken city is its local university and technical college. When things work well, the firms that are attracted to the city and pioneer a new cluster are linked up with the pertinent parts of the local university and college, to work together in the generation of applied research and to train workers. In partnership, firm, university and technical college can develop programmes that retrain older workers in the new skills that they need.

CONCLUSION: 'WHATEVER IT TAKES'

The geographic divide between thriving and broken cities is not inevitable; it is recent and it is reversible. But it cannot be reversed by small adjustments to public policies. Trivially, small is insufficient, but, more fundamentally, spatial dynamics depend upon expectations: firms will locate where they think others will locate. Expectations are currently anchored on the changes of recent decades, and so momentum is self-fulfilling. To change this requires a policy change sufficiently large to shock expectations into a different configuration.

Given the uncertainties over how effective any particular one of the policies discussed above might be, there is no basis for a sudden large adoption of any of them. They need to be tested by a cautious process of incremental experiment. But such a process will not produce the necessary shock. How can the need for cautious experiment be reconciled with the need for a shock? The solution is to make an overarching policy commitment to the goal of narrowing geographic inequalities. In 2011 the Eurozone faced the same dilemma: policymakers did not know what policies would prove effective in defending the currency, and they embarked upon a range of experiments. But these experiments were wrapped in an unambiguous commitment made by the President of the European Central Bank: 'whatever it takes'. This phrase had an instant and enduring impact; speculation subsided because Mario Draghi had left himself no room for failure. We need the equivalent political commitment for cities.

8

The Class Divide:
Having it All, Falling Apart

I and my cousin embody avoidable divergence. Why has it happened? What can be done?

In many families, the adults have acquired more education and skills than ever before in human history; they are more inclined to marry people like themselves than ever before; men have adopted a revolutionary family norm of equality and co-operation never before seen; and parents are nurturing their children more intensively than ever before. Success stabilizes such families; their children inherit the success of the parents. These families are having it all: they are becoming dynasties.

In many other families, the adults have little education, and the skills they laboriously acquired have lost their value. They too are more likely to marry people like themselves, but this is due to shrinking opportunities: assortative mating among the educated has left women with fewer chances of marrying upwards; men have retained the traditional norm of breadwinner but are no longer able to live up to it; and parents have retained the traditional norm of leaving education to the school. The mounting tensions of failure destabilize the family; children inherit the instabilities of their parents. These families are falling apart.

Many of the characteristics that are responsible for successful families are not just good for the families themselves, but good for the entire society. Conversely, many of those that are responsible for failing families are not only private tragedies, but social catastrophes. In reversing the new divergence, the place to start is with strengthening the families that are falling apart. We must face the reality that social paternalism has failed: the state cannot substitute for the family. But families need support as never before, an approach that I am going to call *social maternalism*.* But not all the practices of successful families are benign for society. Since you are reading this, you are likely to be part of this group. In this chapter, you must wait your turn, but your turn will come.

BOLSTERING STRESSED FAMILIES

The people who end up in low-productivity jobs often start their lives with parents ill-equipped to raise them. As we saw in Chapter 5, there has been a sharp increase in the number of children raised in households lacking one or both biological parents. Unfortunately, this often does damage that is irreversible. The implication of these brutal facts is that public policies need to begin early in the child's life, both helping families to stay together, and supplementing parenting with other forms of support.

Putting the family together

Somehow, the proposition that two-parent families are something to be encouraged has become identified with the political right: 'social conservatism'. But only the wildest shores of anarchism have ever espoused free love. As Baroness Alison Wolf, one of Britain's most revered experts on social policy, says: 'no known human societies have ever operated a sexual free-for-all. On the contrary, they have all had a well-recognized institution of marriage ... Society after society has had rules, often draconian, designed to force men who fathered children to wed the mothers.'[1] Such rules are well founded. At the time of their baby's birth, a large majority of unmarried mothers want to marry the father, and most men intend to do so. But five years later, only 35 per cent of these couples are still together, and less than half of these have actually committed to marriage.[2] It matters: at last, hard scientific research is able to supplement social science with evidence from damage to chromosomes. Telomeres are

* A term so new that Spellcheck refuses to recognize it.

the protective caps at the end of DNA: the shorter they are, the more damage is suffered by cells, and health deteriorates. If the mother has unstable relationships, by the age of nine her child's telomeres have shortened by 40 per cent.[3] To understand the sheer scale of this effect, *doubling* family income only increases telomere length by 5 per cent. The damage done by a lack of paternal commitment is so large that it cannot be offset. For many this may be 'an inconvenient truth', but that does not justify denial.

There is nothing intrinsically conservative about encouraging the commitment of both parents to their children; indeed, as a core aspect of our obligations to others it would seem more naturally to be associated with the communitarianism of the left than the individualism of the right. The wariness of the left is due to the confusion of the obligation of parents to children with both the religious obsession that sexual intercourse outside marriage is a sin and with the history of marriage as an institution for the oppression of women. This has been compounded by the delight that part of the right takes in stigmatizing people.

Let's start with sin. Among the many people who regard sin as nonsense, some think that in rejecting it they break the entire link between sex and obligations. Sin is a breach of obligations to God; if there is no God then there is no obligation to be breached. Philip Larkin aptly captured the shift of ideas that happened quite swiftly in the 1960s: 'No God any more, or sweating in the dark / About hell'; we can all 'go down the long slide / To happiness'.[4] But the 'death of God' does not get us off the hook of obligations to others: properly understood, it gets us more firmly onto it. *God* is not responsible for the human misery of failing children: *we* are. Just as social narratives shifted radically in the 1960s as youth rejected the ways of the previous generation, a new generation needs to reset them, decisively unlinking sexual obligations from religious belief. Sex, yes; irresponsible parenting, no. As for marriage as female oppression, the viable solution is not to forgo marriage but to change its norms, as has happened in many marriages. Forgoing marriage does not lead to maternal empowerment but to maternal enslavement, as women struggle solo to meet two necessary roles.

Now for stigma: people make mistakes, and young people facing powerful sexual urges make more than most. While we should do what we can to discourage the mistakes, there will continue to be many of them. Once made, the morally appropriate response of society should be forgiveness, not condemnation. Forgiveness explicitly acknowledges that a mistake has been made, but annuls any need for punishment. Instead of stigma, what two young people with an unplanned child need is encouragement to rear their child as a couple.

The evidence that decisions are heavily influenced by the opinions of others in the social network suggests that the reactions of families and friends matter a lot: we are social animals.[5] But public policy could act as reinforcement. Governments could recognize the huge value added if the two biological parents choose to live together with the child: a tax-credit bonus could reduce the tax burden for those who are taxpayers, and income could be supplemented by an equivalent amount for those who are not. The commitment of young parents to their children benefits us all, and we should be prepared to pay for it. When parents withhold this commitment, the rest of us pay for it – heavily.

Supporting the family when it most matters: prior to school

Why are there 70,000 children in 'care'? Because social paternalism intervenes by waiting until a young woman has a child that she is not equipped to look after, and then removes it from her. This happens repeatedly *with the same women*. For example, a study of child removal in Hackney found that just 49 women accounted for 205 children removed into care. Social maternalism would not wait and pounce; it would recognize that something was badly wrong with the lives of these women and help them to do something about it. In response to those awful statistics, a few people got together and did just that, forming an NGO: Pause.[6] The lives of those forty-nine women were indeed quite desperate. All but one of them were dependent upon drugs or alcohol. Half of them had chronic mental health issues. Half of them had themselves been raised in 'care', the inter-generational syndrome of failure that social paternalism has accentuated. Pause saw that the vital intervention was to change the lives of these women rather than repeatedly to remove their children, a trauma that pushed them deeper into despair and damaged the child they were bearing.* Changing lives requires both empathy and mentoring, and practical support to manage addiction, housing and abuse by violent men. Success depends upon raising self-esteem, not bullying people off benefits. That is what Pause attempted, gradually spreading its organization around Britain's stigmatized towns. Does it work?

Recently, the organization was independently evaluated. It was found that among the 137 women whom Pause had supported, there had been remarkable improvements in lifestyles. Three quarters of those with mental health problems had experienced significant improvements, and substance abuse and domestic violence were both substantially down. In turn, this had led to fewer pregnancies: the best estimate was that each year there were twenty-seven fewer births. Pause was also highly cost-effective: each £1 that the programme cost saved £9 over the following five years. But of course, Pause is tiny: social paternalism still rules the roost, dominating public spending on 'care'.

So why is social paternalism still dominant, despite its manifest failures? It is because dedicated professionals on the front line are trapped in the compartmentalized hierarchy designed for control. Here is an illustration of how it frustrates social maternalism; it comes from a psychotherapist managing a community mental health team in a broken city and its hinterland where his patients led lives of humiliation, isolation and stress. Some mothers didn't dare to take their children to school because of 'the bullying' – the victim not being their child at the school, but the mother at the school gate, assaulted by other mothers fighting over the limited pool of men. The team realized that their patients needed a safe space where they could gradually forge friendships with others facing the same stresses. They set up a project to run cafés on the sink estates, renting shops and converting them into attractive spaces. Each café was organized as a co-operative of volunteers from among patients in the community.

* The practice of pre-announcing to the pregnant mother that her baby will be removed at birth produces a severe increase in maternal stress that irretrievably damages the foetus.

Because they were attractive, they were well used by a wide cross-section of the community, without any hint of stigma. The impact on the mental and emotional health of the volunteers was assessed by their own testimony, by the professionals involved in their care, and by analysis of the health records. People told of how their isolation had been ended by the new friendships that the work facilitated. If someone failed to turn up, a friend would make it their business to contact them: the cafés incubated reciprocal obligations. The friendships that were struck up enabled people to explore their lives at their own pace, thinking beyond crisis response without fear of humiliation. Gradually, some of them restored coherence to their lives. Relapse and hospital stays decreased, and people developed self-esteem. Gaining qualifications and a future became thinkable: they became better parents; they got jobs. An indication that the cafés were valued is that they did not suffer the vandalism that beset other local businesses. As it developed, the project's finances improved and it nearly broke even. Its impact was impressive and it became an example used in conferences. And then it was closed.

Running a café was judged by the mental health team's managerial hierarchy in the NHS as too peripheral to justify the continued claim on the budget: the core activity of the team was treatment. Hospital stays were reduced, but that was a different budget. As people got jobs, they came off benefits, but that was the Social Security budget. As to Social Services, why should they divert money from core activities to fund something that the NHS wanted to discontinue? Better parenting helped the children in school, but the priority for the Education budget was its core activity of teaching. Hierarchies removed from the coalface, managing fragmented specialisms, killed an initiative that addressed the core of the problem, instead of learning from it and scaling it up. For each, the priority was the symptom that it was treating. As the despairing psychotherapist remarked: 'without better interventions this will be perpetuated down the generations with only a relatively few individuals escaping the cycle.'

That is where social maternalism begins; it continues. Young parents struggling with an unplanned child face pressures for which they are unprepared. Most parents feel the duty of care instinctively most of the time, but parenting young children can be immensely stressful: moments inevitably occur in which couples get angry with their children, and angry with each other. It requires skill, self-discipline and forgiveness to prevent such moments escalating into enduring damage. Teenagers scarcely out of childhood are plunged into a situation in which they need to sacrifice their own desires, control their tempers, and plan ahead. Young parents need money, relief and non-judgemental mentoring. This is the core of social maternalism: how can these things be provided?

Households fit their lifestyle to their income: with a little planning and prudence a large majority are able to meet the basic needs of their children. Paternalist largesse can be a two-edged sword. Britain provides free housing for single mothers; Italy and Spain don't. Britain has one of the highest rates of teenage pregnancy in Europe; Italy and Spain among the lowest. In 1999 Britain introduced increased benefits for those low-income families with children. Modern statistical methods enable us to tease out the consequences of this policy change: low-income families responded with a massive increase in births, estimated at an extra 45,000 children each year.[7] So, as a result of this free housing and enhanced benefits, many children are being raised in households that have a bit more money. But many women were encouraged to bear children who will not be raised well. These are hugely expensive benefit programmes with ambiguous effects, whereas other uses of public money are unambiguously beneficial, yet under-provided. Here is an example.

Young couples have not had the time to build up a cushion of savings, so they are vulnerable if hit by an adverse shock. Cushioning such shocks is therefore a valuable use of public money. The most evident shock is unemployment. In the USA, the financial crisis of 2008 caused a large and prolonged surge in the unemployment rate. New research by one of my doctoral students shows convincingly that this increased the neglect of young children.[8] The effect was large and it was causal. For each 1 per cent increase in the unemployment rate in a county, the incidence of child neglect rose by 20 per cent, affecting young children the most. But public policy can help mitigate the damage caused by unemployment. Counties vary in their rules for the duration of unemployment benefits; in those counties where benefits lasted longer, the impact of unemployment on neglect was substantially reduced.

So much for the money to raise children; now for relief in managing tasks that, done properly, are hugely demanding. Relief starts with the extended family: there is an obligation on other family members to rally round, but the extended family has shrunk. My father was one of seven siblings, my mother one of four, and so there was an army of aunts and uncles to support them in rearing me. Now, parents have fewer siblings, so the obligations of those that remain have correspondingly increased. But parents such as myself are only-children, and in such situations the extended family needs to be revived. Norms need to change; offsetting the horizontal shrinkage, greater longevity is expanding the family vertically. In response to the new need, people are indeed changing their norms appropriately: grandparents are far more engaged with their grandchildren than in the past.

Governments can do much more as well. Most governments have the sense to provide financial support for parents with young children, but increasingly this has been merged with the objective of encouraging people to get a job. In stressed young families, the period while the adults are parenting young children is not the right time to do this. Those people who never have children receive a huge benefit from those who do: the retired are only able to live off their savings because the subsequent generation is putting those savings to work. While parents are struggling to rear young children is the key time for the state to make the transfer payments that reflect this contribution to society.

But the state can do more than give money: it can provide in-kind support both within the household and beyond it. Parenting is difficult for every new parent, but some couples are in such inauspicious circumstances that trouble is all too likely. Where trouble can be predicted, it can also be averted by intensive pre-emptive intervention.

Just as there is a limit to what the market can do, there is a limit to what the state can do through public services of support. However, we are not yet at that limit. There are a few examples of intensive publicly provided support, and to the extent that they have been evaluated they show signs of success. One example is the Dundee Project, a modest experiment in unconditional support for stressed families.

Practical, day-to-day support for a young family is expensive, but far cheaper than the consequences of family breakdown.

A vital feature of the Dundee Project was that it was completely separated from the service that scrutinized the family. Scrutiny is necessary: *in extremis*, a child should be removed from its parents. But without such absolute separation of functions, the basic conditions for building a trusting relationship between the parents and the workers providing support are not met. In Britain, the Dundee Project inspired a massive scale-up into the Troubled Families Programme (TFP), but while well motivated, this was contaminated both by the additional objective of getting young mothers into work and by being run by the existing social services, with their role of scrutiny. This overload blunted the TFP's efficacy.

Although integrating support with scrutiny undermines each service, integrating physical support with mental support could be reinforcing. Often, the parents in those families that are predictably liable to become troubled have incipient mental health problems. Mental health interventions, such as cognitive behavioural therapy and anger management programmes, have been rigorously evaluated and show impressive success rates. Such pre-emptive support costs money, but it may avert behaviours that are much costlier to society in the long run. While the *provision* of child support, mental health care and scrutiny should be joined up, their *functions* need to be kept sharply separate.

Teenage couples expecting a baby are parents with L-plates and need non-threatening guidance. The occasional evening class is unlikely to be enough. Grandparents can help, but quite often the couples most liable to become dysfunctional parents are from families that are themselves dysfunctional. Young couples need some source of mentoring and informal support beyond the family. One way to supplement dwindling or dysfunctional extended families is to create a new resource: a modern analogue for our own societies of the Peace Corps or Voluntary Service Overseas that once inspired many thousands of American and British youth. Then, the new social resource was a growing pool of educated young people looking for a sense of purpose beyond their own enrichment. Today's equivalent is the growing pool of fit and savvy retired, financially comfortable with their pensions but with a hole in their lives left by an empty nest. These people have been equipped by life with the non-cognitive skills with which to become the unthreatening helpers for the stressed young couples who are in need of support. Rising to a duty of rescue can bring a deeply satisfying sense of purpose into life at a stage when otherwise it can become wistful or complacent. As with all support, the role would have to be sharply delineated, and participants trained, to ensure that it could not deteriorate into a patronize–blame–scrutinize–report relationship. Maybe it should be paid; if so, payment should depend on the authorization of the young parents, so that they would feel empowered. Maybe young parents could be given a budget that they could draw upon for such a purpose. Rather than being government-organized, a new crop of NGOs could recruit the capable-with-time to help the thousands of young families that are not coping with their obligations. Whereas governments are terrified of failure, and so ill-equipped to experiment, NGOs are ideally equipped to try new approaches.

There is good reason for the phrase 'the terrible twos': young children are periodically impossible, stressing even experienced parents to the limits of endurance. From that age, children benefit from being socialized into groups beyond the family – kindergartens. There is a strong case for these to be provided by the state and open to all without charge. All states provide school-age education, and the case for state provision of kindergartens is stronger than for any other level of education. In general, as children get older their educational needs become more complex and differentiated. The main advantage of states over other forms of provision is in those activities that lend themselves to standardization and are more cheaply done at scale. Kindergartens are not complex: the key feature that society should want them to offer is to provide a standardized forum in which young children meet others drawn from a wide cross-section of society. Standardization and free provision has the vital advantage that by making the parental decision to send the child to the kindergarten normal for the entire society, those parents who are least equipped to take good decisions will be more likely to do so. The universal provision of free public kindergartens thus achieves two highly desirable outcomes: they are socially mixed at a time when children are at their most readily shaped by social influence, and the children most in need of pre-schooling are likely to attend them. Instead of public kindergartens, however, many countries have a complex plethora of subsidy schemes for private provision that have accumulated incrementally with each new ministerial initiative to meet an evident need. For example, the British Sure Start programme prioritized getting mothers into work, and was readily gamed by targeting recruitment on the easiest 'successes' who just ticked the criteria: complexity almost guarantees that schemes will tend to be used by those who least need them, and private provision guarantees differentiation of intake. The exemplar of free, state public provision of kindergartens is France, with its *écoles maternelles*. We experienced it first hand while living in a low-income Breton town; in neither Washington nor Oxford were we able to find its market-provided equal.

Schools as sites of support

Recall that the most important activity that happens in a school is not the teaching but the interactions within the peer group; the differences that begin in the family are replicated and amplified by the differences in the social composition of schools. Silicon Valley think that their technology has opened the world of knowledge to the children of the less educated. But the evidence is quite contrary to their hopes: the internet has widened rather than narrowed differences in opportunities. Everyone now has access, but recent research shows that the children of the educated learn to use the internet for expanding their knowledge, whereas the children of the less educated use it for distraction.[9]

The most valuable change that could happen to schools would be to make them more socially mixed. The key impediment to social mixing is school catchment areas. Because where people choose to live has become so socially stratified, catchment areas have the effect of mirroring this stratification in schools. One way of breaking free of this trap for post-primary schooling is to create publicly funded schools that have city-wide catchment areas, differentiated by purpose rather than location. One school might promote itself as the best place for aspiring sports professionals; another for aspiring actors; another for the children of parents who value discipline. Drawing on the concepts introduced in Chapter 2, the idea here is that heads and school governors would be trying to build schools with somewhat distinctive *belief systems*: they become networked groups in which distinctive narratives circulate. The schools would know they had to be good at what they did, otherwise parents living in affluent catchment areas would continue to send their children to the local, affluent-only school in preference. New rules have now enabled such schools to be established in Britain, and I was part of a team that tried to start one in Oxford, a city whose catchment areas are grotesquely skewed. Our plan for city-wide, lottery-based access met with a predictable response: a wall of vested interests and ideology. The outraged local educational elite, led by the school in the most affluent catchment area, rose up in fury. They succeeded in blocking us; perhaps you might have better luck.

Schools as organizations

The teaching activity of schools could be improved. This is a heavily researched topic with a vast literature, but the dominant motif is that teacher quality is far more important than money. Four simple things can raise teacher quality: attract a better intake; base training on the pragmatism of evaluated experiments; assign the best teachers to the most difficult settings; and weed out the weakest teachers.

In Britain, the Teach First programme has had a dramatic impact. Its aim is simple: to induce good students graduating from universities to spend their first few years teaching before switching to another career. The approach has potential for analogous targeted recruitment: how about Teach Last? Upon retiring from his chair in Amsterdam, Professor Jan Willem Gunning, my co-author for many an article, became a maths teacher in a local school. He tells me it has been the most rewarding experience of his life. But the Teach First programme was restricted to teaching in London, the area of the country that least needed it. The schools that need Teach First are in the provincial towns and cities, where good teachers are often wary of taking jobs lest they become marooned. Precisely because those who plan to teach for life are deterred by fear of getting stuck, those who don't plan to remain a teacher should be the easiest to recruit. The London-bias in Teach First is compounded by a wage premium currently paid to teachers in London, where schools receive far more funding per pupil than those elsewhere. London has the best school results in the country. Teach First, the wage premium and the funding premium per pupil should all be closed in London and be switched to the places that need them. Teach First was precisely the right programme, targeted at precisely the wrong place.

Deciding between teaching methods is well-suited to learning from randomized trials. But politicians and the educational establishment are wary of such experimentation. Pragmatism is an admission of ignorance, and the confidence that comes with an ideology is much more satisfying. However, the wide variations in the PISA scores between countries and schools suggest that there is much still to learn, and that will only come from evaluated experiments. Teacher training should be built around this evolving evidence, and students should be taught how to keep learning from it.

Weeding out the weakest teachers can have a dramatic effect.[10] While it takes some very fancy social science technology to establish that the worst teachers are doing massive damage, it does not require much research to understand why nothing is done about it. The vested interests of the teaching profession, represented by various unions, threaten annihilation for any politician who dares to suggest it. Understandable? Yes. Ethical? No.

There are a few classroom policies that appear to help address attainment problems, although fashions change and ideology again impedes analysis. In addition to teaching, student effort is crucial: the question is how best to induce it among those least inclined to try. Economists at the University of Chicago are using lab experiments to test different approaches,[11] and have found that quite simple techniques can have substantial effects. One is that, in order to be effective, any rewards need to be delivered almost immediately after the effort – within minutes, not months. As to the sorts of reward, esteem works better than money (once again, we are revealed to be more social animals than greedy ones). But rewards turn out not to be the best motivator. People are much more motivated to avoid losses than to acquire gains – the technical term is 'loss aversion' – so swift, esteem-related losses for low effort may pack the biggest punch. Yet this is not a message prominent in teacher training colleges.

The issue of streaming is beset by ideological disputes, and is an issue desperately in need of pragmatism. A credible psychological theory is that children seek peer esteem, and are willing to put in some effort to get it (or avoid losing it). The most potent peer group is likely to be the other students in the class. If the year group is streamed, so that the ability gap between stronger and weaker students in the class is narrow, then it becomes worthwhile for weaker students to put in the effort; similarly, the strongest students have to try harder to stay ahead. But if the gap is very wide, as it will be if the year is divided randomly into classes rather than streamed, then effort by the weaker students is pointless and by the stronger students unnecessary. There is some empirical support for this idea, but it needs more thorough testing than I have yet seen. What we most need in schools is not dogma, but experimental variations that are rigorously and independently evaluated.

Finally, there is the issue of money. The differences in public spending per pupil currently tend to *amplify* other differences in attainment. The most substantial differences are geographic: the metropolis has a booming tax base and vocal lobbies; broken cities have neither. In Britain, the differences are predictably extreme. London has by far the highest spending of public money per pupil, while my own home region of Yorkshire and Humberside has among the lowest. Yet London already has the best exam results in the country, while my home region has the worst: the gap is recent, large and widening. Expect motivated reasoning: the vested interests currently defending this gross misallocation of funds should be shamed into decisive defeat.

Beyond the school: activities and mentoring

Most activities outside the school are for teenagers, but most of the divergence in attainment and life chances occurs earlier. For pre-teens, the key differentiating behaviour is pitifully simple: reading. The children of the educated class read; the children of the less-educated class don't. Reading opens doors and the children of the elite go through them. School is supposed to fix this problem; children are taught the mechanics of how to read, but this is very different from acquiring a habit of reading. We now know how to encourage these habits in the children of non-reading parents, we just haven't yet got round to doing much about it. But any concerned group of citizens with some gumption can make a difference: here is what works.

Rotherham is a much-stigmatized town that in Britain has become emblematic of marginalization. Like nearby Sheffield, it is a steel and mining town where the jobs have disappeared.* Amidst this tragedy and the associated demoralization, a small group of citizens determined to raise literacy standards among the children of the most marginalized families. They searched for an example they could use, and chose one that seemed to have worked in an American town. Adapting it to their own context, they partnered with one of the universities in Sheffield to conduct a quantitative evaluation in parallel with their efforts. That's why we know it works: it came through on the test scores in the schools. They set up a charity, found a disused site in the town centre – there were plenty of them – and persuaded local firms to adapt it from a bar into something quite magical. I use the word 'magical' both figuratively and literally: this was a centre where children could go to learn magic. The name over the door, 'Grimm and Co', the sign on the door, 'no grown-ups', and the blacked-out windows all tempt children in, usually either dragging their hesitant parents after them, or coming for a pre-booked visit with their classmates. Once inside, they encounter a giant beanstalk, a further sign saying 'please do not eat the staff', and a myriad of other stimuli to enchantment. All this is a prelude to being lured through a concealed door to mount the book staircase, past the office of the momentarily absent Mr Grimm, to the room where the loose pages of his new story are read to them. And then disaster! The last page is missing! The completed story is urgently needed: please can someone help? Here are a few pencils if you can finish it.

Invariably, the reaction is a stampede. Teachers have broken down in tears as children who have never willingly picked up a pencil write

---

* Consistent with marginalization, Spellcheck refuses to recognize the name despite its population being double that of Oxford, a name to which it raises no objection.

as if their lives depended on it. And everything gets followed up: Rotherham classes have published collections of poems distributed around the world; the Royal Shakespeare Theatre Company has come and performed for them; Bob Geldof has written a story for them. Appetites can be ignited; habits can be changed. This brilliant initiative – the creation of one impassioned woman – can be scaled up and modified to fit different local contexts. Already it has attracted delegations from China and South Korea. Yes, this is *Rotherham* that East Asians are learning from, not Hampstead. If they can do it, so perhaps can you.[12]

There are many other such actions that can help children outside school. The non-cognitive skills are formed not by study, but by people who become trusted mentors, and by group activities such as sports where children can learn co-operation and leadership. Finding a mentor who is both usefully knowledgeable and trusted depends upon the breadth of the child's social network, which in turn will reflect that of the family. The single most important decision in my own career was taken in the month before going to college: having been accepted for law, I wrote asking to switch to economics. In reaching that decision I was desperate for advice, as I realized that it would chart two different lives.* But my family network included nobody with pertinent experience: in desperation, I asked my dentist (unsurprisingly, he was useless). Nowadays, children from the two divergent classes face huge differences in their span of social networks. The Pew Research Center measures nine types of people that a family might have as part of its network. On eight of them, educated households have more connections than less-educated ones: the ninth is janitors, where the less educated have an advantage. Of the eight, the largest divergence of all is in what I lacked for that decision: 'do you know a professor?' For the family in which I grew up, such a question would have been tantamount to 'do you know the Queen?', but my children are awash with them: when Daniel, my seventeen-year-old, got interested in nanotechnology, his first port of call was next door.

But mentoring by someone whom a teenager has chosen to listen to is not just useful for information: it is a source of the narratives

---

* Instead of writing books, I could have been a rent-seeking barrister.

that people use to guide their lives. Teenagers going wrong can be redirected by the gentle influence of healthy narratives delivered outside the context of parental rewards and punishments: paternalist power impedes the willingness to listen.[13]

Diverging skills, diverging firms, diverging pensions

School is not really a preparation for life: it is a preparation for training. At its best, it will have equipped some people with cognitive abilities that can be honed into skills that are highly productive in some occupations. But the non-cognitive abilities will not have received the same attention. Many productive occupations depend less upon good cognitive abilities, and more upon well-honed non-cognitive abilities such as perseverance. In the changeover from school to training, those who are going to remain on the cognitive track have a less-demanding passage than those who will be jumping from cognitive to non-cognitive skills.

Post-school skills

We know what works, and we know what doesn't work. Most high-income countries get some aspects of post-school skills development right, but the parts they get right differ, and there has been little willingness to learn from each other.

For those with the best cognitive abilities and an interest in developing them, America and Britain provide the finest skill development that the world has ever had: good universities. Each country has many of them, including five American universities and three British ones in the world's top-ten. In contrast, the twenty-seven countries of the post-Brexit European Union have not a single top-ten university between them, and this is symptomatic of more widespread failings in their university systems. The reason for the difference is how universities are run. High standards are achieved by competition and decentralized management: the same ingredients that have made modern capitalism so productive. In France, by way of contrast, the same centralized control of education that has worked so brilliantly in the standardized, low-complexity setting of its pre-primary schooling has been dismal at the university level.

However, for those other than the elite-educated minority, America and Britain are poor environments for skills development. Recall that the majority of young people should be switching tracks from the sort of training that merely deepens cognitive skills to the sort that develops the neglected non-cognitive skills. Since this is a more demanding transition, it should be the primary focus of post-school policy. From the perspective of the young student, being a leap into the unknown, it is more demanding psychologically. From the perspective of the government, since the required skills are so different from those that it manages through the rest of the education system, it is more demanding organizationally. Per student, it should have a larger budget than studying for a university degree.

The professionals know what is needed: high quality technical vocational education and training (TVET) that young people choose to do in preference to plodding on down the familiar track of cognitive-focused training. Fortunately, they even know how it can be achieved, because Germany has been doing it for a long time and the result has been a highly productive and well-paid workforce. So, what does Germany do? How do they organize such training, and how have they induced millions of young people to make the implied psychological leap? More importantly, why have others not copied them?[14]

The key organizational components in Germany are local partnerships between firms and colleges within a specific industry. The college designs its courses around these skills, and the firms provide on-site work experience and mentoring from its skilled workforce, with the student's time being split between the college and the firm. The student typically undertakes this training for three years, after which she takes a job in the firm. The training has several aims, none trivial and some quite subtle; indeed, the list of how to be an employable young worker sounds almost as demanding as Kipling's famous list of how to be a man. One is to build routine expertise: skills developed through practice and honed through feedback. Another is to be able to think for yourself when necessary: the knowledge and confidence to be resourceful. Craftsmanship brings an ethic of excellence, and a sense of pride in a job well done. It is learned through working with someone who becomes a role model. Then come the functional capabilities: numeracy, literacy, communications technology and graphics.

Since most jobs are in the private sector, young people need business-like attitudes, including recognition that jobs depend upon customers being willing to pay for what is produced. Similarly, the young worker needs the life skills of self-presentation and to complete a task in a timely and respectful way. Finally, the ability to adapt: inquisitive and resilient attitudes such as self-belief, empathy, self-control, perseverance, collaboration and creativity. Reading that, the average student at Oxford might be daunted, yet this is what is needed to make the half of the population less gifted with cognitive skills productive in twenty-first-century work.

Building those skills is both a local and a national undertaking. To be effective, public policy needs to be complemented by a sense of purpose among firms. We are back to the concept of the ethical firm, a team of people who have internalized a mission larger than their individual enrichment. An ethical firm recognizes its responsibilities to its young recruits and devotes time and money to training them properly, not just in the narrow skills of the trade, but in the wider panoply of capabilities covered by those German TVET. In Britain, the contrasting attitudes of firms to their workforce has been exemplified by two giant retailers – John Lewis and BHS; in America, the equivalent has been Toyota and GM. Recall that ethical need not mean stupid; it was BHS and GM that went bankrupt, not John Lewis and Toyota.

We also know what is ineffective: training that is detached from the real world of work. Two common public policies that ostensibly address the skill problem fall foul of this requirement.

In response to concerns about a lack of skills, some governments have encouraged courses that are ostensibly vocational, but last only a few months, are not linked to a future job in a specific firm, and do not go beyond the technical rudiments of a vocation. These miss all the broader skills necessary for technical competence to become really useful to a firm.

More grandiosely, and certainly more wastefully, there has been a huge expansion in low quality vocational courses in universities. In both America and Britain, half of young people now go to university – a response to the excessive prestige of a degree. In Britain, a third of these students end up in jobs that used to be filled by non-graduates, and whose skill requirements have not changed. Their degrees have not made them more productive.[15] At school, many children dream of the glamour professions they see on social media. There is a massive mismatch between the exposure of various professions and their frequency among the workforce. Children should indeed dream and plan and aspire, but in aggregate these aspirations have to mesh with reality. The adjustment of dreams to jobs is part of the pain of becoming an adult. As the Norwegian writer Karl Ove Knausgård has so beautifully expressed, the passage from sixteen to forty, 'that which is now so vast and so all-embracing, will inexorably dwindle and shrink until it is a manageable entity which doesn't hurt so much, but nor is it as good.'[16]

Adults should not connive to exploit this passage. People working in the glamour professions – forensics being an example – have painfully explained to me that university courses ostensibly training for their profession are recruiting on false promises. Students graduate from these programmes with large debts: in America, their debts are often larger than those of students taking valuable academic courses at top universities. They have been lured into an expensive cul-de-sac by the word 'degree' attached to a dream profession, when what they needed was a launch pad into a productive, albeit less seductive, career.

In both America and Britain, the huge pool of under-trained people looking for jobs have found them in firms designed to run profitably on modest productivity and correspondingly modest pay. Such firms economize by laying workers off as soon as demand dips; by skimping on training; by excluding unions. They learn to cope with the high staff turnover resulting from disaffection, relying on the desperate and the gullible to replace those who quit. In some sectors, this low-productivity–low-cost business model will be more profitable than the high-productivity–high-cost model in which firms invest in their workers. Where it is more profitable, low-cost firms will drive out high-cost firms from the market. But although in their role as consumers people are better off, in their role as workers they are worse off; their incomes are lower because they are less productive. More formally expressed, there is a market failure in the process of skill formation. People would be better off if they paid a little more for what they buy, but earned a lot more from their work, but there is no mechanism that induces the chain of commitments to transactions that would in aggregate result in this superior outcome. Expressing the problem in such language does not make it go away: society needs to do something about it. Minimum wage laws, compulsory training levies and union rights all have a role constraining the scope for firms to drive labour costs down at the expense of productivity. To take a simple example of regulation and its consequences, a restaurant chain operating in Paris and London faces a substantial difference in the minimum wage laws. In Paris, where the minimum wage is much higher, it organizes its menus and its staff, training them in more complex service routines, so that each waiter can serve more people than in London. As a result, the productivity of its waiters in Paris is higher than of those in London. Meal prices are no different, though a diner in Paris receives less attention than one in London. But the crucial social difference is that the waiters in Paris earn more. Yes, London has a lot of jobs, but they are lousy ones.

Having set out what good non-cognitive training looks like, and the alternative track down which many young people are currently lured, we can finally turn to the psychology: what determines whether young people prefer this option? The crude psychology of *The Wealth of Nations* suggests that people only care about money. The more accurate psychology of *The Theory of Moral Sentiments* tells us that people also care about their position in society: they give and receive esteem. The evidence on regrets supports our intuition that esteem trumps money. But even on the criterion of money, many young people in America and Britain are being lured down cognitive culs-de-sac. They are doing so because that, currently, is the choice that generates the most peer esteem. When they tell their friends that they are going to university, those who are not look sheepish. When they tell their friends that they are studying forensics, their friends recognize the role model from Netflix. The nub of the problem is the mis-ranking of esteem between cognitive and non-cognitive training. It runs deep through the Anglo-Saxon societies; young people learn it from the narratives related to them by the rest of us. It is so deep that you may well be thinking that it is inevitable. But it isn't; again, Germany has shown that rankings can be different.

I could give you the data, but the way that I learned about this was more personal. For a year we had a highly capable German au pair living with us, who was at precisely the stage in her life at which she was facing the choice between continuing on to university, or switching to vocation-specific training. Should she have wanted, she had sufficient cognitive aptitude to continue her academic education: she had offers from universities. But her aspiration was a vocational course run jointly by a company and a college in her home town.* The training programme on which she embarked was so impressive as to be daunting. Her chosen vocation was in marketing: the product that the firm produced, and which she would need to be able to market, was a technically sophisticated piece of equipment. For week one of her first year she worked on a lathe, alongside the workers making it. By year three she was in Latin America learning Spanish. She is now an employee, well paid and secure. Perhaps she will compete head to head with a British salesman whose post-school training was a degree. In making that crucial choice our au pair was surprised by our surprise. The track she took was not just more challenging than staying in the classroom, it was more prestigious. Esteem and material rewards steered her in the same direction.

To create equivalent influences in America and Britain we must waive farewell to the symbols of cognitive privilege. The word 'degree' needs to be defanged: lathes and Latin America can become more glamorous than three more years of the classroom. Germany has done this well, but the leader is Switzerland. Vocational training in Switzerland is serious: courses are typically three to four years long, and firms are closely involved because they pay half of the costs, which are considerable. It is also popular: 60 per cent of young people choose vocational courses, partly because they are paid while studying on them, but also because such training is an accepted avenue to top jobs.† The achievement is all the more remarkable because this world-beating vocational training coexists with a university in the global top-ten: the cognitive paths do not have to be weakened in order for the non-cognitive paths to thrive.

* Britain used to have such colleges, called polytechnics. Symptomatic of the British bias to academic prestige, they were all turned into universities.
† In Britain during 2016, among those in further education only 4,000 people achieved a technical level award: less than one for every 10,000 of the British population (Alison Wolf, *Financial Times*, 28 December 2017).

Vocational training needs enhanced kudos, not only for those who take the courses, but for those who give them. Teaching cognitive skills provides easy kudos: we have titles like 'professor', and belong to a 'university'. Vocational training is currently too fragmented to offer such easy kudos. Perhaps the many vocational courses need to be given the common enhanced status of meeting a vital national purpose: a National Skill Service in which all staff can take pride.

Securing the job horizon

Once in a productive job, how much security of employment should a worker have? Workers take on long-term obligations, such as mortgages, and so need as much job security as possible. In contrast, firms face periodic shocks to the demand for their products and so will want as much flexibility as possible. The compromise they reach will depend upon their relative bargaining power, but this in turn is heavily influenced by government policy. At one extreme, exemplified by France, governments legislate to make job security a requirement of employment. At the other extreme, exemplified by America in the 1920s, governments legislated to restrict unions. In between, sector-by-sector differences in the bargaining power of workers produce a patchwork. Every professor, however pedestrian, has lifetime job security: otherwise we might get anxious and this could interfere with our ability to think great thoughts (doubtless, other professors will come up with further justifications). Meanwhile, my award-winning actor nephew, working in a sector saturated with job-seekers, looks forward to a lifetime of transience.

In rethinking employment rights, ideology is not going to help: while the ideologues of the left abhor a *market* for labour, those of the right sanctify it. The most common free-market critique is that minimum wages cause unemployment. Unemployment is the most salient indication that something is amiss, but it is not always the most important. A labour market has two distinct functions. The one that matters for unemployment is to pair up job-seekers with a particular skill with the jobs that firms create for those skills: what is going on is *matching*. But the function that matters for mass prosperity is the creation of those skills: *investment*. There is an inherent tension between these two. Being able to make binding commitments can make the investment more viable. The training that a worker needs in order to acquire a skill is costly, and someone has to pay it. To the extent that the worker pays for it, she worries whether the firm will employ her on a higher salary for long enough that her investment in training is worthwhile. But to the extent that the firm pays for it, it worries that, once trained, the worker will quit and take a better-paid job with another firm. Guaranteed job security can give the worker the confidence to overcome that first worry. The unemployment generated as a side effect of wage controls can give the firm the confidence to overcome the second one, so between them they are likely to increase investments in training. But guaranteed job security and wage controls discourage firms from hiring workers, and so impede the matching function of the labour market. That is why it is better to solve the firm's investment problem not by using high unemployment to discourage workers from quitting, but by paying for the training through a government-imposed levy.

But workers need job security not just to recover their investments in skill, but because they take on commitments that anticipate their future salary. This ability to take on commitments such as raising children, or buying a home, is beneficial to society, so job security is socially valuable. It may be more efficient for the firm to adjust to the need to pay the worker during periods of slack demand than for the worker to bear the risk of being laid off. If the firm has to keep the worker, it may train her in several tasks so that when the demand for one task drops it can switch her to another.

There has, however, to be a limit to such security; while firms should be able to cope with temporary fluctuations, they cannot adjust to a large, permanent drop in demand without shedding labour. At the limit, the firm goes bankrupt. Yet the fact that job loss is unavoidable in no way mitigates the cost to the worker. For this class of shock, we need an entity larger than the firm – the state. Nobel Laureate Jean Tirole has proposed a smart way for government to induce firms to retain workers through market troughs, while still enabling them to shed employees when faced by a permanent contraction. This is to impose a charge on labour-shedding to reflect the extra costs to the state of welfare payments and retraining.

The governments that have reputedly best responded to such job shocks are those of Denmark and Sweden, which developed the concept of *flexicurity*. The policy is closely related to the challenge of reviving broken cities: if an industry has collapsed, it will have hit some specific locations hard and its workers will need retraining. *Janesville* is a rare study of retraining programmes in an American town hit by the closure of its major plant.[17] It reveals that the retraining was a decisive failure. Those among the redundant who took the programme were *less* likely to get work than those who didn't and, if they did find work, earned *less* than those who didn't retrain. Why did the programme fail so resoundingly? I think that three key things were neglected. Moreover, the neglect went right back to schooling: the men made redundant had never been taught things that are basic for modern learning. The neglect then continued through their long period of employment at the plant. Not having been faced with the prospect of the penalties of redundancy proposed by Tirole, the firm had had no incentive to equip the men with a broader range of skills that could have made them more employable. But above all, retraining was not co-ordinated with any targeted stimulus designed to attract a new industry to the town. Instead, the cluster effect triggered a downward spiral in which the closure of the plant led to corresponding contraction among the other local employers so that there were few jobs for retrained workers to chase. The experience recounted in *Janesville* suggests that, without such a high-profile co-ordinated effort, retraining is a snare offering the illusion of hope. But most likely, even with better education, a wider endowment of prior skills and a big push to form a replacement cluster, redundant workers will hesitate to sink their newly needed savings into retraining. Two professors at Chicago's Business School, Luigi Zingales and Raghuram Rajan, have proposed that all workers should be given a lifetime credit that they draw on for retraining as needed.*

The incipient robotics revolution, and whatever further technological revolutions lie beyond it, will require many people to retrain. Robotics is, I think, unlikely to reduce the need for work – our wants are probably insatiable. But it will change the composition of tasks for which workers will be needed. This is the essence of a valuable insight.

---

* In May 2018 the French government introduced such a policy.

Think of the typical job as made up of a series of tasks. Even the most seemingly routine job invariably involves moments that require judgement, the ability to interact with other people, and some non-routine action. Robotics will eliminate some tasks, and in doing so will sharply reduce the cost of the output currently produced during a working day. By redeploying to the remaining tasks that do not lend themselves to robotics, and to new tasks that reliance on robotics create, the typical worker can become much more productive.[18] Because different jobs have very different compositions of robotic-suited and unsuited tasks, the skill composition of work is likely to keep changing substantially; periodically, people will need to retrain to be able to perform new packages of tasks. Just as Parisian waiters earn more than their counterparts in London, tomorrow's workers will earn more than today's, but only if, like those Parisian waiters, they learn different skills. A corollary is that one of the highly labour-intensive sectors that will need to expand massively is the training sector.

Security in retirement

I would like to retire, but please not yet. But I already know the incomes I will receive from my state and university pensions: I am secure until death. Not so, many others.

Risks can easily be pooled, and for most types of risk, if they are pooled they evaporate. The reason for caution in pooling risks is 'moral hazard'. In some situations, once the risk is shared, everyone takes greater risks: because we all have fire insurance we are more careless. But one risk borne by many pensioners involves no moral hazard whatsoever: it is the risk involved in all defined-contribution pension schemes. Virtually all firms have decided that defined *bene-fit* schemes such as my own are ruinously expensive. My own scheme, for British universities, bears this out; it has accumulated the largest deficit in a pension fund ever recorded. Fortunately for me, this will not affect my own entitlement, which will be borne by the next generation of academics and by students who will pay higher fees. They will be heartened to know that I am truly grateful.*

* Just in case, let me assure them that I have them over a legal barrel: thank God for barristers.

Meanwhile, everyone else has been shunted into the defined *contribution* pension schemes. Here they find themselves bearing three risks. One is that the entire pension fund into which they are contributing may perform worse than other funds; in contrast to a defined benefit scheme, the shortfall is no longer the liability of their employer. Another is that their choice of investments within the fund may do worse than the average choices of other employees. Finally, on the day on which they retire, when their benefit is cashed out, the market may have dropped below its long-term average: stock markets are sometimes highly volatile. As a result of these three risks, two workers with the same history of pension contributions can end up with considerably different pensions.

While the defined benefit schemes such as my own are too generous, shifting all the risk on to society, the defined contribution schemes are needlessly exposing people to avoidable risks just when they are least able to bear them. They have shifted from pooling risks so that they evaporate, to dumping them on individuals at a time when they are vulnerable. This is an eminently fixable error of design.

But the people facing the most serious retirement insecurities are those whose working life is spent shuffling between the firms from hell. They do not even accumulate entitlements to defined contributions. Dumped on to society when they are too old to work, they become society's liability. Again, this is a market failure: their employers have been allowed to cut their employment costs excessively in not making adequate payments into a pension scheme. As with minimum wage laws, French policy looks to be superior to the Anglo-Saxon model: the high contributions required from employers ensure that as long as people work they build up an adequate entitlement to a pension. That proviso of course implies that the economy must be run in such a way as to generate enough productive jobs for everyone. This is the critical benchmark that must be met by training programmes; mopping up the unemployed with lousy jobs is a failure, not a substitute.

Belonging to society

While I have emphasized family, workplace and nation as the cornerstones of belonging, in all healthy societies there is also a dense web of networked groups to which people become attached. Robert Putnam's celebrated book *Bowling Alone* lamented the decline of these forms of belonging in America. Such attachments encourage people into habits of acknowledging reciprocal obligations, as well as countering isolation and its corollaries of loss of self-esteem, and depression. The decline in America is neither inevitable nor universal across the West. In Germany, formally registered civil society groups, *vereine*, are common and increasing. Half of all Germans belong to at least one such club, and the number of clubs has increased by a third in the past twenty years. The proportion of Germans taking part in such groups is around triple that of southern Europe.[19]

CURBING THE HAVING-IT-ALL'S

The rise of the new educated class has certainly widened social inequality. But most of the behaviours that have made it so successful have not been at the expense of the rest of society. Their strategies would be better emulated than curbed. But some aspects of the educated class's success *are* at the expense of others: zero-sum housing demand; zero-sum work; and zero-sum social behaviour.

Housing: homes versus assets

People have two motives for buying a house. For most people it is a home; for some it is an asset. In the Britain of 1950, half of the entire housing stock was owned as an asset and rented to people needing a home. Only 30 per cent of people actually owned their home. One of the triumphs of social democracy was to transform this situation. By 1980 the private rented sector had shrunk drastically, to only 10 per cent, while owner-occupation had nearly doubled. In the early 1980s a further twist in public policy raised owner-occupation to a high point of 70 per cent, by enabling tenants in social housing to buy their homes at a discount.

This increase from 30 to 70 per cent was a cumulative triumph of public policies. *Owning* a home enhances the sense of belonging, and that, as I have suggested, is a vital social good. Belonging is the foundation for reciprocal obligations. Home ownership also gives people a greater sense of having a stake in society, and inclines them to be more prudent: psychologists have discovered that, once people have something, they become highly averse to losing it. And owning a home anchors people. A street in Oxford was once divided halfway along between rental and owner-occupation; the divide is still visible because of the height of the trees – only owners planted them.

Four public policies kept house prices affordable for families on median income. A building programme run by local government increased supply; restraints on net immigration limited the rate of increase in households; curbs on buy-to-let restricted the pure asset-demand for housing; and curbs on the ratio of mortgages to income restrained what people could bid. The asset-transfer to tenants in social housing complemented these policies, by enabling families whose incomes were below-median to own their house.

From the late 1980s this progress began to unravel. Home owner-ship has already fallen to 60 per cent and is still declining; young families can no longer afford to buy a home. Over the past twenty years, the price of the average house has jumped from 3.6 times aver-age earnings, to 7.6 times. This is not surprising: all four of the policies that had restrained house prices have been reversed. Local government building programmes were stopped in the hope that pri-vate firms would replace them (they didn't, partly because acquiring land with planning permission was far more difficult for them than for local government). Immigration controls were relaxed, becoming the main driver of household growth. The rules that had curbed buy-to-let were replaced by those that encouraged it, unleashing a huge new asset-demand for housing. Buy-to-let properties have doubled to around 20 per cent of the housing stock. Finally, the curbs on mort-gage finance were lifted, giving way to the lending frenzy that seized the banks in a bonus-hungry race over the cliff. That is why there was an explosion of house prices. Nor, as new below-median income families formed, was there any equivalent to the asset-transfer programme.

As a result of high prices and unrestricted credit, the people who wanted housing as an asset were able to outbid the people who wanted housing as a home, who typically were young families. Twenty years ago, over half of young families took out a mortgage; now it is around a third. Those squeezed out were not the high-skilled assortative maters, but those in the less-educated class. Their inability to buy a home, and the diminishing prospect of ever being able to do so, is central to the new anxieties. But who are the people who outbid them? With house prices rising, everyone wanted to buy a house: the people who were able to do so were those who could borrow the most. The winners in this race have been the older members of the educated class, and smart people who exploited the borrow-and-let opportunity to the hilt. A spectacular case was a couple of teachers who quit their jobs and accumulated a vast housing empire. The affluent and the smart have benefited from a double bonanza: being better able to borrow than young families, they can charge rents that exceed their interest payments. On top of this, as house prices have risen, they have accrued huge capital appreciation.

So, what can be done about it? Again, ideology is a menace. Those on the left want to return to the rent controls of the 1940s, as then, this would freeze people into the home they are currently renting, reducing job mobility. Those on the right want to increase finance for first-time house purchase; by further fuelling demand, this would jack prices up yet further. Yet addressing this problem is not difficult, because we know what worked: the same policies would work again.

It makes sense to increase supply, and the most credible way of doing so is to break the planning log-jam. Local governments are best placed to plan new building programmes, while execution can be in partnership with commercial developers. Local authorities could plan build-to-buy, instead of build-to-rent. But an increase in the supply of housing needs to be gradual: a quantum increase would risk crashing house prices, plunging many young home owners into negative equity. Correspondingly, it makes sense to curb household growth by restoring restrictions on immigration. The credit frenzy unleashed by financial deregulation did not usher in nirvana – it ended in the regulatory disgrace of a bank run. The sight of depositors besieging the branches of Northern Rock was the first such spectacle in Britain for 150 years. As with a house building programme, change will need to be gradual, but its direction is unambiguous: we need to return to ceilings on the ratios of mortgages to income and of mortgages to deposits. It also makes sense to curb buy-to-let. The public benefit from home ownership warrants giving priority to those who want a house-as-home, over those who want a house-as-asset.

All the above policies are gradual. But it is feasible to achieve a quantum recovery in home ownership without jeopardizing house prices. This is by means of a stock transfer analogous to the discounted purchases of social housing that raised home ownership during the 1980s. Currently, the equivalent to the social housing of the 1980s is the policy-inflated stock of buy-to-let. Many such owners are sitting on huge and undeserved amounts of capital appreciation. The necessary public policy is a stock transfer from these landlords to their tenants, through legislating an entitlement to purchase, probably on similar terms to the deep discounts of the 1980s. To avoid inflicting financial distress on landlords, discounts could be bounded by any outstanding mortgage.* Evidently, this conflicts with the immediate self-interest of landlords. But re-assigning the rents of price appreciation on a home to those who live in it is both ethical and, given the benefits of enhanced belonging, consistent with the enlightened self-interest of the affluent.

Working to some purpose

Many of the educated people who are highly productive are hugely beneficial to society. But many are using their skills to enrich themselves at the expense of others.

The nexus of jobs in finance and law is the core of this diversion of talent. Return, for a moment, to the astounding volume of trading in financial assets. While active transactions can be useful to make assets liquid, much of the trading is zero-sum: were the volume of transactions reduced there would be no loss to society. If they are zero-sum, why do they happen? The answer is that the very smart outwit the slightly less smart. Asset markets are largely 'tournaments' in which the winners have some small informational advantage over the losers. The winners are those with the exceptional abilities and

---

* This would be the mortgage outstanding at the date the policy was first announced, so as to avoid it being gamed by remortgaging.

resources to outsmart others; as a result, they earn staggering amounts of money. Given the potential benefits of gaining an informational advantage, there is constant pressure to get access to information. A company invested in a high-speed cable between Chicago and New York that skims milliseconds off the transmission of price information between the two markets.[20] The commercial return on the investment depended upon this generating a tiny advantage in computerized trading, so that it could be sold to a few companies that would exploit it at the expense of those that received the same information milliseconds later. A society in which investment in such a cable is undertaken while bridges are left to collapse due to lack of maintenance has not got its priorities right.

Excess asset transactions inflict several social costs beyond their damage to the horizon of firms, discussed in Chapter 4. One is that they widen inequality to no good purpose. The super-smart work for themselves: this is the implication of the bonus system in investment banks, where the stars in effect pay the firm a modest share of their individual profits for the services it provides. Deutsche Bank, the most extreme example of an investment bank run for stars, paid €71 billion in bonuses, dwarfing the €19 billion paid to shareholders.*

Power is no longer in the hands of owners of capital, nor even of the managers of their wealth. Pension funds cannot pay the mega-salaries that would be required to recruit stars, and so they are managed by the slightly less smart. Transactions between the two groups generate a gradual transfer from future pensioners to the super-smart.

A further loss is that these zero-sum tournaments tie up some of the smartest people in society doing work that is of no use to anyone else. Yet such people are potentially hugely valuable to others. At the opposite end of the spectrum from asset management is innovation. Economists estimate that typically an innovator captures only around 4 per cent of the overall gains from their innovation: the remaining 96 per cent accrues to the rest of us. So, the incentives that the market provides for the super-smart to deploy their scarce

---

* The shareholders ended up bearing losses that far exceeded these dividends, as the share price collapsed.

abilities on innovation are far too weak, while the incentives to use them for trading assets are far too strong. I have not seen any attempt to quantify this form of social cost, but my sense is that it is considerable: innovation and asset management are both huge sectors. In America, the profits generated by the financial sector are around 30 per cent of all corporate profits. Looked at another way, the financial sector is supposedly providing services that make the economy more productive, but it would need to be raising the profitability of the rest of the economy by 43 per cent* just to pay for the profits that it captures for itself, before the rest of us break even. This seems unlikely: would we really notice that much difference, were our financial sectors leaner?

What is true of asset managers is true of lawyers. Willem Buiter, former Chief Economist for Citigroup, puts it aptly: the first third of lawyers produce the immense social value we know as the 'rule of law'. The next third are working on legal disputes that are essentially zero-sum games: each side over-invests in winning the tournament and so they are socially useless. The rule of law is a huge public good, but no commercial lawyers are working to achieve 'justice'; they work to win a case in a tournament. The last hour of such legal effort purchased by a party to a legal dispute yields its return not by generating more justice, but by increasing the chances of winning the tournament at the expense of the other party. The final third of lawyers are socially predatory: they are employed in the legal scams that fleece the productive. They are the ultimate rent-seekers. In America, one of these scams, in which redundant patent rights were bought up and twisted into law suits that extorted money from firms that innovated, was so egregious that even a gridlocked Congress had the gumption to close the loophole. In Britain, when lawsuits that relied upon a medical insurance scam were outlawed, the market value of the law firm that specialized in it halved overnight.

Lawyers are valuable, but there are too many of them. Young people are attracted into the profession by a multitude of incentives. I recall that my initial choice of law as a degree course was because I naïvely imagined that lawyers were the modern equivalent of

* $30/70 = 0.43$.

pastors, advising, adjudicating, helping, and sometimes they are just that. But I changed my choice once I found out that 70 per cent of the incomes of British lawyers came from their monopoly on housing transactions: the profession was dominated by rent-seeking. Far from being a pastor, I would be a parasite. Nowadays many young people are attracted by the idea of battling for justice – courtroom battles are a staple of Netflix. The seven-figure incomes of City lawyers may also have a certain appeal. But, like actors, there are too many of them. The eminent Harvard economist Larry Summers once produced a correlation between the ratio of engineers to lawyers in a society and the nation's rate of growth: it was a neat metaphor for the larger issue that market forces do not deliver the right balance between those activities that are socially predatory and those, like innovation, that are socially valuable.

So, what can be done about it? As with the metropolis, part of the answer is tax, but there is an important difference. The rents generated by the metropolis are socially valuable; they are just unfairly shared. The purpose of taxing the highly skilled workers in the metropolis would not be to curtail their activities but to redistribute the rents. In contrast, the rents captured by asset traders and lawyers are not socially valuable; it is the activities themselves that need to be curbed. Hence, it is the purpose of the activities, rather than the location, that should be the target.

There have been many proposals for taxes on financial transactions. Any such taxes need to be carefully designed to hit the right transactions; for example, trading in the shares of companies needs curbing much more that trading in currencies. It is not remotely socially useful for the shares of the typical large company to change hands seven times in a single year, which is the current norm.

As for taxing private litigation in courts, it could be designed both to reduce the volume of disputes and to reduce the large rents on them that lawyers currently capture. Lawyers are not immune to the lure of self-interest. When contracts were paid by the word, lawyers deemed it necessary for them to be very long; once they were paid by the contract instead of the word, they rapidly became radically shorter. Legal costs escalate to eat up the rents involved in the dispute. To take a recent dispute that is familiar to many British people, consider what happened when the politician Andrew Mitchell sued a newspaper for defamation. The substance of the dispute was the precise words he had used in an altercation with a policeman who had stopped him from wheeling his bicycle through a gate. Since there were no decisive witnesses, the case was resolved by a judge determining which of two testimonies to trust: that of Mr Mitchell or that of the policeman. In the process of this trivial matter, the lawyers on each side ran up costs of £3 million, which became the liability of the losing party. In other words, this trivial legal task ate up the equivalent of the *average lifetime earnings of three British households*. By taxing such disputes, we can encourage more of them to be settled more simply, and also shift some of the rents from the inflated costs of lawyers to society. Lawyers will explain why such a proposal is an affront to justice.*

There is another approach: shame. Just as *ethical citizens* are needed to shame firms into more purposive behaviour, so the power of social sanction can strip the rent-seeking professions of their glitzy veneer. Talented young people need to be brought face-to-face with the social implications of their career choices: how are mega-incomes actually being generated?

Curbing social divergence

Until 1958 Buckingham Palace held an annual ball for debutantes, a forum for match-making among the top echelons of British society. It stopped when enough people recognized that perpetuating class divisions in this way was a menace, not a service. The greater porousness of the old upper class is symbolized by the marriage of Prince William to Kate Middleton, whose mother had been an airline stewardess: Kate would not have been invited to a debutante ball. But 'assortative mating' among the old upper class has been replaced by even more effective assortative mating among the new elite.[21] Prince William

---

* But not necessarily: as part of the reality checks for this book, I asked a highly experienced lawyer to comment on these proposals. His response was 'I like the idea of targeting the rich City lawyers and their metropolitan ilk.' But perhaps he is atypical: he is a Quaker.

and Kate met while studying at St Andrews, an elite university. Like-marrying-like is a powerful force for social inequality. Such assortative mating, a force that helps stabilize marriages, inadvertently widens class divisions, but there is little that can be done about it.

But some behaviour is exploitative, and could potentially be curbed. In America between 1981 and 1996 children at elementary school increased their hours of study by an astonishing 146 per cent.[22] In Britain during the past decade, suicide rates among university students have risen 50 per cent. Because there are zero-sum aspects of the success on which 'tiger parents' fixate, their stress is transmitted not just to their own children but to others. To an extent, this could be tackled in schools. Heads and their staff naturally try to establish a prevailing culture. Mostly, their struggle is to place a lower limit on academic effort, but perhaps there also needs to be an upper limit. While we cannot afford to fall behind global standards, the teenage years should not be turned into a junior version of the toxic rivalries of an investment bank.

As to those toxic rivalries, a story that hit the headlines in 2013 was of a summer intern at an investment bank, so keen to impress that he worked a twenty-hour day before dropping dead. This is an extreme instance of a race to the bottom that drives groups of people to become workaholics. Everybody would gain from working less, but no individual dares to step out of line: they would lose out in the race for promotion, and by breaching prevailing norms they would lose esteem. This is a classic co-ordination problem and it has a straightforward solution – public policy. Long hours of work can be discouraged by taxation, or curtailed through regulation. When the French government reduced the permitted working week to thirty-five hours it was widely derided. But I recall a harassed manager in a workaholic organization wistfully noting that his own CEO was trying to impose a thirty-five-hour day. Gradual reductions in working hours, and corresponding extensions of vacations, are appropriate and necessary ways of turning rising national productivity into better lives. Without them and the policies proposed above, society will become further divided into a workaholic skilled class with abundant money but little time, confronting an underemployed, unskilled class with abundant time but little money.

CONCLUSION: SOCIAL MATERNALISM WITH A HARD EDGE

Work should bring purpose to the core years of life. Currently, it does so for many of the fortunate, but not for all. Many people find themselves in jobs that offer too little opportunity for self-respect: they contain insufficient skill for it to be a source of pride, or they lack the satisfaction that comes from knowing that what you do contributes to society. This, rather than simply the differences in pay packets, is the crux of the failures by which divergences between families become divergences between jobs. The income inequalities matter and get larger as life progresses through to retirement. But if they are only addressed by redistribution, not only will the required taxation-cum-benefits be enormous, the core deficiency of purpose, or meaning, will be accentuated. Many people will be living on the productivity of others.

The challenge is to reduce the widening dispersion of productivities. Addressing it has taken us through a long march that began with the switch from social paternalism, in which the state polices recalcitrant families, to social maternalism, in which the state cushions them with practical support. The hard edge that social paternalism projects on to those families falling apart is more appropriately wielded, I have suggested, against the damaging activities of a minority of the most successful. Both will be needed to build a capitalism that enables everyone to work with dignity, wherever they live.

9
The Global Divide: Winners, and the Left Behind*

Globalization has been a powerful engine for rising global living standards. The economics profession, divided on many issues of public policy, has been virtually united on this assessment. But the sustained advice of economists has lost the confidence of the public. In part, the profession had forfeited its 'licence to operate' as a result of the global economic crisis. But there is a more focused reason: our enthusiasm for globalization has been insufficiently nuanced. This is odd, because 'globalization' is not even an economic concept. It is a journalistic amalgam of radically different economic processes that are highly unlikely to have common effects, let alone be universally benign.

The profession has been unprofessional, fearful that any criticism would strengthen populism, so that little work has been done on the downsides of these different processes. Yet downsides were apparent to ordinary citizens, and the effect of economists appearing to dismiss them has resulted in a widespread refusal of people to listen to 'experts'. For my profession to re-establish credibility we must provide a more balanced analysis, in which the downsides are acknowledged and properly evaluated with a view to designing policy responses that address them. The profession may be better served by *mea culpa* than by further indignant defences of globalization.

* This chapter has benefited from innumerable discussions with Tony Venables. It draws on Collier (2018a).

THE TRADE *MEA CULPA*

The *mea culpa* starts with trade, which causes powerful redistributions both within and between societies.

Within societies, the proposition of comparative advantage tells us that, because trade brings mutual gains, *with appropriate compensation through redistribution within each society* it would be possible to make everyone better off. As a profession, we have elided from that true proposition to the patently false one that everyone in a society *is* made better off. International economics has shown little interest in internal mechanisms of compensation. This is the more important because of two features ignored in simple models: losses are largely transmitted through the labour market, and they are geographically concentrated. When Sheffield lost its steel industry, the knowledge that somewhere else in Britain the consumption gains more than offset the consumption losses of Sheffield's unemployed would not have been much solace.

Between societies, global trade has driven countries into different specializations. In a one-sentence summary, Europe, the USA and Japan have specialized in the knowledge industries; East Asia in manufacturing; South Asia in services; the Middle East in oil; and Africa in mining. This has enabled both East and South Asia to converge spectacularly on the high-income societies, reducing global inequalities as never before. But natural resource extraction places exceptional stresses on governance because it generates enormous economic rents whose ownership must be determined politically. Some societies manage these stresses, but many suffer from huge diversions into rent-seeking. For example, oil has not benefited South Sudan: it has triggered a conflict-induced famine and mass displacement. The global boom in commodity prices of 2000–2013 appeared at the time to be powering Africa and the Middle East forward, but this now looks doubtful. Remarkable new global data has collated comprehensive measures of national wealth per capita, including not only the conventional components such as the capital stock, but education and natural wealth as well.[1] The data provides two snapshots – 1995 and 2014 – fortuitously spanning the commodity super-cycle. From it, we can see whether the unprecedented temporary increase in the natural resource earnings of many poor countries has led to gains that can be sustained. What it reveals is that the poorest countries fell further behind everyone else. Not just the absolute increase, but the *percentage* increase in per capita wealth was much less in the low-income countries than in all other income groups, and in much of Africa wealth actually fell. As with the effects of trade within societies, the cheery models show only *potential*. Moving from potential to realization depends upon public policies that the models finesse.

THE REGULATORY *MEA CULPA*

Corporations have globalized, morphing into legally complex networks of subsidiary companies that trade with each other but are controlled by a parent. For such companies, tax has become voluntary. In Britain, this was exemplified by Starbucks: despite selling billions of cups of coffee, during an entire decade the British subsidiary made virtually no taxable profits. It transpired that another subsidiary, based in the Dutch Antilles, was making remarkably large profits despite not selling any coffee at all; instead, it was selling the rights to use the name 'Starbucks' to the British subsidiary. As the company indignantly announced, it had paid all taxes due in the Dutch Antilles, although it omitted to mention that the tax rate there was zero. In poor countries, the equivalent is natural resource extraction: in Tanzania, a gold-mining company contrived to report losses to the Tanzanian tax authorities, while distributing huge dividends to shareholders.

An even less salubrious aspect of corporate globalization is the growth of shell companies and havens of banking secrecy. A shell company, established by highly skilled lawyers in a metropolis – typically London or New York – is one whose true ownership is concealed. If such a company opens a bank account in a secrecy haven jurisdiction, the money deposited is shielded from scrutiny by a double wall of obfuscation. This structure has become a major means of protecting corrupt and criminal money from detection. Bitcoin has recently added a further option.

As with trade itself, for the potential gains from corporate globalization to be realized, public policy must react. In practice, it hasn't: the globalization of companies has not been matched by the globalization of regulation. The capacity to tax and regulate remains firmly lodged at the national level. As I discussed in Chapter 6, our supranational co-ordination mechanisms – the OECD, the IMF, the EU, the G7 and the G20 – have lost the capacity to forge binding reciprocal obligations underpinned by enlightened self-interest. Each nation prefers to compete in a race to the bottom. This defeat of governance has been the ugliest reality of modern globalization. Having been the epicentre of the problem, in its presidency of the G8 in 2013, Britain began to lead the way in trying to address it.* For example, the UK pioneered a crackdown on 'shell companies' through which lawyers conceal asset ownership; the country now has a compulsory public register of the true ownership of all British companies, closing a major conduit for corrupt money.

THE MIGRATION *MEA CULPA*

Corporate interests have become highly influential in economic policy-setting, one of its focal points being the benefits of immigration. It is evident why business should favour immigration: it enlarges the pool of workers from which to recruit. However, the interests of business and citizens are not coincident. While some immigration benefits both firms and citizens, it benefits firms even when it reduces the welfare of citizens.

Globalization has conflated trade and the movement of workers, but there is a fundamental analytical distinction: trade is driven by *comparative* advantage, whereas the movement of labour is driven by *absolute* advantage. In consequence, although on the standard textbook assumptions migration is *globally* efficient, there is no reason to expect it to be mutually beneficial for host societies and countries of origin. Migration introduces a third category of beneficiary, migrants themselves, who are the only unambiguous

* I seized my opportunity to contribute to that effort (Collier, 2013).

beneficiaries (if they did not gain, they would not migrate). They receive the absolute productivity differential that drives labour movement. Migration is globally efficient, so that, in principle, transfers from migrants to hosts and those left behind could leave all better off. But in the absence of such transfers migration can be mutually damaging. It is privately rational for migrants, but this does not necessarily aggregate into collective benefits for societies. For example, despite the evident misuse of a scarce skill, global GDP rises if a Sudanese doctor moves to Britain and works as a taxi driver.

Once immigration is set in the context of the rents of the metropolis, introduced in Chapter 7, its potential for costs to citizens becomes apparent. The metropolis generates 'rents of agglomeration' which get captured partly by landowners, but mainly by those workers with high skills and low housing demand. If the nation opens its borders to immigrants, the pool of potential workers will expand. For the typical country, the global workforce is around a hundred times larger than the national workforce, so the effect of fully open borders would be dramatic. Many foreigners will have higher skills and lower housing demand than nationals. Since they have an incentive to compete for these high productivity job slots, these immigrants will displace nationals.

The process is globally efficient: the metropolitan economy will grow, and with it the rents of agglomeration. But who now gets the rents? With a workforce that has less demand for housing, and more skill, the rents will shift from landowners to skilled workers, making them harder to tax. Among the skilled, those current citizens who *retain* their high-skill jobs in the metropolis will gain; they will have become yet more productive by working with people who are more highly skilled. But those citizens who are *crowded out* of the skilled metropolitan job slots will lose the rents that they would otherwise have had: instead they will work less productively in provincial cities. This transfers rents from citizens to immigrants. If citizens expressed political attitudes reflecting their self-interest, we might expect these two effects to manifest themselves as pro-immigration sentiments among highly skilled metropolitan citizens, and anti-immigration sentiments among citizens in the provinces.

Something a little like this may have happened in Britain. The population of London is the same today as in 1950, but its composition has changed considerably. As of 2011, 37 per cent of its population is first-generation immigrant, whereas in 1950 it would have been negligible. Without immigration, it is unlikely that London would have shrunk by 37 per cent: no metropolis has done so. More likely, immigration brought people with lower housing demand and higher skills than many citizens and so outbid them for the London job slots. Nationally, the Brexit vote revealed the divergence of identities captured in the discussion of *rational social woman* in Chapter 3. But the differences between London and the rest of the country may reflect the diverging economic effects of immigration on the two new classes within the city. Indeed, by analysing the Brexit vote, two somewhat counter-intuitive predictions can be tested.* The theory predicts that those members of the educated class who were not crowded out of London jobs would have become more productive due to the influx of skilled immigrants to the city, and so should have been *less likely to vote Leave* than the provincial educated. We find this to be correct: they were 25 per cent less likely. In contrast, Londoners from the less-educated class, who faced competition from low-skilled immigrants but had not left the city, would actually have lost from the influx and so should be *less likely to vote Remain* than people from the same class living elsewhere. Correct again: they were 30 per cent less likely. So, perhaps within London, *rational economic man* was still alive and well. Differences in class composition, and these different economic consequences of immigration, may be a better explanation of the vote than the prevailing metropolitan narrative of provincial xenophobia.

A very different cost of immigration to citizens is its tendency to undermine the reciprocal obligations that had built up within the society. Recall that the genius of the period 1945–70 was to harness shared identity for many new reciprocal obligations. Those whose

---

* The statistics that follow are by the psephologist Dr Stephen Fisher, of Oxford University, based on the most reliable of the Brexit survey data. We realized the scope for testing these hypotheses too late to write up the research prior to the publication deadline for this book, but our intention is to submit it for professional scrutiny and publication. In the interim, the results must be treated as provisional.

lives turned out to be fortunate accepted an obligation to help those whose lives turned out less well. This narrative of obligation was reinforced by a narrative that made compliance purposive: who could tell, perhaps in the next generation, whether the offspring of the fortunate would be among those less fortunate, so it was in everyone's enlightened self-interest. Immigrants miss out on these narratives of shared identity, reciprocal obligations and enlightened self-interest, and so citizens may doubt whether they have accepted them. Those citizens whose lives have been fortunate may, consequently, be less willing to pay taxes that benefit immigrants as well as citizens. Such an effect would be particularly bad news for anxious provincials with few skills; just as they need to call on obligations, their fellow-citizens walk away from them because of immigration. Unfortunately, the evidence for such an effect is now compelling.

New survey evidence from across Europe records attitudes on the part of those with above-average income towards redistributive taxation designed to help those who are badly off.[2] Unsurprisingly, across Europe those who have incomes above the average tend to be less enthusiastic about redistribution than those whose incomes are below average. But when these responses are matched against the proportion of immigrants in the population a clear pattern emerges: the higher the proportion of immigrants, the lower the willingness of those with above-average income to support redistributive taxation. People on above-average incomes evidently still retain some sense of obligation to their poorer fellow-nationals, but that erodes as the identity gap is widened to non-nationals. Surveys of opinion are old social science technology. A more recent methodology is to simulate medical experiments by randomly dividing people into two groups and subjecting one group to a 'treatment' not given to the other group. In new work that investigates the same issue using this entirely different approach, two Spanish researchers asked the same question, but make immigration more salient for one group by 'priming' them with discussion of it, while priming the other group with some anodyne topic.[3] They found the same tendency as the other study: the group that has been reminded about immigration is significantly less willing to pay redistributive taxes.

Hence, while some migration is likely to benefit host societies and countries of origin, as well as migrants themselves, there is no reason to think that the amount of migration generated by market-driven self-interested private decisions is socially ideal. As usual, ideologies mislead. The left is instinctively sceptical of market-driven processes except for migration, while the right makes the corresponding exception to its blanket enthusiasm for the market. Pragmatism and practical reasoning are more nuanced, asking how much migration benefits a society, and by whom?

CONCLUSION: A PROFESSIONAL
MEA CULPA

Economists such as myself have been too keen to defend globalization against its critics. The net effects are positive, but globalization is not a unified phenomenon that has to be adopted wholesale or rejected in its entirety. It is a ragbag of economic and social changes each of which is potentially separable. The task of public policy is to encourage those components that are unambiguously beneficial; to arrange compensation for those that are predominantly beneficial but which inflict significant losses on identifiable groups; and to limit those that cause redistributions that cannot readily be compensated.

PART FOUR
Restoring Inclusive Politics

10

Breaking the Extremes

Capitalism is generating divided societies in which many people lead anxious lives. Yet it is the only economic system that has proved to be capable of generating mass prosperity. What has happened recently is not intrinsic to capitalism; it is a damaging malfunction that must be put right. This is not a simple matter, but, guided by prudent pragmatism, evidence and analysis that fit our current context can shape policies that would gradually be effective. During the era following the Great Depression, pragmatic policies put capitalism back on track; they can do so again. Yet our political system is not generating such policies. It has become as dysfunctional as our economies. Why is it no longer capable of thinking pragmatically about solutions to problems?

Capitalism last worked well between 1945 and 1970. During that period, policy was guided by a communitarian form of social democracy that had suffused through the mainstream political parties. But the ethical foundations of social democracy corroded. Its origins had been in the co-operative movements of the nineteenth century, created to address the urgent anxieties of the time. Its narratives of solidarity became the foundation for a deepening web of reciprocal obligations that addressed these anxieties. But leadership of the social democratic parties passed from the co-operative movement to Utilitarian technocrats and Rawlsian lawyers. Their ethics lack resonance with most people and voters have gradually withdrawn their support.

Why did political parties not turn to pragmatism? Most probably, this was the fault of voters. Pragmatism calls on people to attend to the evidence of context and to use practical reasoning to assess whether proposed solutions would actually work. That requires effort. An informed electorate is the ultimate public good, and as with all public goods each individual has little incentive to provide it. Most public goods can be provided by the state, but this one can only be provided by people themselves.

Instead, the vacuum created by the implosion of social democracy was filled by political movements that offered voters a bypass to effort. Pragmatism has two enemies: ideologies and populism, and each seized its opportunity. The ideologies of both left and right claim that context, prudence and practical reasoning can be bypassed by an all-purpose analysis spewing out truths valid for all contexts and all time. Populism offers an alternative bypass: charismatic leaders with remedies so obvious that they can be grasped instantly. Often, the two fused, becoming yet more potent: once-discredited ideologies refurbished with impassioned leaders peddling enticing new remedies. Hail to the herald: from the radical left, Bernie Sanders, Jeremy Corbyn and Jean-Luc Mélenchon; from the nativists, Marine Le Pen and Norbert Hofer; from the secessionists, Nigel Farage, Alex Salmond and Carles Puigdemont; and from the world of celebrity entertainers, Beppe Grillo and Donald Trump.

Currently, the political battlefield is seemingly characterized by alarmed and indignant Utilitarian and Rawlsian vanguards under assault from populist ideologues. This is the political menu from hell. In escaping it, the fundamental change will come through infusing our politics with a different ethical discourse. But there are also some changes to the mechanics of our political systems that have led to the current polarization, as we will see in this chapter.

HOW POLITICS POLARIZED

Our political systems are democratic, but the details of their architecture have increasingly inclined them to polarization. Most of our voting systems favour the two largest parties. So, the menu of choice facing voters depends upon what these two parties offer. The key dangerous step has been that, in the name of greater democracy, in many countries the major political parties have empowered their members to elect their leaders. This has replaced a system in which the leader of a party was drawn from among its most experienced people, and often chosen by its elected representatives.

The people most inclined to join a political party are those who have become adherents of some political ideology. Hence, this change has tended to tilt the selection of leaders towards ideologues. Of the three major ideologies, social democracy has proved to be the most vulnerable, for reasons I set out in Chapter 1. Its combination of Utilitarian and Rawlsian philosophy is not securely grounded in our common values. This has left the polarizing ideologies of Marxism and Nativism to dominate the field. Marxism had appeared to be mortally discredited by the collapse of the Soviet Union and the Chinese switch to capitalism, but a new generation has grown up for which these are merely historical events, at best skimmed over in history lessons. Nativism was utterly discredited by the Holocaust and this memory has been kept alive. But where the mainstream party of the centre-right has adopted the hybrid of Utilitarian and Rawlsian ethics for its immigration policy, Nativist parties have found an opening.[1]

The rise of the ideologues has left the many voters who are pragmatists facing a menu which has been selected by the extremes. Further, as many people disengage from politics because they find this menu unappealing, the winning strategy for leaders has changed from adopting policies that attract the wavering voter in the middle of the spectrum, to ensuring that the ideologically motivated voters all turn out to vote. To promote 'inclusion', the minimum age for voting and party membership may be lowered, but, lacking responsibilities and experience, teenagers are the most prone to ideological extremism. Those non-ideological voters who feel themselves to have been disenfranchised have been left to the pickings of the populists.

Several recent major elections have exemplified this process in action. The American election process of 2016 enabled ideological populists of left and right to dominate the campaigns with simplistic critiques of how they would address the failings of capitalism. On the left, Bernie Sanders was narrowly held at bay but in the process severely weakened the attachment of the Democratic base vote to the archetypal Rawlsian lawyer Hillary Clinton, who systematically pursued the 'victim' vote blocks.[2] On the right, Donald Trump, using the superior media skills of a celebrity, displaced all the more centrist candidates. In the election itself, Trump maintained his simplistic critique while Clinton failed to articulate a more sophisticated one, appearing almost as the apologist for the current system.

The French election of 2017 eviscerated all the potential leaders of the two main parties. On the left, the incumbent President Hollande, an archetypal social democrat, recognized that he was too unpopular even to run, and his prime minister, Manuel Valls, another social democrat, was eliminated in the primaries in favour of Benoît Hamon, an ideologue of the party's left. On the right, the past president, Nicolas Sarkozy, was eliminated, as was the centrist Alain Juppé, in favour of an ideologue of the Republican Party's right, François Fillon, whose campaign subsequently imploded for personal reasons. This left the first round of the French election, through which the contest was to be reduced to two candidates, a tight race between five maverick leaders – four ideologues and a pragmatist. Neither of the two mainstream party candidates went through to the second round, and the final contest was between the pragmatist, Emmanuel Macron, and a Nativist populist of the right, Marine Le Pen. However, had a mere 3 per cent of French voters chosen differently, the contest would have been between two ideologue populists – Le Pen on the right, and Jean-Luc Mélenchon on the left. France survived its voting system, but narrowly. In contrast to Hillary Clinton, Emmanuel Macron was able to articulate a clear, non-ideological yet sophisticated critique of the current system, aimed not at 'victim' groups but at the average French citizen, while exposing the emptiness of the populist remedies. His programme was a prime example of pragmatism, in which good communication skills enabled a complex argument to triumph over the snake oil of populism.

Between the British elections of 2010 and 2017, the Labour Party changed its process of selecting a leader. In 2010, its archetypal Utilitarian social-democrat leader, Gordon Brown, had come to the leadership as the unopposed choice of Labour Members of Parliament. By 2017 the party was led by a Marxist populist, Jeremy Corbyn, who had minimal support from Labour MPs but had been elected by passionate young idealists who had been given the right to easy membership of the party.* This measure had almost completely changed the Labour Party's composition. On the right, David Cameron, the centrist leader in 2010, had been replaced in 2016 by the unknown quantity of Teresa May, a desperate measure by Conservative MPs designed to avoid following the new constitution of the party, which required that the leader be elected by party members. This appeared likely to elect a maverick ideologue, as it had done when first used in 2001. Currently, Britain's two main political parties have leadership selection systems that, if used, almost guarantee that the menu of political choices will consist of polarizing ideologues – vegan or veal, sir? In the 2017 election, Jeremy Corbyn pitched an ideological populism of the left, whereas Teresa May failed to articulate a coherent strategy, leaving voters bereft of choice and resulting in a hung parliament.

Even in Germany, Chancellor Merkel's brief flirtation with a curious blend of Rawlsian legalism and populism that opened Germany's borders for a few months, was sufficient to drive one-in-eight voters to a new Nativist party in the 2017 election. The vote share of her Christian Democrat party of the centre-right collapsed to its lowest level since its foundation in 1949. Yet the collapse of the centre-right did not help the centre-left. The vote share of the Social Democrats collapsed even more sharply, also to its post-1949 low. The centre is shrinking, leaving the field to populist ideologues.

RESTORING THE CENTRE: SOME POLITICAL MECHANICS

We need a process by which the mainstream parties are driven back to the centre. Here are two possible rule changes to leadership selection, both far more democratic that the present systems.

The most straightforward is to confine the selection of a party

---

* Formal Marxist theory has long recognized that the vanguard is dependent upon attracting a category of fans termed 'useful idiots'. Mr Corbyn's insightful innovation was to refine this into 'youthful idiots'.

leader to the elected representatives of that party. Elected representatives have two features that make them better suited to selecting a leader than leaving it to members of the party. For a start, they have an interest in appealing to a wide group of voters; this pushes them towards centrist candidates. Secondly, as insiders, they are less likely to be deceived by celebrity tricks of the trade: they are informed voters. For example, in Britain, the Conservative leader in 2001 would have been Ken Clarke, a centrist with huge ministerial experience; the Labour leader in 2015 would have been a centrist; and had elected Republicans chosen their party's presidential candidate, Donald Trump would not be in the White House.

Elected representatives have more democratic legitimacy than party members; in aggregate, they represent *far more supporters* of the party than the number on official membership registers. But if the winning criterion continues to be the system that offers the largest number of active selectors then an inferior alternative might be to open the leadership vote, at least for major parties, to *all* voters, although the record here is unpromising. Since ordinary voters know little of candidates, there is a bias towards charismatic populists.

Failing the reform of party leader selection, the safest alternative is probably a voting system based on a degree of proportional representation. There are drawbacks, but coalitions constrain parties from implementing their ideologies, and encourage evidence-based pragmatism. Norway, the Netherlands and Switzerland, which have long been governed by coalitions generated by proportional representation, have all avoided the worst excesses of modern capitalism. The period of British coalition government, 2010–15, and the American political gridlock of 2011–17, in retrospect both look somewhat superior to the governments that preceded and followed them.

RESTORING THE CENTRE: INFORMED SOCIETIES

Tinkering with our political systems may help to make them more amenable to strategies that are ethically grounded and pragmatically designed. But politics can be no better than the societies it reflects. A politics that is ethical and pragmatic can only be generated once a society has a critical mass of citizens who demand it. That is why this book has been written primarily for citizens, not politicians. A critical mass does not mean everyone; it means enough to give politicians the courage to act. Fortunately, social media can be used to spread good ideas as well as bad ones. As an aide-memoire, I have summarized below the proposed policies that can directly address the new divergences, and the more fundamental strategies for restoring ethics in organizations.

Pragmatic new policies

In a short book with a wide remit, new policies cannot be developed in detail. All the proposals in this book are grounded in academic analysis, but require considerable further work before they are ready to be implemented. Nevertheless, the impediments are liable to be political, not technical.

Reversing the new divergence between the metropolis and broken cities will cost money, which can be raised by taxing the huge increase in the rents of agglomeration generated in the metropolis. Chapter 7 set out why much of the productivity bonanza of the metropolis is a form of rent rather than being genuinely earned by the people who capture it. But it also highlighted the difficulty in taxing the rents: many of them accrue not to landowners, as has been thought to date, but to the high-earning skilled. Precisely the same rationale that justifies taxing land in the metropolis more highly than land elsewhere applies to these skilled workers. I anticipate the impassioned outrage of threatened self-interest: push back. How is this money then best spent in reviving broken cities? The key is a co-ordinated push to attract a rising industry, perhaps one suited to the particular city's traditions. Co-ordination depends upon relationships: to build common knowledge, firms that might potentially locate in the city need to know what other firms are doing. The city will probably need to court an entire group of interconnected firms. Training is worthless unless it is tied to the specific requirements of such firms and preferably co-managed by them.

Reversing the new class divergence between the highly skilled educated and the deskilled less educated also requires policies that tackle both sides. Being stuck in a low-productivity job is often the end-point of a lifetime of disadvantage that starts in infancy. I have proposed a strategy of *social maternalism*: intensive practical assistance and mentoring for young families at risk of breaking up, followed by mentoring for children during their school years. Mentoring is to social maternalism what monitoring is to social paternalism. But reversing the divergence is not only about enabling the less educated to succeed. Some behaviours of the highly skilled need to be curbed because they are predatory: the ability to win a 'tournament' can bring huge private gains at the expense of those who lose. Too many of our most talented people devote their abilities to such zero-sum games, while activities such as innovation, with large benefits for the entire society, are drained of talent. The sectors most prone to zero-sum games should be taxed more heavily than those in which little of the benefit accrues to those working in them.

Narrowing the global divide between the rich societies of the world and those still stuck in poverty demands more than a big heart. The private responses of people living in societies that are poor and stagnant are to get their money out if they are rich, and emigrate if they are educated. These responses are rational, but in aggregate they are often damaging to their own societies. Africa loses $200 billion of capital flight each year; Haiti loses 85 per cent of its young educated workers. Framing these behaviours as a 'human right' belittles the obligations that they breach. Most people are not saints: while they recognize their obligations, if they are presented with enticing temptations, they take them. When this happens, the moral responsibility is on those who tempt. For decades, much of the capital flight out of Africa was facilitated by lawyers in London and banks in Switzerland. Similarly, the human capital exodus from Africa is an understandable response to public policies that create opportunities. To illustrate with an extreme example: Norway has accumulated a sovereign wealth fund worth $200,000 per person. If a family of five leaves its poor homeland and settles there, it gains an entitlement to a pro rata share of assets worth $1 million, over and above any income that the family members earn. The government of their homeland lacks any means of countering such an incentive to leave. However, two groups of people have a much better claim to that $1 million: the Norwegians who saved the money, and the thousands of poor people among whom it could be shared. Poor societies need to catch up with rich ones. To do so, they need from our rich societies what we have and they lack: firms that make people productive. We could do far more to encourage our firms to perform this mundane-seeming magic in the poorest countries.

Ethically renewed organizations

This book began with ethics and that is where it will end. I have tried to sketch the foundations for a moral politics that can replace the weird and divisive tenets of Utilitarian ethics with one that is both better grounded in human nature and leads to better outcomes.

In contrast to the Utilitarian vision of autonomous individuals, each generating utility from their own consumption, and counting equally in the great moral arithmetic of total utility, the atoms of a real society are relationships. In contrast to the psychopathic selfishness of economic man restrained by the Platonic guardians of social paternalism, normal people recognize that relationships bring obligations, and that meeting them is central to our sense of purpose in life. The toxic combination of Platonic Guardians and economic man that has dominated public policy has inexorably stripped people of moral responsibility, shifting obligations to the paternalist state. In a bizarre parody of medieval religion, ordinary people are cast as sinners who need to be ruled by exceptional people – the moral meritocracy. With the rise of the Utilitarian vanguard, the saints came marching in. As obligations have floated up to the state, rights and entitlements to consumption have showered down: we are all children now.

But in the process, the state has acquired responsibilities that exceed its capacities, ones that can only be properly met by firms and families. Parents, whose sense of obligation to their children derives from love, outclass all the substitutes provided by the paternalist state; firms whose sense of obligation to their employees derives from prolonged reciprocity outclass all training provided by the paternalist state. The state has a role, but it is in devising the meta-policies that restore these obligations to where they belong. It was a cultural shift that weakened a sense of obligations within families. The ethical family was supplanted by the *entitled individual* engaged in the single-minded pursuit of desires. But the state connived at this shift, changing laws, taxes and benefits from privileging families to privileging individuals. The state can change its narratives, laws, taxes and benefits to restore the *ethical family*. It was a cultural shift that weakened a sense of obligations to employees and society in firms; business schools taught a generation of managers the corporate equivalent of economic man, that the sole purpose of the firm was to make profits for its owners. But again, this cultural shift was compounded by changed material incentives driven by the rise of investment fund managers chasing quarterly profits. The state can use narratives, laws, taxes and subsidies to restore the *ethical firm*.

The inherent arrogance of Utilitarian paternalism achieved its apotheosis when applied at the global level. Duties of rescue that should have been met unconditionally became instruments for ethical imperialism. International clubs that had gradually built reciprocal obligations within a specific domain of policy were over-expanded into 'inclusive' organizations with vastly enlarged domains, in which reciprocity gradually disintegrated. We have never had an *ethical world*, but in the period from 1945 to 1970 we made more progress towards this goal than during any other period of history, progress that has been unravelling. In restoring forward momentum we need to return to the realistic approach of prudent pragmatism. Providing effective redress for those in need of rescue is affordable and feasible; the looming global anxieties are best met not by Utilitarian moralizing, but through clubs that build new reciprocal obligations among the affluent societies to meet the duties of rescue.

The web of reciprocal obligations enabled by shared belonging delivers states that are more trusted, and so more effective. With the myriad tasks of meeting obligations distributed widely across society, not only are they better met, but people are more engaged and fulfilled. In consequence, we end up with happier societies than have been achieved by the Utilitarian paternalists. Even on their own criterion, the paternalists are skewered. The 'maximization of utilities' is an example of what John Kay describes as obliquity: you don't achieve it by aiming directly for it. Willing reciprocity is superior.

THE POLITICS OF BELONGING

Politics is predominantly national. For politics to perform its potential for building a dense web of reciprocal obligations, the people of a nation need to accept some sense of shared identity. For identity to bind together, rather than dividing, to be British, or American or German cannot mean belonging to a particular ethnic group. Nor, despite the wishful thinking, can it mean to adhere to some distinctive common values. What common values do Donald Trump and Bernie Sanders share that distinguish them both from Nigel Farage and Jeremy Corbyn? An identity shared by all those who grow up in a culturally diverse country can only be defined on place and purpose. It can tap into the hardwired attachments to home and territory; it can highlight the mutual gains from common, purposive actions. It is the basis for a shared 'we'. But an ethical politics can reinforce the instinctive drive for common belonging, and the rationality of shared purpose, through other influences.

It is strengthened by undertaking some collective endeavour towards a common objective, however trivial: even the victory of the national football team has been shown to do this.[3] It is strengthened by the interwoven social interactions that naturally happen within the shared space. Groups that are entirely disconnected from each other may not feel much of a shared identity, so a degree of social integration is desirable, setting a limit to cultural separatism, whether resulting from education, ideology or religion. We need to meet each other. But above all it is strengthened by supportive political narratives of belonging. Communicating such narratives is a core role of our political leaders: by forsaking narratives of belonging based on place and purpose, they have created an opening for the divisive narratives of belonging that claim national identity for some to the exclusion of others.

Leaders can promote new narratives, but the decline of trust in political leaders has inverted authority; people pay more attention to those at the hub of their social networks than to the talking heads on the television. The networks, however, have become self-contained echo-chambers and so we even lack the common space in which to communicate. This is enormously damaging because participation in a common network constitutes the common knowledge that we all hear the same narratives. Without it, even narratives of shared identity struggle to create the conditions for people to be confident that the obligations they accept will be reciprocated by others. Far from circulating narratives of shared belonging to place, echo-chambers more typically vilify 'the other'. Salman Abedi, who in 2017 mass-murdered children at a Manchester concert, grew up in the city, but was raised within a hermetic network of Islamic hatred of 'kaffirs' and so lacked even rudimentary empathy with those around him. Echo-chambers are destructive of the social fabric, but I see no real-istic way of restoring a common arena for discourse. In its absence, the newly influential in each of these echo-chambers – the comedians, the actors, the imams, the exhibitionist extroverts – have acquired a responsibility that they must now exercise. They are the decentral-ized leaders of society, better placed than anyone else to build the shared identity of place across these fragmented networks. The nar-ratives that they spread should become a focus of public attention. They should face pressure to desist from peddling the divisive nar-ratives of ideology that have become their metier.

Like other shared identities, a shared sense of belonging to place, or of common purposive action, is valuable because of the oblig-ations that it can support. Politics is predominantly national because public policy is predominantly national. Some policies are set at local level, some are set regionally, and a few globally, but in all advanced economies, nations are overwhelmingly important. In the United States, despite the obsession with states' rights, around 60 per cent of public spending is done through the nation, not the states; in the European Union, despite the obsession with the power of Brussels, 97 per cent is done through the nation, not the Commission. Nations and their citizens are the essential frame for public policy and will remain so for the foreseeable future. The foremost political function of shared identity is to make nations work as vehicles for a growing web of reciprocal obligations. It is the erosion of that web that has permitted the anxieties thrown up by the recent direction of capitalism to fester into deep wounds in our societies.

Just as narratives of common belonging based on place and purpose can strengthen shared national identity, so narratives of the reciprocal obligations of citizens can strengthen that ethical web. Unsurprisingly, Salman Abedi never absorbed even elementary reciprocal obligations: his neighbour reported that Abedi's car would often block his driveway. In turn, reciprocal obligations can be reinforced by the purposive narratives of enlightened self-interest. Citizens can come to recognize causal chains showing that behaviour that is not in their immediate self-interest, such as paying taxes, can contribute to outcomes that are in the long-term self-interest of everyone. Abedi did absorb such a narrative: he sacrificed his immediate self-interest for the prospect of paradise. Narratives are powerful; we should be crafting better ones.

Reduced to a sentence, *shared identity becomes the foundation for far-sighted reciprocity.* Societies that succeed in building such belief systems work better than those based on either individualism or any of the revivalist ideologies. Individualist societies forfeit the vast potential of public goods. The revivalist ideologies are each based on hatred of some other part of society and are culs-de-sac to conflict. In a healthy society, those who become successful have been reared into acceptance of that web of reciprocal obligations. Being fortunate, these trigger support for those whose lives have turned out to be less fortunate. The successful comply with these obligations because they are rewarded with the self-respect and peer esteem that comes from fulfilling them. More coercive powers are legitimized for use against a recalcitrant minority.

This is the moral pragmatism that can guide our politics from polarized failure to co-operatively working to address the divisions that beset our societies. We have unmet duties of care to refugees fleeing catastrophe; to those mired in despair in the world's poorest societies; to men in their fifties whose skills have lost their value; to teenagers about to be trapped in dead-end jobs; to the children of broken families; to young families despairing that they will ever own a home. We must meet them. But we must also restore the vastly more demanding reciprocal obligations that once arose from our shared identities.

This may send shivers down the spines of those on the right, because of the prospect of redistributive outcomes superficially analogous to those envisaged in Marxist ideology. Similarly, it may send shivers down the spines of those on the left, because it recognizes distinctive obligations within families and nations that offend Rawlsian and Utilitarian norms. Each of these concerns is misplaced.

What I advocate is not a variant of Marxism. Marxist ideology relies on a hate-filled narrative that replaces shared identity with extreme divisions of class identity. It replaces mutual obligations with the assertion of the rights of one class to expropriate what belongs to the other. Like radical Islam, its version of enlightened self-interest invokes a distant paradise in which the state 'withers away'. The actual outcome of Marxist ideology, which has been invariably proved, is social conflict, economic collapse and a state that, instead of withering away, imposes overweening and brutal power. It is currently playing out in the flight of refugees from Venezuela, there to see for anyone who bothers to look. The difference between a society that pragmatically steers capitalism on a foundation of rational reciprocity, and one run by Marxist ideologues, is that between one at peace with itself, and one that is lacerated by mounting hatreds.

As to Rawlsian and Utilitarian dreams, discrediting family obligations in favour of equal obligations to all children, or national obligations in favour of obligations to global 'victims', would not build Eden. It would bequeath to the next generation a society sliding into the pit of entitled individualism. In retrospect, the period of Utilitarian and Rawlsian dominance of the centre-left will come to be recognized for what it was: arrogant, over-confident and destructive. The centre-left will recover as it returns to its communitarian roots, and to the task of reconstructing the web of trust-based reciprocal obligations that address the anxieties of working families.* Similarly, the period of domination of the centre-right by assertive

* In December 2017 I was invited to address Denmark's Social Democrats. Mette Frederiksen, its remarkable new leader, had arrived at precisely this diagnosis and was vigorously returning the party back to its co-operative, communitarian origins. Reversing a long period of decline, its vote share was already rising, with the exception of highly educated metropolitans: the WEIRD were indignantly shifting to the hard left.

individualism will come to be recognized as the seduction of a great tradition by *economic man*. As it recovers its ethical bearings, it will return to 'one nation' politics. The new anxieties are too serious to be abandoned to the far left. Belonging to place is a force too potent, and potentially too constructive, to be abandoned to the far right.

Faced with the new anxieties, it should be evident that the pertinent *economic* menace is the new and virulent divergence in geographic and class fortunes. Faced with the rise of extremist religious and ideological identities, it should be evident that the pertinent *social* menace is the fragmentation into oppositional identities sustained by the echo-chambers of social media. After Brexit and the rise of Donald Trump it should be evident that the pertinent *political* menace is exclusionary nationalism. By eschewing shared belonging, and the benign patriotism that it can support, liberals have abandoned the only force capable of uniting our societies behind remedies. Inadvertently, recklessly, they have handed it to the charlatan extremes, which are gleefully twisting it to their own warped purposes.

We can do better: we once did so, and we can do it again.

Notes

I. THE NEW ANXIETIES

1. See Case and Deaton (2017).
2. Chetty et al. (2017)
3. Chua (2018), p. 173.
4. See, for example, Mason (2015), and my review of this recent literature in the *Times Literary Supplement*, 25 January 2017.
5. See Norman (2018), ch. 7, for a clear historical account of the disastrous distortions to the analysis of economics pioneered by Adam Smith that were introduced by Bentham and Mill.
6. Haidt (2012).
7. Reported in the *Financial Times*, 5 January 2018.
8. A readable new account is Roger Scruton's *On Human Nature* (2017).
9. Cited in Chua (2018).
10. George Akerlof is a Nobel Laureate in Economics. Together with Rachel Kranton and Dennis Snower we have founded an association: Economic Research on Identities, Narratives and Norms. Tony Venables is a world-renowned economic geographer. For the past three years we have been co-directing a research project on the economics of urbanization. Colin Mayer is Professor of Finance at Oxford, former head of its business school, and director of the British Academy programme, The Future of the Corporation. His book *Prosperity: Better Business Makes the Greater Good* (2018) is a virtual companion to this book. For the past three years we have been working together on catalysing investment in poor areas. Professor Sir Tim Besley is currently President of the Econometric Society, a past-president of the European Economic Association, and past-editor of the *American Economic Review*. We are currently co-directing the British Academy Commission on State Fragility. Professor Chris Hookway is the world's foremost scholar of Peirce

and the origins of the Pragmatist school. He has been President of the Peirce Society, and editor of the *European Journal of Philosophy*. On his retirement in 2015, the conference in his honour was entitled 'The Idea of Pragmatism'. Fortuitously, he is my oldest friend.

11. Tepperman (2016).

2. THE FOUNDATIONS OF MORALITY

1. A good case can be made that even our emotions are ultimately socially constructed. See Feldman Barrett (2017).
2. See Etzioni (2015).
3. Just as I had finished *The Future of Capitalism*, Tim Besley introduced me to the philosopher and politician Jesse Norman, who had himself just completed a book on the thought of Adam Smith. With a degree of trepidation, we exchanged manuscripts. I learned much, some of which will be reflected in later notes, but I was relieved to find that Smith will not be turning in his grave at my account of his ideas.
4. Norman (2018).
5. Towers et al. (2016).
6. This was the disagreement between Hume and Kant.
7. Haidt (2012).
8. Mercier and Sperber (2017).
9. Gamble et al. (2018).
10. The Leninist concept of 'democratic' centralism.
11. As Haidt (2012) remarks, 'Deontology and Utilitarianism are "one receptor" moralities, appealing to people with a lack of empathy.'
12. See Dijksterhuis (2005), and Christakis and Fowler (2009).
13. See Hood (2014).
14. See Thomas et al. (2014).
15. See, for example, Cialdini (2007).
16. Akerlof and Shiller (2009), p. 54.
17. Mueller and Rauh (2017).
18. On taboos see Bénabou and Tirole (2011).
19. I have set these ideas out more fully in Collier (2016).
20. A good introduction is their book *Identity Economics*, Akerlof and Kranton (2011).
21. Besley (2016).
22. If you are interested in the details, I have recently surveyed this new literature: Collier (2017).

23. *World Happiness Report, 2017.*
24. The sentiments are those of John Perry Barlow and Mark Zuckerberg, respectively.
25. The technical term is homology.
26. As argued in the seminal study by MacIntyre in 1981, the essence of moral language is to treat others not just as means to a self-interested end, but rather as ends in themselves. See MacIntyre (2013).
27. I have explained shared identity, reciprocity and purposive actions as an analytic sequence, but the *empirical* evidence that the three components are *jointly* necessary for ethical collective behaviour comes from the work of Nobel Laureate Eleanor Ostrom (1990) and her successors.
28. For a fuller discussion of the underlying theory and evidence, see Collier (2018d).
29. A phenomenon known as the political business cycle; Chauvet and Collier (2009).
30. Putnam (2016), p. 221.

3. THE ETHICAL STATE

1. This 'existential crisis' was recognized as such by the leaders of Europe's socialist and democratic parties in inviting me to address their annual conference in October 2017 and their youth conference in June 2018.
2. I set out the model more formally and develop its normative implications in Collier (2018b).
3. Wolf (2013), p. 32. This one sentence not only captures the shift of salient identity to work, but also the emphasis upon personal fulfilment, which I take up in Chapter 5.
4. See the Edelman Trust Barometer. Its *Annual Report* for 2017 opens with 'trust is in crisis around the world': https://www.edelman.com/trust2017/.
5. The exemplar of reciprocal co-operation to address anxieties is the co-operative insurance movement, born in Rochdale, an industrial town like Sheffield and Halifax in northern England. In November 2017 the P and V Foundation, part of the giant Belgian insurance co-operative, presented me with its Citizenship Award and I learned of its origins. The Rochdale pioneers had visited Flemish-speaking Ghent, inspiring the birth of the movement in Belgium, but it had swiftly spread across the language barrier to French-speaking Wallonia, and gradually scaled up to become national. The award ceremony was trilingual.
6. Elliott and Kanagasooriam (2017).

7. David Goodhart (2017) has enlarged on this contrast between national and global identities.
8. The quotation is from *The Making of the British Landscape* by Nicholas Crane (Weidenfeld & Nicolson, 2016), p. 115.
9. Johnson and Toft (2014).
10. Elliott and Kanagasooriam (2017).

4. THE ETHICAL FIRM

1. The survey data are for Britain in 2017. For reasons that will become apparent later in the chapter when I discuss the power of finance over firms, Britain rather than the USA is the supreme exemplar of the Friedman doctrine and its consequences.
2. Gibbons and Henderson (2012).
3. The words are those of a former senior employee, as reported in 'The Big Bet', *Financial Times*, 11 November 2017.
4. Quoted in the *Financial Times*, 23 October 2017.
5. Again, it is a matter of the erosion of professional ethics. The accountancy profession has mislaid its moral compass. See Brooks (2018).
6. 1.7 per cent of GDP, versus an OECD average of 2.4 per cent.
7. See Kay (2011).
8. See Haskel and Westlake (2017).
9. Hidalgo (2015).
10. See Autor et al. (2017).
11. See Scheidel (2017).

5. THE ETHICAL FAMILY

1. I am indebted to Robbie Akerlof for this insight on the change in family norms.
2. Even as late as 1975, working women such as my mother, who left school before completing high school, spent the same amount of time on child care as those who were graduates. By 2003 both had increased, but the less educated were now spending barely half as much time as the graduates; Sullivan and Gershuny (2012).
3. I am indebted to Professor Roger Goodman, a specialist in the modern sociology of Japan, for this intriguing insight.
4. Wolf (2013), p. 236. The data are for white graduate mothers.
5. Ibid., p. 183.

6. See Putnam (2016), p. 67.
7. Eliason (2012).
8. Putnam (2016), p. 70.
9. Ibid., p. 78.
10. Heckman, Stixrud and Ursua (2006).
11. Clark (2014).
12. Bisin and Verdier (2000).
13. Brooks (2015).
14. Seligman (2012).

7. THE GEOGRAPHIC DIVIDE

1. See Venables (2018a, 2018b).
2. See the recent work of Jed Kolko.
3. The underlying research for this disturbing fact is by the OECD. For an accessible discussion see *The Economist*, 21 October 2017.
4. I would like to thank Tim Besley for confirmation and clarification of this point.
5. See Arnott and Stiglitz (1979).
6. See Collier and Venables (2017).
7. Greenstone, Hornbeck and Moretti (2008).
8. Lee (2000).

8. THE CLASS DIVIDE

1. Wolf (2013), p. 240.
2. From the Fragile Families and Child Wellbeing Study Fact Sheet: www.fragilefamilies.princeton.edu/publications.
3. See 'Effects of social disadvantage and genetic sensitivity on children's telomere length', *Fragile Families Research Brief* 50, Princeton, 2015.
4. Philip Larkin, 'High Windows' (1974).
5. A proposition brilliantly explored by David Brooks in *The Social Animal* (2011).
6. Pause has a website. Visit it; join in. The data in the text are taken from http://www.pause.org.uk/pause-in-action/learning-and-evaluation.
7. Wolf (2013), pp. 51–2.
8. Brown and de Cao (2017).
9. Putnam (2016), p. 212.
10. Hanushek (2011).

11. Levitt et al. (2016).
12. If you find this as remarkable as I do, may I encourage you to contribute to Grimm and Co, which is a registered charity. You can visit its website at http://grimmandco.co.uk/.
13. A good source here is Wilson (2011), whose book is indeed called *Redirect*.
14. See http://www.winchester.ac.uk/aboutus/lifelonglearning/Centrefor RealWorldLearning/Publications/Post2014/Documents/Lucas%20 (2016)%20What%20if%20-%20vocational%20pedagogy%20%20RSA-FETL.pdf on which the following paragraph is based.
15. Alison Wolf, *Financial Times*, 28 December 2017.
16. *Dancing in the Dark*, Knausgård (2015), p. 179.
17. Goldstein (2018).
18. Acemoglu and Autor (2011).
19. *Financial Times*, 10 September 2017.
20. Michael Lewis and Dylan Baker (2014), *Flash Boys*.
21. In Britain, there has been a strong increase in assortative mating by education, with the biggest increase being graduates marrying graduates: Wolf (2013), p. 232.
22. See Harris (2018).

9. THE GLOBAL DIVIDE

1. World Bank (2018).
2. The following results are from Rueda (2017).
3. Muñoz and Pardos-Prado (2017).

10. BREAKING THE EXTREMES

1. Pardos-Prado (2015).
2. See Chua (2018).
3. People like to identify with success. Depetris-Chauvin and Durante (2017) show that, following the victory of the national football team, national identity becomes more salient.

Bibliography

Acemoglu, D., and Autor, D. (2011), 'Skills, tasks and technologies: implications for employment and earnings'. In *Handbook of Labor Economics* (Vol. 4B). Amsterdam: North Holland/Elsevier, pp. 1043–1171.

Akerlof, G. A., and Kranton, R. E. (2011), *Identity Economics: How Our Identities Shape Our Work, Wages, and Well-Being*. Princeton: Princeton University Press.

Akerlof, G. A., and Shiller, R. (2009), *Animal Spirits: How Human Psychology Drives the Economy, and Why It Matters For Global Capitalism*. Princeton: Princeton University Press.

Arnott, R. J., and Stiglitz, J. E. (1979), 'Aggregate land rents, expenditure on public goods, and optimal city size'. *The Quarterly Journal of Economics*, 93 (4), pp. 471–500.

Autor, D., Dorn, D., Katz, L. F., Patterson, C., and Van Reenen, J. (2017), *The Fall of the Labor Share and the Rise of Superstar Firms*. Cambridge, Mass.: National Bureau of Economic Research.

Bénabou, R., and Tirole, J. (2011), 'Identity, morals, and taboos: beliefs as assets'. *The Quarterly Journal of Economics*, 126 (2), pp. 805–55.

Besley, T. (2016), 'Aspirations and the political economy of inequality'. *Oxford Economic Papers*, 69, pp. 1–35.

Betts, A., and Collier, P. (2017), *Refuge: Transforming a Broken Refugee System*. London: Penguin.

Bisin, A., and Verdier, T. (2000), ' "Beyond the melting pot": cultural transmission, marriage, and the evolution of ethnic and religious traits'. *The Quarterly Journal of Economics*, 115 (3), pp. 955–88.

Bonhoeffer, D. (2010), *Letters and Papers from Prison* (Vol. 8). Minneapolis: Fortress Press.

Brooks, D. (2011), *The Social Animal: The Hidden Sources of Love, Character and Achievement*. London: Penguin.

Brooks, D. (2015), *The Road to Character*. New York: Random House.

Brooks, R. (2018), *Bean Counters: The Triumph of the Accountants and How They Broke Capitalism*. London: Atlantic Books.

Brown, D., and de Cao, E. (2017), 'The impact of unemployment on child maltreatment in the United States'. Department of Economics Discussion Paper Series No. 837, University of Oxford.

Case, A., and Deaton, A. (2017), *Mortality and Morbidity in the 21st Century*, Washington, DC: Brookings Institution.

Chauvet, L., and Collier, P. (2009). 'Elections and economic policy in developing countries'. *Economic Policy*, 24 (59), pp. 509–50.

Chetty, R., Grusky, D., Hell, M., Hendren, N., Manduca, R., and Narang, J. (2017), 'The fading American dream: trends in absolute income mobility since 1940'. *Science*, 356 (6336), pp. 398–406.

Christakis, N. A., and Fowler, J. H. (2009), *Connected: The Surprising Power of Our Social Networks and How They Shape Our Lives*. New York: Little, Brown.

Chua, A. (2018), *Political Tribes: Group Instinct and the Fate of Nations*. New York: Penguin Press.

Cialdini, R. B. (2007), *Influence: The Psychology of Persuasion*. New York: Collins.

Clark, G. (2014), *The Son Also Rises: Surnames and the History of Social Mobility*. Princeton: Princeton University Press.

Collier, P. (2008), *The Bottom Billion: Why the Poorest Countries are Failing and What Can Be Done About It*. New York: Oxford University Press.

Collier, P. (2013), 'Cracking down on tax avoidance'. *Prospect*, May.

Collier, P. (2016), 'The cultural foundations of economic failure: a conceptual toolkit'. *Journal of Economic Behavior and Organization*, 126, pp. 5–24.

Collier, P. (2017), 'Politics, culture and development'. *Annual Review of Political Science*, 20, pp. 111–25.

Collier, P. (2018a), 'The downside of globalisation: why it matters and what can be done about it'. *The World Economy*, 41 (4), pp. 967–74.

Collier, P. (2018b), 'Diverging identitites: a model of class formation', Working Paper 2018/024, Blavatnik School of Government, Oxford University.

Collier, P. (2018c), 'The Ethical Foundations of Aid: Two Duties of Rescue'. In C. Brown and R. Eckersley (eds.), *The Oxford Handbook of International Political Theory*. Oxford: Oxford University Press.

Collier, P. (2018d), 'Rational Social Man and the Compliance Problem', Working Paper 2018/025, Blavatnik School of Government, Oxford University.

Collier, P., and Sterck, O. (2018), 'The moral and fiscal implications of anti-retroviral therapies for HIV in Africa'. *Oxford Economic Papers*, 70 (2), pp. 353–74.

Collier, P., and Venables, A. J. (2017), 'Who gets the urban surplus?' *Journal of Economic Geography*, https://doi.org/10.1093/jeg/lbx043.

Crosland, A. (2013), *The Future of Socialism* (new edn with foreword by Gordon Brown; first published 1956). London: Constable.

Depetris-Chauvin, E., and Durante, R. (2017), 'One team, one nation: football, ethnic identity, and conflict in Africa'. CEPR Discussion Paper 12233.

Dijksterhuis, A. (2005), 'Why we are social animals: the high road to imitation as social glue'. *Perspectives on Imitation: From Neuroscience to Social Science*, 2, pp. 207–20.

Eliason, M. (2012), 'Lost jobs, broken marriages'. *Journal of Population Economics*, 25 (4), pp. 1365–97.

Elliott, M., and Kanagasooriam, J. (2017), *Public Opinion in the Post-Brexit Era: Economic Attitudes in Modern Britain*. London: Legatum Institute.

Epstein, H. (2007), *The Invisible Cure: Africa, the West, and the Fight against AIDS*. New York: Farrar, Straus and Giroux.

Etzioni, A. (2015), 'The moral effects of economic teaching'. *Sociological Forum*, 30 (1), pp. 228–33.

Feldman Barrett, L. (2017), *How Emotions are Made: The Secret Life of the Brain*. London: Macmillan.

Gamble, C., Gowlett, J., and Dunbar, R. (2018), *Thinking Big: How the Evolution of Social Life Shaped the Human Mind*. London: Thames and Hudson.

George, H. (1879), *Progress and Poverty: An Enquiry into the Cause of Industrial Depressions, and of Increase of Want with Increase of Wealth. The Remedy*. K. Paul, Trench & Company.

Gibbons, R., and Henderson, R. (2012), 'Relational contracts and organizational capabilities'. *Organization Science*, 23 (5), pp. 1350–64.

Goldstein, A. (2018), *Janesville: An American Story*. New York: Simon and Schuster.

Goodhart, D. (2017), *The Road to Somewhere*. London: Hurst.

Greenstone, M., Hornbeck, R. and Moretti, E. (2008), 'Identifying agglomeration spillovers: evidence from million dollar plants'. NBER Working Paper, 13833.

Haidt, J. (2012), *The Righteous Mind: Why Good People are Divided by Politics and Religion*. New York: Vintage.

Hanushek, E. A. (2011), 'The economic value of higher teacher quality'. *Economics of Education Review*, 30 (3), pp. 466–79.

Harris, M. (2018), *Kids these Days: Human Capital and the Making of Millennials*. New York: Little, Brown.

Haskel, J., and Westlake, S. (2017), *Capitalism without Capital: The Rise of the Intangible Economy*. Princeton: Princeton University Press.

Heckman, J. J., Stixrud, J., and Urzua, S. (2006), 'The effects of cognitive and noncognitive abilities on labor market outcomes and social behavior'. *Journal of Labor Economics*, 24 (3), pp. 411–82.

Helliwell, J. F., Huang, H., and Wang, S. (2017), 'The social foundations of world happiness'. In *World Happiness Report 2017*, edited by J. Helliwell, R. Layard and J. Sachs. New York: Sustainable Development Solutions Network.

Hidalgo, C. (2015), *Why Information Grows: The Evolution of Order, From Atoms to Economies*. New York: Basic Books.

Hood, B. (2014), *The Domesticated Brain*. London: Pelican.

International Growth Centre (2018), *Escaping the Fragility Trap*, Report of an LSE–Oxford Commission.

James, W. (1896), 'The will to believe'. *The New World: A Quarterly Review of Religion, Ethics, and Theology*, 5, pp. 327–47.

Johnson, D. D., and Toft, M. D. (2014), 'Grounds for war: the evolution of territorial conflict'. *International Security*, 38 (3), pp. 7–38.

Kay, J. (2011), *Obliquity: Why Our Goals are Best Achieved Indirectly*. London: Profile Books.

Knausgård, K. O. (2015), *Dancing in the Dark: My Struggle* (Vol. 4). London and New York: Random House.

Lee Kuan Yew (2000), *From Third World to First: The Singapore Story 1965–2000*. Singapore: Singapore Press Holdings.

Levitt, S. D., List, J. A., Neckermann, S., and Sadoff, S. (2016), The behavioralist goes to school: leveraging behavioral economics to improve educational performance'. *American Economic Journal: Economic Policy*, 8 (4), pp. 183–219.

Lewis, M., and Baker, D. (2014), *Flash Boys*. New York: W. W. Norton.

MacIntyre, A. (2013), *After Virtue*. London: A&C Black (first published 1981).

Martin, M. (2018), *Why We Fight*. London: Hurst.

Mason, P. (2015), *Postcapitalism: A Guide to Our Future*. London: Allen Lane.

Mercier, H., and Sperber, D. (2017), *The Enigma of Reason*. Cambridge, Mass.: Harvard University Press.

Mueller, H. and Rauh, C. (2017), 'Reading between the lines: prediction of political violence using newspaper text'. Barcelona Graduate School of Economics, Working Paper 990.

Muñoz, J., and Pardos-Prado, S. (2017), 'Immigration and support for social policy: an experimental comparison of universal and means-tested programs'. *Political Science Research and Methods*, https://doi.org/10.1017/psrm.2017.18.

Neustadt, R. E. (1960), *Presidential Power*. New York: New American Library (p. 33).

Norman, J. (2018), *Adam Smith: What He Thought and Why it Matters*. London: Allen Lane.

Ostrom, E. (1990), *Governing the Commons: The Evolution of Institutions for Collective Action*. Cambridge: Cambridge University Press.

Pardos-Prado, S. (2015), 'How can mainstream parties prevent niche party success? Centre-right parties and the immigration issue'. *The Journal of Politics*, 77, pp. 352–67.

Pinker, S. (2011), *The Better Angels of our Nature*. New York: Viking.

Putnam, R. D. (2000), *Bowling Alone: The Collapse and Revival of American Community*. New York: Simon and Schuster.

Putnam, R. D. (2016), *Our Kids: The American Dream in Crisis*. New York: Simon and Schuster.

Rueda, D. (2017), 'Food comes first, then morals: redistribution preferences, parochial altruism and immigration in Western Europe'. *The Journal of Politics*, 80 (1), pp. 225–39.

Scheidel, W. (2017), *The Great Leveller: Violence and the History of Inequality From The Stone Age to the Twenty-First Century*. Princeton: Princeton University Press.

Schumpeter, J. (1942), *Capitalism, Socialism and Democracy*. New York: Harper and Bros.

Scruton, R. (2017), *On Human Nature*. Princeton: Princeton University Press.

Seligman, M. E. (2012), *Flourish: A Visionary New Understanding of Happiness and Well-being*. New York: Simon and Schuster.

Smith, A. (2010), *The Theory of Moral Sentiments*. London: Penguin.

Smith, A. (2017), *The Wealth of Nations: An Inquiry into the Nature and Causes*. New Delhi: Global Vision Publishing House.

Spence, A. M. (1974), *Market Signalling: Informational Transfer in Hiring and Related Screening Processes*. Harvard Economic Studies Series, vol. 143. Cambridge, Mass.: Harvard University Press.

Sullivan, O., and Gershuny, J. (2012), 'Relative human capital resources and housework: a longitudinal analysis'. Sociology Working Paper (2012-04), Department of Sociology, Oxford University.

Tepperman, J. (2016), *The Fix: How Nations Survive and Thrive in a World in Decline*. New York: Tim Duggan Books.

Thomas, K., Haque, O. S., Pinker, S., and DeScioli, P. (2014), 'The psychology of coordination and common knowledge'. *Journal of Personality and Social Psychology*, 107, pp. 657–76.

Towers, A., Williams, M. N., Hill, S. R., Philipp, M. C., and Flett, R. (2016), 'What makes the most intense regrets? Comparing the effects of several theoretical predictors of regret intensity'. *Frontiers in Psychology*, 7, p. 1941.

Venables, A. J. (2018a), 'Gainers and losers in the new urban world'. In E. Glaeser, K. Kourtit and P. Nijkamp (eds.), *Urban Empires*. Abingdon: Routledge.

Venables, A. J. (2018b), 'Globalisation and urban polarisation', *Review of International Economics* (in press).

Wilson, T. D. (2011), *Redirect: Changing the Stories We Live By*. London: Hachette UK.

Wolf, A. (2013), *The XX Factor: How the Rise of Working Women has Created a Far Less Equal World*. New York: Crown.

World Bank (2018), *The Changing Wealth of Nations*, Washington DC.

World Happiness Report, 2017 (2017), edited by J. Helliwell, R. Layard and J. Sachs. New York: Sustainable Development Solutions Network.

Acknowledgements

The origin of this book was an invitation from Toby Lichtig of the *Times Literary Supplement* to write a 'state of society' essay for the first issue of 2017. The unsettled times had triggered a clutch of books diagnosing various ills and Toby offered me licence to draw on them as I judged fit. Through the Christmas period, books, children and laptop alternated on my knee, resolving into a diagnosis: the book that was needed for the times was *The Future of Capitalism* but, unfortunately, nobody had written it. The article produced a remarkable reaction, culminating in Andrew Wylie bearing news from New York that three publishers had pre-emptively bid for a book that I had not proposed to write. My British publisher, Penguin, asked me to defer the book for which I was contracted and write this one first.

Intellectually, the task was daunting, my proposition being that what was needed was a synthesis of moral philosophy, political economy, finance, economic geography, social psychology and social policy. Each of these disciplines has laid minefields around itself, designed to deter and destroy intruders. I have been fortunate that some brilliant academics have been willing to work through drafts of the manuscript commenting on it. Their suggestions have undoubtedly greatly improved the final version, but my gratitude to them does not imply that they share any liability for the result.

Among philosophers I would particularly thank Tom Simpson, for going through the entire manuscript and explaining subtle issues with exemplary clarity and patience; Chris Hookway, for many hours of discussion on Pragmatism; Jesse Norman, for his masterful knowledge of Adam Smith; and Konrad Ott, for hours of discussion on reciprocity and the Kantian perspective.

Among economists, Colin Mayer and I discovered with delight that we had written what are effectively companion books, to be published at the same time, his being *Prosperity*. I have long been in intellectual awe of John Kay, who combines the skills of a polymath with the pragmatism of good judgement. With great kindness, he worked through the entire manuscript in detail and gave me hours of comment and suggestions. Tim Besley, at the forefront of modern analytic economics, yet astonishingly erudite on moral philosophy, not only commented on the manuscript but organized a seminar on it at All Souls, Oxford, persuading Alison Wolf to be the discussant for the proposals on 'social maternalism'. Tony Venables, whose profound influence on Chapter 7 is evident, also commented in detail on the entire manuscript. Finally, Denis Snower, President of the Kiel Institute for the World Economy, not only commented in detail on the manuscript but has been invaluable in encouraging and contributing to what we have come to regard as 'behavioural economics, generation 2': the attempt to bring the insights of social psychology into the economic analysis of group behaviour, as distinct from individual decision biases. Our colleagues in the network Economic Research on Identity, Narratives and Norms will in various places recognize my intellectual debt to their work.

One of the least-appreciated explanations for Oxford's continuing intellectual pre-eminence is that the college system generates random social interaction across disciplines. In my case this is augmented by the generous anomaly of having rights at two different colleges. It is thanks to a lunch at St Antony's College that Roger Goodman, professor of the sociology of Japan, began my illumination in the attitudes of elite Japanese women to children. And it is thanks to a lunch at Trinity College that Stephen Fisher, Britain's foremost academic psephologist, came up with the test of Brexit attitudes presented in Chapter 8. Steve also provided the most exhaustive of all the written academic comments on the manuscript, in a determined and generous bid to save me from myself. The indefatigable Laura Stickney of Penguin performed a complementary and equally vital service in nudging the manuscript into readability.

Finally, I am indebted to the many people who have contributed the evidence of their own experience: Bill Boynton, Chairman of

Keele World Affairs, who has built a brilliant forum for the people of Stoke-on-Trent; Deborah Bullivant, the dynamo behind Grimm and Co; Paul Cornick of Unite; the sociologist Professor Mark Elchardus and the people of the P and V Co-operative Movement in Brussels; Ian Moore, who for many years led a team of cognitive behavioural psychotherapists in Sheffield; Gianni Pittella, President of the European Socialists and Social Democrats, and his advisor Francesco Ronchi; and Alan Thompson, lawyer and Quaker.

A book that is easy to read is hard to write, and my family have had to live with the process of struggle. As ever, Pauline has combined holding us all together with providing the eagle eye of the honest reader. Brought up to shun prominence, it has been a difficult decision to write such a personal book; but without it, the edge of passion in the writing would have seemed contrived.

Index